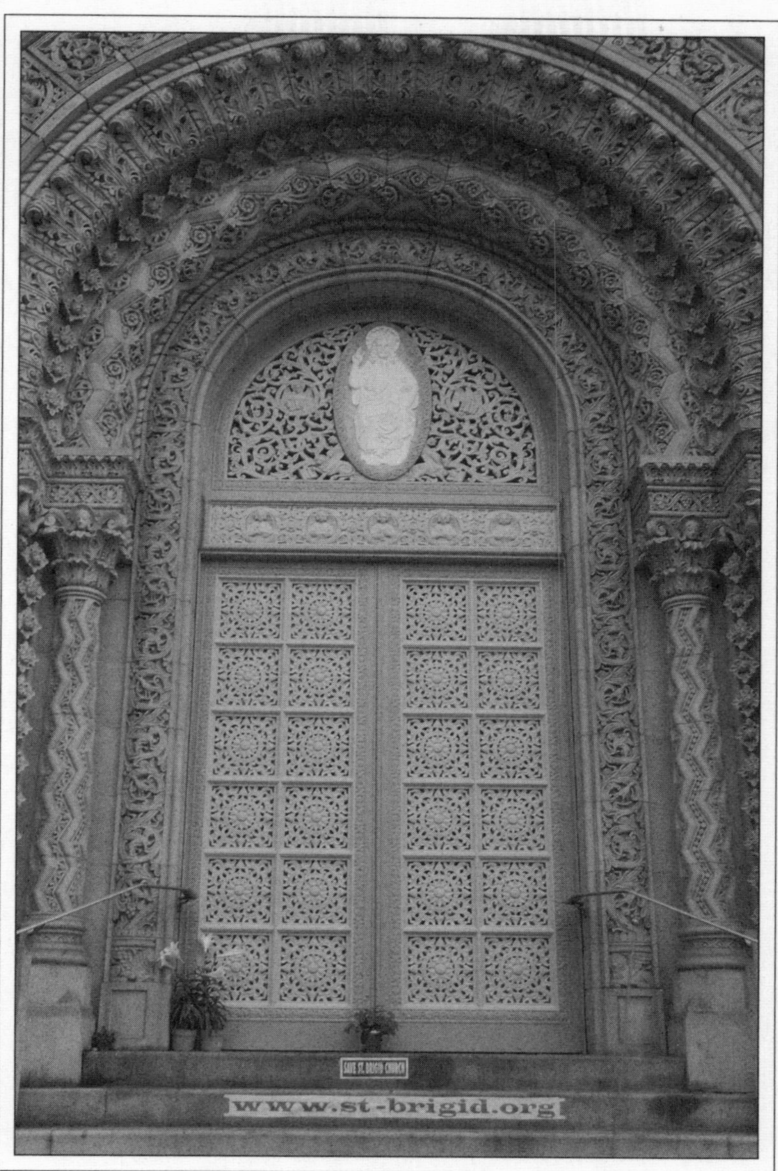
www.st-brigid.org

HOW A BAND OF BELIEVERS LOST THEIR CHURCH AND FOUND THEIR FAITH

✦

THE GRACE OF EVERYDAY SAINTS

✦

JULIAN GUTHRIE

HOUGHTON MIFFLIN HARCOURT

BOSTON ✦ NEW YORK

2011

www.hmhbooks.com

Library of Congress Cataloging-in-Publication Data
Guthrie, Julian.
The grace of everyday saints : how a band of believers lost their church and found their faith / Julian Guthrie.
p. cm.
ISBN 978-0-547-13304-1
1. St. Brigid Catholic Church (San Francisco, Calif.)—History.
2. San Francisco (Calif.)—Church history. I. Title.
BX4603.S5G88 2011
282'.7946109049—dc22
2010049819

Book design by Boskydell Design

Printed in the United States of America

DOC 10 9 8 7 6 5 4 3 2 1

Dedicated to Joe Dignan

Contents

Introduction

THE STORY OF ST. BRIGID began for me one morning in December 2004, when I was driving along one of San Francisco's busiest thoroughfares. Stopped at a light, I saw a small white candle burning on the front steps of a Catholic church. Surrounding it were bouquets of beautiful fresh flowers.

The church's name was St. Brigid.

Taking the same route home night after night, I saw the candle burning there on the steps. Over time, I came to learn that the Romanesque building erected more than a century before by Irish immigrants had been closed a decade earlier by an archdiocese in turmoil. I learned that parishioners had kept the candle burning since the night they were locked out of the place they loved. They met every Tuesday night in the basement of a nearby Russian Orthodox church that had offered them sanctuary. They gathered each week, without fail, to discuss how to reopen St. Brigid.

I was drawn into the story of this church and its believers. The parishioners had waged a quiet crusade for all this time and showed no signs of giving up. I began attending the group's weekly meetings and was charmed by the innocence of the St. Brigid faithful. They had come to San Francisco from across the globe—from Burma, China, Mexico, Ireland, Colombia, the Philippines—and seemed to be from another era, one devoid of celebrity- and attention-seekers, one filled with simple desires and acts of goodness.

I remember smiling as I listened to an elderly woman suggest they hold bake sales in the parking lot to raise money—even though the costs to upgrade the church were said to be in the millions of dollars. The parishioners talked of picketing at rush hour, armed with rosaries and signs: WE LOVE ST. BRIGID and HELP US REOPEN OUR CHURCH. They talked of writing to the pope and reminded one another to send birthday cards to the archbishop. There was a quiet rhythm to the meetings, beginning with the praying of the rosary and ending with coffee, cookies, and catching up.

On the surface, this sort of devotion may seem normal. Churchgoers across the country are remarkably committed to their own houses of worship, helping out with everything from construction and repairs to teaching Sunday school and volunteering in the front office.

But the story of St. Brigid and its parishioners is so much more. Their struggle takes them from a sunlit sanctuary in San Francisco to the steps of the Vatican in Rome. It involves private investigators, attacks and counterattacks, the pursuit of truth and the exposure of lies. It unfolds as one of the darkest periods in the two-thousand-year history of the Catholic Church, pitting laity against clergy, faith against doctrine. And the darkness descends on the people of St. Brigid before it hits Catholics worldwide, opening eyes here and upending ways of life and systems of belief.

Full of twists and turns, tragedy and triumph, the story of St. Brigid is replete with lovable characters who are funny and flawed, humble and heroic, and with leaders who are dramatic in their differences. One leads with his soul, the next with his mind, the last with his heart. All are changed by the battle. The first, a young Irish priest, risked his collar to fight for the life of St. Brigid; the second, a fiery death-penalty attorney from the South, endured the trial of his life; the third, a lapsed Catholic, was forced to confront his painful—and secret—past.

Their saga represents the longest parish protest in Catholic America. In many ways, the epic fight waged from one corner of San Francisco is a microcosm for the struggles of Catholics today: There is the beauty and resiliency of everyday believers versus the ossified problems of a well-meaning institution. There is the forgiveness of the followers contrasted to the denial and silence of those who lead.

Working on this book has made me think of the places we hold sacred. Everyone has somewhere, some corner of the world, worth holding on to. For me, it is a winding dirt road around the lake in Idaho where I spent summers growing up. When I go home to visit my family, I can't wait to head out on a jog along the road, its towering pines framing the glistening lake. It is where I can find—inexplicably—peace.

I never imagined I would write a book about a group of Catholics trying to save a church. I was brought up in a family that attended an Episcopal church a few times a year. My dad, Wayne, liked the sunrise service on Easter. My mom, Connie, enjoyed the candlelight spectacle on Christmas. The thing I remember most about church has nothing to do with a sermon or priest or pretty building. It has more to do with the small moments, the single interactions. What I remember most is my dad's terrible singing. I inherited his inability to sing on key, so we would sing fearlessly and boisterously until we glanced at each other and broke into laughter. Recently, about a year after my father died, I went to an Easter service at Grace Cathedral, a magnificent Episcopal church on San Francisco's Nob Hill. When it came time to sing, I launched into the hymn. In that moment, something happened that I'll never forget: I felt my father's presence. He was to my right, singing, smiling, and looking so happy, when the end of his life was anything but. He was there with me, healthy and handsome. Truly with me. I wondered later if I was blessed with that moment in church because I was somehow more receptive there, if my mind slowed and my heart opened.

The story of these parishioners' quest to hold on to their sacred place is for believers and nonbelievers alike. For, in a world that can seem increasingly isolating, this story asks: Where do we find community? Importantly, it asks: What in *your* life is worth fighting for?

Recent polls show that an astounding 92 percent of Americans believe in God. Yet faith is not a part of everyday conversations, even among close friends. For me, and I hope for readers, this book opens the door to that kind of conversation.

I have spent six years now learning about the faithful from St. Brigid. I have been invited into their homes and meetings. I have attended their birthday parties, anniversaries—and their funerals. I have seen them work in obscurity and watched them seize the spotlight. And I have seen them come back from defeat after defeat. I was there, too, when they lost one of their own—when tragedy ended a vibrant life.

What has struck me most, though, is that these are everyday people who represent the best in humanity. They believe in something bigger than themselves, and they are never going to let go—despite the powerful opposition and despite the appearance of getting nowhere. Through their years of wandering, layers of rejection, and unthinkable betrayals, they do not believe that they have lost. For them, too much was gained along the way.

As the Irish priest involved in their struggle told me: "They have the spirit of fighters, the grace of saints."

Over the years of reporting this story—first for a series that ran in the *San Francisco Chronicle,* where I work as a journalist, and now for this book—one other image has been especially powerful. It is something that says everything about love and faith, about deeds over words. It is something I happened upon, like the burning candle on the church's front steps. In this case, what remains with me is the devotion of a certain housepainter, who continued to physically care for St. Brigid long after it was closed.

When I first met him, he declined even to give his name, saying he didn't want any recognition. Slowly he warmed up, apologizing for his paint-splattered coveralls. I learned that he lived three blocks away from St. Brigid and carried his equipment to the steps of the church.

"I've always figured if the church looked loved, it would be harder to keep it closed," he said of his work, which on this day involved sanding one of the church's three main doors.

Over the years, he shared stories of his happiest times attending St. Brigid with his only son. It was the place where the single dad connected with his shy boy. Working on St. Brigid was the place where old memories were exposed for him—memories of attending Mass with his wife, who would laugh aloud at the kneel-sit-kneel-sit motions. She was a nonpracticing Jew and found the Catholic traditions farcical. After their divorce, and after the housepainter finally got his life together, his son started spending weekends with him. Mass was something the two of them shared, something that was just theirs. Often, they would walk home talking about Bible passages mentioned during Mass, thinking of how the writings were relevant to their lives.

Although he had volunteered in the spring of 1994 to picket during the morning rush hour, holding signs that he'd made himself, he hadn't attended committee meetings. He preferred to operate alone, either reflecting on good or not-so-good times or listening to country music on his transistor radio. He tended to different parts of the church but took special pride in the doors. To him, they represented dark and light: dark when St. Brigid was closed at midnight on June 30, 1994, and light when they would one day be pulled open again.

He liked to work in the silence of an early morning or cloaked in fog late at night. He would take time to admire things like the ornamental archway carved in stone and to study the limestone statues by Ireland's great sculptor Seamus Murphy, which depicted the faces of his country's Easter uprising of 1916.

He told me stories about encounters with homeless people and skateboarders who had encamped on the front steps. And he talked of the occasional interaction he had with passersby. One morning when he was refinishing a door, a man and a woman at the base of the church tried to get his attention. Reluctantly, he stepped down off the ladder.

"Can people get married in this church?" the man wanted to know.

"It's closed," the housepainter replied.

"Why are you fixing the door if it's closed?" the man asked.

The housepainter smiled slightly, revealing a crooked grin. He pointed to the sky and said, "God."

PART I
FAITH

Skepticism is the beginning of faith.

—OSCAR WILDE

1 *God's Will*

November 13, 1993

LILY WONG KNEW the precise number of steps it took to get from her home to the pews of St. Brigid, an old Catholic church in the heart of San Francisco. Navigating the four long city blocks took fifteen minutes. She tapped the uneven sidewalk with her white cane, listening closely to the sounds of the street: the throaty roar of buses, the beeping of a truck as it backed up, the acceleration of a taxi trying to speed through a yellow light, the sputtering buzz of a motorcycle.

Lily always crossed Broadway at Van Ness Avenue, a busy commercial strip ushering tourists and locals out toward the Golden Gate Bridge or down toward the Civic Center. On this Sunday morning, she waited at the corner of Broadway, listening for the hum of the east-west traffic to quiet and the north-south sounds to pick up.

A woman close by asked Lily if she needed help when it was time to cross. Lily smiled in her direction and said she was fine. She was grateful for everything she could do on her own. She had been slowly going blind since she was a teenager, living with her large family in a small, remote village in Burma. By the grace of God, she still had some sight, but it was now blurred, as if she were in a snowstorm.

Standing at the corner, Lily thought of her mother, Dymphna Wong, who had just celebrated her eighty-third birthday. Before leaving for church, Lily had visited her, telling her as always how her family loved and needed her. She had kissed her mother's soft, powdery cheek before leaving and said she'd be back in two hours. Lily, the sixth of Dymphna's eleven children, was awed by how her mother found contentment in what she had. When her mother started having difficulty getting around, she adapted to a walker. When she could no longer use the walker, she said cheerfully that God was telling her the time had come to rest.

Years earlier, Lily had traveled to England, where her brother lived, to see whether her sight could be saved. The answer was no. Her brother's eyes had welled with tears, but Lily accepted what she was told. She did not even feel angry. She would follow her mother's example. And she trusted the Lord to watch over her. She learned Braille—albeit poorly, with one finger—and took classes on the Dictaphone. Her hearing grew stronger as her sight waned. In a way, the whole family was adaptable like that. They had come a long way from their town in Burma.

Lily's father had died of cancer the year before at the age of eighty-three. Shortly before his death, he had converted from Chinese Buddhism to Catholicism, finally giving in to the pleas and prayers of his children, who had already converted. Back in Burma, the Irish nuns who arrived as missionaries after World War II had showed so much love for Christ that soon the eldest of Lily's siblings converted. Then the next, and the next, just like dominoes. One day Lily, a devoted Buddhist, returned home from school and told her mother, "I think I would like to be Catholic." She had learned the Ten Commandments, and she repeated the words from Deuteronomy: "*You shall have no other gods before me.*"

What Lily missed most today was the sense of trust that came with being able to look another person in the eye. She had to rely on devices, such as her talking clock beside her bed or the gadget she carried to tell her whether she was receiving the correct amount of change. She relied on the same bus line, the kindness of strangers, and her regular places for coffee, groceries, and medicine. She relied on furniture not being moved, on roadways and sidewalks being even, on drivers looking before they pulled out of garages, on others paying attention to where they were going.

Crossing Broadway, Lily heard the wail of an ambulance—a pitch she knew to be higher than the sound of a fire engine. She made the sign of the cross, *signum crucis,* whispering out of routine: *In the name of the Father, and the Son, and the Holy Spirit. Amen.* The street was bumpy, and the crosswalk felt like an uneven bridge. She moved as quickly as she could. *Twenty-seven steps to cross. Twenty-five steps to reach the bottom step of St. Brigid.* From the sidewalk, she paused to take in the outline of the massive stone church. Her sister Janie had pointed out the large, ornate cross about twenty feet up and the year 1900 engraved just below. In Burma, she had gathered in people's homes, the way Catholics did in the early days of the Church. Until she came to San Francisco, she had never had a building that held her faith. And she had never been anywhere as grand as St. Brigid. To Lily, this was the barque of Peter that the nuns had talked about, a steadfast place representing a journey of faith. She had memorized every detail of the church in the same way she had memorized the lines on the faces of those she loved. She worked hard at remembering, knowing the details would remain when her sight was gone. Her sanctuary was glorious, with soaring coffered ceilings, solid oak pews, stained-glass windows, and stations of the cross, showing Christ's suffering, death, and rebirth. Lily found comfort in the culture of Catholicism, with its elaborate rituals and its predictability.

She relied on St. Brigid now and loved the independence it gave her. She could get there on her own.

It was a mild November morning, and Lily took her time with the church steps. Tilting her face toward the sun, she removed a rosary from her purse. The sunshine felt healing, like one of her favorite sacramentals. Her hands moved knowingly along the beads. *Outward and visible signs of an inward and invisible grace.* That is how the nuns in Burma had defined sacramental. She climbed the remaining steps slowly, already looking forward to being with those who, like her, had chosen to spend their Sunday morning in church.

So many people said hello to her. She smiled in their direction, making out their silhouettes and reading their friendly gestures. She greeted Helen and Tillie Piscevich, sisters who had attended St. Brigid for fifty years. Tillie stood slightly taller than Helen, something Helen joked had more to do with hairstyle than height. Lily knew their routine. After Mass, Tillie walked to the back of the church—past the "poor boxes" for offerings—to pray before the statue of the Virgin Mother. Helen ventured to the opposite corner to have a quiet conversation with the statue of Saint Anthony. The women believed the saints interceded on their behalf in answer to their most urgent prayers.

Lily said hello to Siu-Mei Wong, another convert from Buddhism, who had arrived from Singapore in 1983 knowing no one, but she now seemed to know all by name. The petite thirty-four-year-old had come to San Francisco to attend graduate school in part because of her devotion to Saint Francis, the city's patron saint. Siu-Mei was energetic, introducing her to new people and inviting her to events. Lily settled into her usual pew, about halfway to the altar. Not far away was a pretty, elegantly dressed woman named Cleo Donovan. Lily had learned that Cleo chose the same seat each Sunday because it was where she found comfort. It was where she felt closest to her only daughter, Leslie, who had died of a heart attack when she was twenty-six. In that pew, Cleo could see the flip of her daughter's ponytail, could feel the warmth of her smile. Her daughter had been baptized, confirmed, and eulogized at St. Brigid.

To Lily, St. Brigid was a place of transcendence, a place where differences were erased. For this hour, there would be no fear, no barriers, no stumbling. Here the pathway was even.

* * *

Robert Bryan checked his watch under his starched Brooks Brothers sleeve. It was time to leave the caffeinated confines of his neighborhood coffee shop on Union Street and head to St. Brigid for Sunday Mass. He had his usual double latte and a scone.

He was exhausted, having worked most of the night on the appeal of a death row inmate at San Quentin State Prison. He had death penalty appeals pending in nine states. Dozens of boxes had just arrived in his office on the ten-year appeal of the conviction of Bruno Hauptmann, put to death in 1936 for the kidnap-murder of Charles Lindbergh's son. He had recently begun representing Hauptmann's widow, and the case came with a mountain of files urgently needing review.

Robert, who was fifty and had been raised a Southern Baptist, was in the process of becoming a Catholic. His wife was Catholic, and his daughter, Auda Mai, had been baptized Catholic. But Robert's interest in the religion was complicated.

He struggled with many of the positions of the Catholic Church, finding it out of touch with much of what was happening in the world. He was at odds with its view on women's roles, sexual orientation, birth control, and abortion. He found the patriarchal clericalism discriminatory. But he admired its stand against the death penalty. And, as a young man in Birmingham, Alabama, he had watched Catholic priests stand up for the rights of the oppressed when other men of the cloth did nothing. He had watched with admiration as a small group of Catholic activists, notably Daniel and Philip Berrigan, met with Thomas Merton and began the Catholic peace movement during the Vietnam War. He also loved the Church's respect for creation, its liturgical beauty, and its tradition of welcoming immigrants.

After weighing the good and the bad, he had decided he could do more by working within the Church than remaining outside. It would bring his faith in line with the rest of his life, which was about righting wrongs and fighting injustice. It felt right to convert, to join a church that had done so much for social justice.

Robert had made a study of churches and cathedrals throughout the United States and Europe. He had visited cathedral after cathedral in France, where his wife was born. St. Brigid held its own with its history, and Robert reveled in it. The church had been established when Abraham Lincoln was president and opened as a parish on September 10, 1863. St. Brigid was dedicated the following year by a Spanish priest, Joseph Sadoc Alemany, who in 1853 had been appointed San Francisco's first archbishop by Pope Pius IX. St. Brigid was the eighth Catholic church established in the City of Saint Francis, and its first priest was Father James Aerden, an Irish Catholic who was followed by a long line of cherished Irish priests, or FBIs—foreign-born Irish—as church insiders came to call them. St. Brigid's dedication, as reported in the newspaper, said: "There were a remarkable number of prelates in attendance. Never before have so many gathered in a sanctuary in California at the same time. St. Brigid Church had no seat unoccupied when services began, and latecomers were content with the only accommodation they could get—standing room."

When St. Brigid opened, San Francisco was a city of around 50,000 people, most of whom had poured into the area during the Gold Rush. Now, the church that had begun life as a simple wooden structure was a striking Romanesque edifice with awe-inspiring interiors. The building had survived major earthquakes, the Great Depression, and two world wars. During the 1906 earthquake and fire, the building had been damaged, but services continued nearly uninterrupted, and the sanctuary served as a shelter for the displaced.

As Robert approached St. Brigid on this November morning, he remembered how the names of parishioners who served in World War II were carved into the stairway inside the front door. He thought of the secret note about the early life of the church that was tucked into a cornerstone of the building, placed there by nuns who taught at the school next door.

Entering the church, he ran a comb through his thinning strawberry blond hair and smoothed his mustache. The death penalty cases and mountain of work could wait. In a way, being in St. Brigid was wonderfully selfish. Here, the bare-knuckled lawyer would kneel to show humility. He would stand to show respect. And his mind would rest.

Father Cyril O'Sullivan—Father O to parishioners and schoolchildren—pulled on his baggy pants, oversized fisherman's sweater, and tennis shoes. He stopped before the mirror in his bathroom in the rectory to check his dark curly hair, reminded that the older priests found his locks long and unruly. He went for a haircut once a year, right before heading home to see his mother in Ireland. The priests' disapproval was one thing; the stern look from Evelyn O'Sullivan was quite another.

From his bathroom, he heard a loud knock at the front door. He looked at his watch. Parishioners usually came to the back door, which was closest to the parking lot. He grabbed his coat and headed to the front door. Peering outside, he saw homeless men with a shopping cart and a dog. He greeted them with a smile. The men wanted to know whether the church had a soup kitchen.

"Regretfully no," Father O said, in his lightsome Irish brogue. One of the men said something about the impressive size of the church.

"Yes, St. Brigid is grand," Father O said, smiling. "You are invited to stay for worship, which is about to begin."

The men looked at one another. They mumbled their thanks and said they were in search of food.

As they turned to leave, Father O called after them, "Wait a minute. Wait there. I'll be right back. Don't go away."

He closed the door softly behind him and bounded into the kitchen. He found shopping bags and began filling them with all the food in the refrigerator—milk, yogurt, cheeses, deli meats, macaroni salad—and much that was in the freezer. It was there for the priests, purchased once a week by a woman who came to clean, shop, and cook.

He carried the heavy bags down the steps and set them in the cart. The men looked on with a mix of wariness and gratitude.

"That's really nice of you, good Father," one man said.

"I'm happy to do it," Father O replied. "And if you feel like it, join us for Mass."

Returning to the kitchen, Father O ran into Pastor Kirby Hanson, the priest in charge, who had been at St. Brigid for five years. Father Hanson looked confused.

"What happened to our food?" Hanson asked. "It's gone."

Father O knew that the other priests were not amused by his habit of giving away all of their food. They feared there would soon be a line out the door when word reached the street.

"Well, you see," Father O began, "there were some homeless at the door. They were hungry. How can you not give a handout of food?"

"You gave away the food?"

"Yes," Father O said. "They were hungry, so I fed them. Oh, and they had a dog." He added that in hopes of softening Hanson, who loved animals and had a yellow Lab—a failed guide dog.

Hanson shook his head and left. It was his turn to celebrate Mass.

Father O shrugged it off. He had never expected rectory life to be a model of heaven. As a relatively young priest, he was still going through a sort of initiation, a normal process where younger priests were occasionally treated as second-class citizens. The older pastors got the big funerals and big weddings, leaving the smaller, less significant ones to the young priests. Father O didn't mind. He was a servant to the church and in service to the archdiocese. He could replace the food in the fridge. Besides, he wondered, where would he be if he talked about helping those in need but didn't do so when they came knocking at his door? Deuteronomy 15:7 instructed: *"If there is a poor man among your brothers . . . do not be hardhearted or tightfisted."* And Psalm 146:7 advised: *"He upholds the cause of the oppressed and gives food to the hungry."*

Some detail seemed to come up with his superiors at least once a week. He didn't wear his clerical garb enough. He introduced himself as Cyril rather than Father O'Sullivan. He told jokes that were a bit too colorful. Now the refrigerator caper. He was sure he would hear about this one for weeks to come.

Father O headed to the side entrance. Smiling as he walked, he made his way to the back of the church. Even after all these years, he found beauty in the simple Sunday Mass, in the reliability of this hour that began with the penitential prayer of forgiveness and ended with the words "Go in peace." When Father O wasn't preaching, he liked to observe from the back, taking in the routine and rhythm. As a young boy in Cork, Ireland, he had stared wide-eyed at the mob of people at Mass and at the impressive choir, which was sixty strong. He had found the ornate robes, incense, and elaborate prayers magical. It was his theater. When he became a priest, his parents were congratulated and assured they had earned their place in heaven. Father O's friends cheered him, saying he had become a "soldier of Christ" and was joining "the world's oldest military."

Father O stood below the large rose window in the choir loft. It was where he stopped when he had entered St. Brigid for the first time in September 1990 through the same side door. The church had carpets and statuary from Ireland, including works by Cork's foremost stone carver, Seamus Murphy. The walls were made of thick squares culled from San Francisco streets at the turn of the century. The stones, in hues of silver and sand, reminded him of heavy fog and dwindling daylight.

Watching the parishioners pass by, he remembered something else that had captivated him that first day: St. Brigid had the scent of a church. And it had the silence of a church. It had all of the trappings of God, all of the ornamentation designed to turn one more deeply inward.

Father O had found a home in America. Here, he was reminded

of his church in Cork, where great oil paintings lined the cathedral-like walls.

On this Sunday morning, the pews at St. Brigid were about half full. He and Father Hanson had been working to bring in more parishioners, and they were making progress. But the demographics of the neighborhood and the city had changed, moving away from its strong Irish and Italian Catholic roots to more Asians. Still, they had a robust new soccer program that he led, a thriving parochial school, and a strong young-adults program. About a thousand people attended weekly Mass.

The Mass began. Father O liked the tradition of beginning with a recognition of sin. It was not about kicking oneself but about thinking of one's strengths and weaknesses. Father O looked at the faithful. There were bowed heads. Bouncy kids. Note-takers. Watch-checkers. Snoozers. It was a scene being played out in churches across the country, around the globe, in houses of worship large and small, rural and urban. To him, the service was an offering, a movement into the sacred of life. It was a period when time stood still.

Father O watched Pastor Hanson, a kind man who never stayed angry for long. Soft-spoken and formal, he was always in his collar, even when he wasn't working. In recent months, he had appeared distracted to the point of being detached. Father O had asked whether he was okay, but he didn't want to pry.

At the pulpit, Hanson, in his slow and methodical speaking style, began with a reading from Ephesians 4:1–16 about the need to find and maintain unity in the midst of growing diversity and differences of opinion. He then prepared for the Eucharist. It was a sacrament Father O loved, believing the presence of the Lord was there. As a new priest, he had felt the least comfortable with the sacrament of the funeral. He hadn't been mature enough to deal with other people's grief. But now he jumped at the opportunity to do any funeral, knowing it was a time like no other for families in need.

After the Eucharist came the announcements. Typically, there was something about a birth, death, or wedding or news of an upcoming event. Recent announcements had included news about a Thanksgiving food drive, a potluck at a parishioner's home, and the church's new program, sending skilled nurses into the homes of the isolated elderly. On this day, Father Hanson put his notes down. He cleared his throat, telling the gathering he had something difficult to say.

Father O wasn't aware of any announcement. Generally, Hanson would at least brief him on what was coming up, but he had said nothing earlier in the week.

Again, Father Hanson cleared his throat. His expression was troubled. Finally he spoke. He said it had been decided. . . . He started again. It had been decided, he said, speaking quickly now, that St. Brigid would be "suppressed."

The church, he said, needed to be closed.

Father O's gentle smile vanished. He saw the parishioners recoil. Silence filled the sanctuary.

This church had served Catholics since congregants began arriving in horse-drawn carriages. It had been a beacon of faith for generations of the city's founding families and newest immigrants. It had existed before the Model T Ford, before radio, and before even the Statue of Liberty. Now, it was to be shuttered?

Looking over the pews, Father O saw Carmen Esteva, a woman from the Philippines who had moved into a condominium a half-block from St. Brigid so she could attend Mass every day. She believed it was the only way to ensure the safety of her soul. He saw an older Italian couple, Guido and Mary Alacia, who had attended St. Brigid from childhood, walking in their Sunday finest with other Italian families in the neighborhood. He saw the single dad who had his son on weekends and enthused that his recalcitrant boy with the mop of brown hair was beginning to enjoy Sundays at St. Brigid. He saw Eleanor Dignan, a stylish woman who had shared with him stories of her troubled marriage and fears over her beloved son, who was falling away from the church.

Hanson, looking flustered and red-faced as he stood at the pulpit, urged the assembly to accept the cost-cutting move as "God's will."

The church would be closed on June 30—in seven months. He said the archbishop had made this decision with difficulty. It was due to declining attendance, fewer men entering the priesthood, and aging buildings requiring seismic strengthening since the 1989 Loma Prieta earthquake. Hanson said that up to a dozen churches across San Francisco were on the closure list and that parishioners of St. Brigid would be well served at other sites.

Father O wasn't listening to the rest of the announcement. He was contemplating the words "God's will." *It was God's will that St. Brigid close?*

Looking at the good people of St. Brigid and the sanctuary saturated with their prayers, he thought, *Like hell it is.*

2 *The Will of the Archdiocese*

IN THE SLEEPY, sunny town of Sonoma, about forty-five miles across the Golden Gate Bridge from San Francisco, George Wesolek sat in church with his wife and three daughters, ages thirteen, twelve, and eight. A fourth girl was on the way, making the forty-nine-year-old father feel like a very lucky man.

But today, Wesolek kept checking his watch, falling out of sync. When others stood, he sat. When others knelt, he stood. He went over numbers in his head. Something about the figures consoled and reassured him, like a familiar prayer. In 1962, San Francisco had fifty-four parishes, with 250,000 people attending weekly Mass. Now there were fifty-four parishes, with 125,000 people attending weekly Mass. Other statistics played in his mind. Twenty full- and part-time positions had recently been terminated. Twelve service offices, including the offices of AIDS education, peace and justice, and separate groups devoted to Hispanic, African-American, Chinese, and Filipino ministries were cut back and combined into three offices.

Wesolek had put two years of his life into planning for this day, November 13. As head of special projects for the San Francisco archdiocese, the tall Pole with the bright green eyes, athletic build, and shaved head was the point person for church closures in San Francisco. Appointed by Archbishop John Raphael Quinn, head of the Catholic Church in San Francisco for sixteen years, Wesolek had organized a committee of canon lawyers, a council of priests, and a bevy of consultants. Nearly 150 people had participated on different committees, and fifteen thousand people had responded to surveys. Self-surveys of parishes had been done, resulting in the weekly Mass tally that now ran through his mind. Pastors had been asked to describe the life of their parishes: the numbers in youth and senior ministries, the numbers of baptisms, confirmations, and deaths each year, the numbers in adult conversion classes, the types of community outreach programs. The city had ordered the archdiocese to seismically strengthen old churches—at an estimated cost of more than $60 million. A dollar figure had been placed on every property. On top of this costly retrofitting, everyday costs piled up: Roofs needed replacing, boilers needed fixing, floors needed redoing, walls needed painting.

Archbishop Quinn, a taciturn and centrist theologian, and the Wesolek team had decided that the best approach was to deal with the churches not one by one but as an entire archdiocese and devise a strategic plan to guide them ten years out.

Sitting in the small Spanish-style church just off the old Sonoma Plaza, Wesolek rubbed his brow. It was a momentous time in the life of an archdiocese established on July 29, 1853, by Pope Pius IX. Change was needed but would not come easy. He let his eyelids close. Parishioners in San Francisco would be struggling with the news of the morning. But he reminded himself that it was time to be practical, not sentimental.

As a young man, Wesolek had been a priest, attending seminary in Detroit in 1968 just as civil rights battles were erupting, taking the priest-in-training out of the seminary and into the volatile streets to support racial equality. He had lasted seven years before voluntarily deciding to leave the priesthood. Coming from a big and gregarious family, where get-togethers attracted a hundred of the closest relatives, he had found rectory life unbearably lonely.

So he understood the power of a church. Growing up in Owosso, Michigan, he went to St. Joseph's, the center of a tight-knit Polish community. He went to Catholic school and attended Mass daily. His confirmation name was Michael, after Saint Michael the archangel, whose role was to protect and defend. Going to church was like putting on his shoes: He did it without thinking. In the same way, he and his classmates knew to stand when a priest entered the room and utter the words "Praise be Jesus. Good morning, Father." Even the Wesolek family's food was blessed at St. Joseph's. On Easter and Christmas Eve, his grandmother Anna, short and chubby with silvery hair that was always pulled back, would have eleven children to dinner—one chair was left empty for baby Jesus. After dinner, a large square sheet of unleavened bread, called *oplatki,* was passed around. Each person would break off a piece of the wafer, ask forgiveness of the others at the table, and then give forgiveness. It wasn't until the sixth grade that George learned there was such a thing as a Protestant. When he and a friend were mad, they assailed the other as "Catholic!" or "Protestant!"

His wife squeezed his hand. Mass was ending. Wesolek again checked his watch. He needed to head to San Francisco to meet with the priests whose churches were slated for closure to get a sense of the parishioners' reactions. He expected tense days ahead.

But after the shock wore off, he anticipated parishioners would accept the decision. Under canon law, parishes were operated by the people but owned by the Church.

And, he reassured himself, leaving his church in Sonoma and heading into the sunshine, Catholics were an obedient people.

3 *Order of Execution*

THE MASS AT ST. BRIGID in San Francisco had ended more than an hour earlier, but the parishioners remained. They milled around the sanctuary in shock, some heading to their beloved statues to kneel and pray, others lighting votive candles. Robert Bryan stood in the center aisle. Here was a church with all of the pageantry and magisterial ritual in the arsenal of the Catholic Church. He looked up at the stations of the cross. He looked toward the altar and around at the brilliantly colored stained glass. He went over Father Hanson's words. Now, four years after the 1989 Loma Prieta earthquake, the church was suddenly deemed unsafe?

He caught the eye of two men he had gotten to know in recent weeks: John Ross, a tax attorney at Chevron, and Richard Figone, a San Francisco Superior Court judge. He motioned to them, asking in a hushed tone if they could meet in the school library, which would give them privacy.

Even before the library door closed behind them, Robert began framing his case. Something else was at play, he intoned, his blue eyes flashing as he paced the library. Loosening his tie, he questioned the timing of the decision to close the churches; attendance had been down at most parishes across San Francisco for thirty years. And he was suspicious about why St. Brigid would be targeted. The church had a dynamic young associate pastor in Father O and one of the largest young adult groups in the city, with

120 members. It had a great choir, a winning men's soccer team, a strong parochial school, and outreach to the elderly and the homeless. It also had more than $700,000 in its account—money raised or donated by parishioners. The building itself was on one of the city's busiest streets, a reminder of heavenly things in the midst of mundane pursuits, a giant, hard-to-miss ad for the Roman Catholic Church.

Robert looked imploringly at Figone and Ross. He felt a connection to the church, but he wasn't even a Catholic yet. He wondered why the men appeared so calm as they looked at him quizzically, saying little.

Finally, after what seemed like minutes of silence, he asked what they thought. Figone, a lifelong Catholic, replied, "I believe that our best approach is to request a meeting with the archbishop."

"You think he'll tell us the truth?" Robert asked.

"He's the archbishop," Figone said. Ross nodded in agreement.

It was all Robert could do not to roll his eyes.

He had seen clerics who were heroic and clerics who were hypocrites. In college, he had been impressed by the priests leading civil rights marches in Washington, D.C. On the other hand, when he was a boy, sitting in the family's Baptist church in Birmingham, he had wondered what would happen if a black person walked in for a service, for the church, like the city, was segregated. When he asked the pillars of the church why blacks weren't allowed, he was told that's just the way things were. When a bomb went off in the 16th Street Baptist Church in Birmingham in 1963, killing four black girls—with the Ku Klux Klan claiming responsibility—he watched as church leaders, including men of the cloth, remained unforgivably silent.

As the meeting in the library ended, the men agreed that Figone would place a call to Archbishop Quinn. The judge said it was important to be conciliatory and ask what the St. Brigid faithful could do to keep their church open. Robert nodded. But as they parted, he had a different thought: They could pursue their plan, and he would pursue his.

Walking the few blocks home, Robert looked at the storied Victorians, Edwardians, and elegant apartment buildings. The parish boundary ran from the San Francisco Bay to the north to California Street to the south, from Buchanan to the west and Jones to the east. It encompassed parts of several fashionable neighborhoods, Cow Hollow, the Marina, Pacific Heights, and Russian Hill, as well as the commercial strip along Van Ness. St. Brigid was on prime property worth tens of millions of dollars. If the church were closed, what would the archdiocese do with the building?

Robert crossed the street and looked down Broadway. He could see St. Brigid's bell tower, its gold-colored steel cross jutting high into the sky. If the bigger and taller the church, the closer to heaven, then St. Brigid was with the angels, he thought.

There had to be an angle. Robert had sources across San Francisco, and he had recently met a woman who worked in the archbishop's office. Maybe he could mine some information there. He also had plenty of friends who were cops, and he kept private detectives on retainer. He would get at the truth, no matter what. One of his favorite passages from Scripture was John 8:32: "*And ye shall know the truth and the truth shall set ye free.*" Unlike that of many of his new friends at St. Brigid, his approach was not to sit back and pray the rosary.

Arriving home, Robert tossed his keys in the dish on the table. He eyed his briefcase stuffed with death penalty cases. The last thing he needed was another one, but St. Brigid's closure felt like a wrongful order of execution.

Joe Dignan was at home when his mother, Eleanor, swept through the door. His year-old daughter, Mary, with soft golden hair and bright blue eyes, had finally fallen asleep. His wife, Polly, was in Golden Gate Park at the riding stables, where she worked.

"Hello, Mother," Joe said.

"You can't believe what's happened," she said, out of breath, her perfume wafting through the air. Eleanor always wore Chanel No. 5 to Sunday Mass.

"Would you like tea?" he asked. He had been consuming ridiculous amounts of caffeine since his latest attempt to stop smoking.

"Joe, you can't believe what's happened," Eleanor repeated.

"I heard you, Mother. I'm waiting for you to tell me," he said, fingering the small silver hoop in his left ear and adjusting the black rubber bracelets around his wrists.

"They announced today that St. Brigid is going to be closed. In June. That's in seven months. They're going to close our church in seven months!"

Joe stared at his mother in surprise, straightening his lanky frame.

"What?" he asked. "They can't *close* St. Brigid. How do you *close* St. Brigid?" His mother must have gotten it wrong.

Removing her red cashmere shawl, Eleanor repeated what she had heard at Mass. She said she had stayed afterward to talk to other parishioners. Everyone was taken by surprise. Everyone was devastated. Some talked about trying to change the archbishop's mind. Some said they would have to accept the decision. "The word of the archbishop is the will of God? Isn't it, Joe?"

Joe looked at his mother. The older she got, the more devout she became. It had been the opposite for him, not that he had ever felt particularly devout in the first place. His earliest memories of St. Brigid were of faking colds and coughs so he could get out of attending Mass. He wanted to stay home in his flannel baseball pajamas and watch *Batman* or *Rocky and Bullwinkle* cartoons. When his mother succeeded in dragging him to church, he would fidget in boredom, read the names of saints on the archway, and talk to himself until his mother elbowed him or shot him a look. When he reached adulthood, church served only to remind him of the sinner he was.

"What are you going to do?" Eleanor asked.

So many years later, his mother was still after him about that old stone building.

"What do you mean?"

"Joe, dear," she said, suddenly collecting her things. "Please go and do something to save St. Brigid." Looking askance at her watch, she said, "I stayed too late after church, getting all the gossip. Now I'm late for my painting class." Joe knew his mother's painting class was a way to relieve stress, and was a form of expression for all she kept silent.

"What can *I* do?" Joe replied, trailing after her.

"Get involved," she said. Before he could say another word, she was out the door.

From the driveway, Joe watched her make the half-block walk to her own home on the tourist-packed, crooked part of Lombard Street, to the home of his childhood, with the lovely garden filled with lemon and pear trees and plate-sized dahlias.

He looked at his mother and shook his head. Why would he get involved in saving St. Brigid?

Three days had passed since the announcement. Calls had poured in to the archbishop's office. Everyone wanted a meeting.

Archbishop Quinn, who was more adept at policy than politics and more comfortable with decrees than handholding, sent a letter to his aggrieved parishioners: "I remain firmly convinced that the decision to close St. Brigid church and parish was the correct decision, and I reaffirm it."

He went on to say, "I am fully aware that this decision will be a grave disappointment to you. At the same time it is basic to my office as Archbishop to consider not only individual parishes but the overall good of the whole Archdiocese. It is obvious that there are too many parishes in the City, and several of them like St. Brigid need expensive retrofitting. We must be architects of the future, not victims."

The parishioners responded by turning to one another and turning to prayer. One prayer disseminated among the parishioners read: "Oh God, we claim St. Brigid Church for our Lord Jesus Christ for his purposes and intentions. Come to the assistance of St. Brigid against the powers of hell. Guard her with your special care and obtain for her and for us the protection of our church in order to carry on the great honor and glory of God."

Distraught laity began calling and visiting Lily Wong, asking what they should do. Helen and Tillie Piscevich, the two sisters who sat near her at Mass, said they had never opposed a priest or challenged an archbishop, even after the Second Vatican Council had supposedly ushered in a new democracy giving greater roles to parishioners. They talked about what they saw as the "aura of priests," of these men who were set apart from others, who served as the intermediaries between man and the Divinity. They said that St. Brigid was the one church that took them back to their childhood and gave them a sense of neighborhood. And it was St. Brigid that made them feel connected to something great: this big spiritual Catholic family that brings men and women from every country, every race and language, into one place and one faith.

Lily understood.

Carmen Esteva, who revered priests as representatives of God incarnate, said that she loved St. Brigid dearly but believed the archbishop's decision had to be supported. "It would be a sin to challenge the archbishop," said the Filipina who had moved into the neighborhood because of St. Brigid. Robert Head, a pipe fitter and welder who sat near Lily during Mass, had said he felt the parishioners were being treated as if they were part of a McDonald's franchise. "If we're not the top producer we're shut down?" he asked. "When you work with your hands, a building is more than a building. The men who laid out the wood for those pews we sit in had to know how the wood would react, how it would expand and contract. There is beauty in those pews, in every detail of the church."

It was midweek when Lily entered the hospital chapel, taking a break from her medical transcriptionist job at San Francisco General. She moved her hands along the railing, which creaked in response. She thought of the irony of prayer, of asking for something only when it becomes threatened. She had never prayed for her eyesight while she had it. In the same way, she had never prayed for St. Brigid until she thought she could lose it. Like her vision, she had assumed the church would always be there. It was something that wasn't supposed to be taken away.

Sitting back into a pew in the chapel, where she sometimes led the rosary for employees, Lily bowed her head. Her life had not been easy. And it had never felt fair. It was delivered in parts: a bit of good, a dollop of bad. As a child, she had perfect vision. By the time she was fifteen, her vision was murky. The diagnosis was retinitis pigmentosa, a progressive disease in which there is damage to the retina. She was told the night vision goes first, then the side vision, and finally, in cases like hers, the central vision. Shortly after coming to San Francisco in 1974, Lily had discovered St. Brigid. She lived nearby, on Nob Hill, and commuted across the Bay Bridge to Berkeley to take courses as a medical transcriptionist. She still had peripheral vision and could see the vibrant colors of the church's stained-glass windows. Her family had prayed and prayed that God would save her sight. But slowly, inexorably, things were going dark. It was a test for her.

Kneeling with her hands clasped on the railing, Lily again asked God to intervene to save St. Brigid. She thought of a conversation she had had with Louisa Stanton, an eighty-eight-year-old woman who lived across the street from St. Brigid and had attended the church from childhood. "We are being treated like throwaway Catholics," she said to Lily, her voice filled with hurt.

Pulling herself up from the pew, Lily considered another irony. Here she was, the only parishioner at St. Brigid who couldn't see, yet people were looking to her to lead.

Father O'Sullivan had retreated to his study in the rectory in the days after the announcement. Every time he ventured outside, parishioners approached him, seeking answers about why St. Brigid had been picked. He had repeated the reasons given by Father Hanson.

The problem was, those reasons weren't sitting well with Father O. The parishioners had maintained this church, paying for new floors, ceilings, and fixtures and turning the old basement into a gleaming gym for schoolchildren. They had paid the bills, raised the money, added structures, and organized events. Masses were celebrated in five languages, and they were held three times a day on weekdays and five times on Sundays. People had worked for their church without pause for more than a century. An enormous block in a busy city held St. Brigid church, rectory, parochial school, and convent. Now its parishioners were being told that their church no longer mattered, that their needs could be met by another parish. To him, that was like telling a happy family member to go and join another family.

Father O had heard talk over the summer of a reconfiguration of churches and programs in the diocese. He had seen administrators walking through St. Brigid, taking notes on clipboards. He knew Mass attendance had declined in San Francisco and that there had been similar drops in attendance in many big cities nationally. But he'd never imagined that St. Brigid would be on anyone's closure list. St. Brigid felt far too alive to die.

Father O was not surprised he had been left in the dark. He knew the Catholic Church to be run consistently top down; he was its voluntary servant. In being a priest, he had committed to giving it his life. And he was sure from the look on Father Hanson's flushed face and from his trembling hand on the day of the announcement that he too was struggling with the news he had been told to bear.

With his Sunday homily rapidly approaching, Father O was torn between this sense of service to his bishop and a desire to care for his flock. He had never faced a decision like this in his career, and it was not one he wished on himself now. Would he support the decree of the archbishop to shut down a dozen churches across the city, including St. Brigid? Or would he side with those like Robert Bryan, who was already talking about challenging the closure? Would he follow his priestly orders, with traditions dating back thousands of years, or would he follow his own definition of being a priest, which was about caring for others?

Father O's Irish roots had trained him to fight. Growing up in the hardscrabble town of Cork, he had come to understand how some of the purest men—like those of his hometown who fought for an independent Ireland—could be branded rebels, while there were men of God who were anything but. He thought of his father, Timothy, a carpenter, and of his father's friends. They were gentle and friendly and predictably the life of any party. But they never yielded and never backed down. They had spines of steel.

But his priestly calling had trained him to follow. He had known as a child that he wanted to be a priest. When he was all of five, his father had hoisted him onto the bar of the neighborhood pub, the Castletown, and announced, "Young Cyril here is going to be a priest." Pints of ale were raised to the future Father O'Sullivan.

He had never stopped loving being a priest. And if he defied the will of an archbishop, he would risk everything. He could be barred from preaching, from the sacraments he loved to celebrate. He had allegiances to his superiors and to his faithful. Now he had to choose.

Father O grabbed his fisherman's coat and cap and headed out for a walk on Union Street. Maybe the fresh air would help. Walking along the trendy street in the Marina District, he looked at the array of shops and restaurants. There were nail and hair salons, restaurants and furniture shops. Bars and cafés dotted every corner, packed with good-looking young men and women in pursuit of other good-looking young men and women. He walked by Perry's, a popular spot for people-watching, Bloody Marys, and brunch, and strolled to the end of the commercial part of the street, turning left and walking one block up. There was St. Vincent de Paul, another Catholic church. Father Hanson had said that the flock from St. Brigid would be welcomed at nearby houses of worship. Father O knew that when a church was closed in America, one ground for appeal was to show that the parishioners would be denied access to the sacraments. He knew, too, that rarely was that the case in densely populated cities. It certainly would not fly here.

Father O had had his share of disagreements with his superiors before but always over minor issues, like giving away the rectory's food. Heading back up Union Street, back toward St. Brigid, he thought of his father, who had left school after eighth grade to start an apprenticeship as a carpenter. Unschooled but street smart, Timothy O'Sullivan was the man others in Cork went to for advice. He was the man the priests visited to borrow the family's car or to share in an evening of libations and laughter. He was a great dad, who died too young—Cyril was in his final year of the seminary. Turning onto Van Ness, Father O remembered something his father had told him: "You always respect the collar, son, but not always the man."

4 *Stand and Fight*

THE FOLLOWING SUNDAY, Father O entered the sanctuary of St. Brigid wearing green silk vestments and an expression that gave nothing away. Standing at the pulpit, he brushed back his hair and unfolded his wire-rimmed glasses. Behind him, the Italian marble angels kneeling in prayer at the altar cast gargoyle-like shadows across the back wall.

Before the Mass, several parishioners had passed around small flyers, about the size of dollar bills, to everyone in the pews: "The light shines in the darkness and the darkness has never put it out." Underneath the inscription was a solitary candle.

Someone had begun placing a white candle on the front steps of St. Brigid at night. Flowers were also left on the steps.

Father O could feel the tension in the sanctuary. His inner turmoil had been replaced by a calm reserve. He knew the parishioners wanted more than a homily.

Robert Bryan was there, about halfway back on the left side. He sat on the edge of his seat, as if ringside, nodding occasionally to Father O with encouragement. Lily Wong was there, too, waiting for something to happen. She believed that whatever Father O did, it would be right by God.

Father O delivered his homily, blessed the offering baskets piled with money, and offered communion, all uneventfully. But just as the Mass was about to end—after the Eucharist and in time for the announcements—Father O made his way closer to the crowded pews. He had something concealed behind his back.

As he looked around the beautiful sanctuary, founded by priests named O'Neill, Doogan, and Callaghan, Father O thought of Cork, where boys were raised to stand up for their position. This servant of the Church needed to stand with his flock.

Unfurling a white towel and holding it high, he cried out, "Are you going to throw in the towel? Or are you going to fight?"

For a moment, the church was still.

Then the normally reserved churchgoers let out a stadium-style cheer.

Robert practically jumped out of his seat. "This," he enthused, "is what religion is supposed to be!" Turning to his wife, he said, "Do you know how radical this is? How radical it is for a priest to do this?" Not far away, Lily sat and smiled. She was moved by Father O's passion. Here was a young man—thirty-eight years old—who was being very brave. She had always thought he was a man to follow into battle, and now, in this moment, Lily could feel lines being drawn between those in the pews and those in power.

Father O waited for the din to subside. He understood that his message would shock some in the congregation. So much was at stake, for him and for them. Many of these parishioners were immigrants who had made their way through hardship to finally find a home in St. Brigid. They trusted the church leaders to do the right thing.

For Father O, being a priest was all he wanted. His ordination at the cathedral in the county of Waterford was the best day of his life. But now he had defied his superiors. The parishioners, likewise, were entering new territory.

At the front of the sanctuary, Father O draped his towel over the communion rail. His hidden prop and rallying cry had been inspired by his short-lived stint as a boxer. When his arms felt as though they would give out, he had found courage in the battle cry to keep fighting, to never throw in the towel.

He turned back toward the pews to talk with the parishioners. Speaking softly, he said there were times in the Gospels when Jesus didn't hesitate to refute church leaders. "What we are hearing from our religious leaders is that we must get out, we must move on," Father O said. "But there is not a passage in Scripture where Jesus tells his followers to get out. It is probably unscriptural." He said that when it came down to it, his decision didn't rest on being Catholic.

"I respect my archbishop," Father O said. "But my conscience will not allow me to agree with him on this issue. In my mind, it's simple: If you love something, you will never give up on it."

The next Sunday, November 28, 1993, the parishioners streamed into St. Brigid. Shafts of golden light filtered through the stained glass, and down in the sanctuary, the sounds of Mozart came from the prized Ruffatti organ. It was not his turn to preach, so Father O stood and watched from the back of the church. Standing under the ornate rose window with petals representing the seven sacraments, he smiled.

Scores of people, young and old, had white towels draped over their shoulders.

5 *Under Fire*

ARCHBISHOP QUINN WAS seated behind a table in the basement of St. Mary's Cathedral, the mother church for Catholics in San Francisco, Marin, and San Mateo counties; Pope John Paul had visited there in 1987. It was January 13, 1994, and the archbishop faced nearly two dozen priests of the archdiocese.

Only days before, he had received a letter signed by forty-one of the diocese's hundred and twenty-five priests, asking that the parishes slated for closure remain open for at least two years. The priests said they believed the process leading to the closure orders had been "deeply flawed." While commending Quinn for his "vision" and for the work put in by the commission led by George Wesolek, the priests wrote: "We believe that there are injustices being recommended in the plan that would produce great spiritual harm." The letter took the archbishop by surprise.

Quinn relied on institutional loyalty, and he sent a prompt and sharp reply. He wanted to meet with the priests who signed the letter, calling the petition a matter of "considerable gravity" with "great symbolic overtones." He set conditions for the meeting: All who signed would be present, and anyone who could not attend for "grave and serious reasons" would send a letter indicating why he signed the petition and describe "precisely his intent in signing it."

Quinn and his top lieutenants filled twelve chairs behind a table. As the meeting began, Quinn heard one priest say: "The language of this room does not suggest a friendly, informal discussion. Just look at the arrangement of those chairs!" Another priest quipped that it was "like Jesus and the apostles."

Quinn told the priests that he did not expect them to always agree with his decisions, but he did expect their support once a decision was made. The diocese, like the Church itself, was based on the absolute authority of clerics and the established hierarchy of priests.

"Why now?" he asked of their letter. "This is very divisive, very harmful to the archdiocese." After reiterating the reasons for the closures and the need to think of the well-being of the entire archdiocese and the future of the Catholic Church in San Francisco, Quinn asked the priests to share their thoughts.

About a dozen hands were raised. One by one, the priests said they did not consider themselves disloyal, but instead they believed the parish consultations and self-surveys were faulty and hasty. And they felt they had never been given the chance to plead their case.

More than thirty minutes passed, and one hand remained up. A priest with curly hair, sitting about halfway back, was being overlooked. Finally, Quinn nodded. He knew the priest before him.

Father O stood to speak. While nervous, he did not mince words, taking a deep breath before starting: "Archbishop, this is criminal. This is not justified. You need to reconsider this decision for the good of our people."

The room was still. The young priest sat down, feeling Quinn's icy stare. The archbishop had heard of his call to action from the altar of St. Brigid—as had the other priests, who moved away from him when he first sat down. Quinn did not need an Irishman fomenting rebellion. And he certainly didn't need anyone calling his actions "criminal."

The archbishop returned to the chancery later in the day to find another letter of protest from yet another priest. In this case, it was from Father Hanson, who had gone along with the closure order and announced the news in a firm but compassionate manner.

Father Hanson began: "The reasons given for closing St. Brigid would have been valid some time ago when we completed our self-study of the parish. They have not characterized the situation here for some time."

The letter continued: "Ever since I arrived at St. Brigid, I have attempted to open up this parish and turn things around. I believe this has happened." Like the other priests, Hanson acknowledged the "herculean" job done by the Wesolek commission. But he said pointedly: "It is inconceivable to me and the parishioners that the Commission would make a recommendation to you concerning the closure of St. Brigid without personally visiting with me and the parish leadership to discuss the recommendation for closure and the reasons. Time and again during the months of cluster meetings when the discussion started to veer into the area of specific parish closures, we were reminded that the forum was intended to allow us to participate in the development of the pastoral plan for the archdiocese and not for the discussion concerning the possible closure of specific parishes." He ended the letter: "Needless to say, Archbishop, this is the most important period in the history of this venerable 130 year old parish."

6 *Organizing for Battle*

On a Wednesday night later in January 1994, more than five hundred people packed the auditorium of St. Brigid School. It was the first official meeting of the Committee to Save St. Brigid, and Robert Bryan was presiding over a sea of commotion. The attorney tried to get the crowd's attention, but the parishioners were busy sharing their ideas on how to save St. Brigid.

Eleanor Croke, a longtime churchgoer who had moved to San Francisco from the East Coast and whose family came from Tipperary, Ireland, suggested sending thoughtful, handmade cards to the archbishop to get on his good side. Nelly Echavarria, a seamstress who lived and worked up the street, had found phone numbers for the Vatican in Rome and had already placed her first call. "I told the man at the Vatican that we have a bishop in San Francisco who is not doing God's work," said Echavarria, small and tightly wound like one of her spools of thread. "I told this man to listen and to listen very carefully: I said I wanted my message delivered to the Holy Father. I said that the Holy Father needed to know about our grievous situation in San Francisco."

Robert noticed that many in the room were introducing themselves to one another for the first time. They had seen each other in church but had never actually met.

Denise Nicco, an executive from the city's gas and electric company, told another parishioner, "The thing that's at loggerheads here is that we belong to a church that's hierarchical, yet we live in a democratic country, and the two elements don't work. They think they can tell us our church is closing and we will accept that."

Siu-Mei Wong, the young woman from Singapore, carried a clipboard and asked people to sign in. Several declined, fearing the archbishop would see the list. Robert smiled to himself. He hoped the archbishop would see the list.

Finally, amid the chatter, a man standing against the back wall let out a piercing whistle. "Time to listen, kids," he bellowed. On the stage, Robert tipped his hat in appreciation.

"I'm new to St. Brigid," Robert began. "I am new to Catholicism. So new that I'm not yet a Catholic. But what I see happening here is not about religion." The crowd murmured. "It is about human rights, about civil rights."

John Ross listened in amazement. Judge Figone was supposed to be taking the lead as chair of the ad hoc committee, but it was Robert who was stealing center stage. Ross thought it was inappropriate to be talking about anything other than how to be conciliatory toward the archdiocese.

Clearly comfortable with his own smooth oratory, Robert told the gathering a bit about his background, explaining that he had chosen to spend his life fighting the death penalty because it was an injustice. He said that one of his first death penalty cases had been in Alabama in 1979, when he represented a black man convicted of murdering a wealthy white woman. He won the appeals case in front of an all-white panel of judges. "This struggle for St.

Brigid is about good versus evil, about the little guy taking on the powerful." There were more murmurs, this time with the shaking of heads. Robert was undeterred. He said he was looking into the legal steps that could be taken to stop the closure order and that he had consulted with a canon law expert in Washington, D.C. "This is a fight over what's right and wrong," he said.

Doris Munstermann, whose family had attended St. Brigid for a century, voiced her concern that if they weren't careful, the parishioners might come across to the archdiocese as the enemy. "We need to do everything with respect," she said. "The archbishop is a good man. This was a difficult decision that he made in the best interest of the church." Applause followed.

Robert nodded. "We can be respectful and still disagree," he said. "We cannot go hat in hand." He smiled and added, "Napoleon once said, 'Luck is on the side of those with the most cannons.' I couldn't agree more."

Munstermann shook her head. "We need to show our love for this place called St. Brigid. We need to share our stories. My father was an usher at the church. My mother used to tease and say she was a 'Sunday widow.' My grandmother was buried from there. My sister was married there, as were my cousins, aunts, and uncles. It's a home, a big home. It's a community where people come together to help and to celebrate." There was clapping.

Maureen "Moe" Frix, tall and slim with short dark hair, was there with her son and daughter. She wore a white towel draped over her shoulders, as did her children. Her husband, an army major general, was overseas. Raising her hand, she said, "I don't know if anyone is aware of this, but the schoolchildren don't have any idea what's going on. Even worse, the teachers say the children are feeling responsible. We need to start explaining to them that good men—yes, even priests—can make bad decisions." There was more loud clapping.

Dunn Silvey, a fifth-generation San Franciscan who ran a copy service store, chimed in that he would keep his office open 24/7 so that the parishioners could use his fax and copying machines and phones. "People may dismiss this as the closing of just one church in one corner of San Francisco," he said. "But there were marriages and deaths and all of life's celebrations here for more than a hundred years. We can't just stand by and let them take that away. Time would never heal that hurt."

Robert, now standing on the floor in front of the crowd, asked for volunteers to lead the committee. Hands shot up. One by one, the positions of vice president, treasurer, community outreach, and archdiocese liaison were filled. Someone suggested a need for a spiritual leader. Only one name was offered: Lily Wong's. Lily, off to the side, tried to demur. Then the chanting began: "Lily, Lily, Lily." Finally she smiled and waved her hands to get people to stop. She agreed to lead.

Still standing against the back wall, apart from the small groups that had clustered together, was the lanky man who had let out the whistle. As the meeting was ending, he raised his hand. "What about starting a newsletter?" he asked. "We need to keep everyone informed. I volunteer to write it."

Robert nodded. "I love it, it's a great idea," he said, asking, "And what is your name?"

After a pause, the man in the khaki pants and green jacket replied, "My name is Joe. Joe Dignan."

Before the meeting broke up, Robert returned to the stage and talked about the challenges ahead. And he vowed to battle for St. Brigid the way he would fight for a death row client: Nothing, and no one, was off-limits.

Within days of the meeting, hundreds of people were gathering nightly on the steps of St. Brigid to circle the church. Clutching candles, rosaries, or flashlights, they walked and they prayed. Bake sales and car washes were organized to raise money to retrofit the church, despite the enormity of the cost. Ads were placed in newspapers, and parishioners picketed in front of the church morning and night.

At Mass, in place of money, parishioners put IOUs in the Sunday offering. The notes said: "IOU $___ payable when our church is restored." Groups spread out across the city to collect signatures of support for St. Brigid. They became fixtures at Fisherman's Wharf, the Financial District, Moscone Center, and City Hall. Congregants organized a "black Sunday," where church attire was all black—save for the white towels over shoulders.

Even the younger children were getting into the act, standing with their parents in front of St. Brigid at rush hour, wearing their school uniforms and waving signs reading: PRESERVE OUR HERITAGE. SAVE OUR FUTURE. KEEP OUR CHURCH OPEN and HELP SAVE OUR CHURCH AND GYM, which was in the basement of St. Brigid.

Entire classes were drawing colorful pictures of their church to send to Pope John Paul II. A picture by a seventh-grader showed the church building inside a heart with a passage from Matthew 16:18: "*And so I tell you Peter: You are a rock, and on this rock I will build my church, and not even death will be able to overcome it.*" A drawing by a fourth-grader included a picture of a forlorn puppy holding a sign: IF THEY CLOSE ST. BRIGID, I'LL BE VERY SAD!

Though Robert was charmed by such efforts, he didn't have time for bake sales or puppy dogs. Within days of the closure announcement, he had hired a private investigator to dig into the behind-the-scenes dealings at the diocese, convinced that the high-ranking men in dark suits and white collars were not forthcoming in the reasons behind the planned closure.

7 *Send Someone from Rome*

ROBERT BRYAN'S LEGAL assistant poked her head in the office door and said he had a call he'd want to take. Robert grabbed the phone. His private investigator was on the line, a man he'd worked with for years on a variety of cases. The no-

nonsense investigator told him he had some major news. He said that a well-placed source had informed him that the San Francisco police were getting ready to file charges against one of the city's highest-ranking priests.

"You're kidding me, right?" Robert said, getting out of his chair. "This is great. Continue."

The priest was said to be a close friend of Archbishop Quinn's, the investigator said, and was believed to have "done a number" on some boys over a period of years. Not only that, the investigator said in his matter-of-fact manner, the archdiocese was rumored to be making secret payments to parishioners who had problems with other clergymen in the area. He went on for another ten minutes, adding more details, sharing more rumors. Robert had one hand clenched, one hand on the phone.

Hanging up, he took a deep breath. He sat back down and began digging through some files he had started collecting when he began considering converting to Catholicism. He found what he was looking for. Two years earlier, in 1992, a priest in Massachusetts had been convicted of sexually abusing a child. Boston's Cardinal Bernard Law had condemned the *Boston Globe* for its reporting of the case. He rifled through the file. A year earlier, there had been another case in which the Boston archdiocese paid about $40,000 to a man who was alleged to have been raped as a child by a priest named Paul Shanley. Almost a decade earlier, a Reverend Gilbert Gauthe was indicted on multiple counts of molestation in Louisiana, admitting he had molested more than thirty children and youths. In the files were abuse reports and rumors on alleged sex abuse claims in Canada and Australia, cases where the "transgressions," as they were labeled, were dismissed and denied by church officials.

Robert picked up the phone to call reporters.

The next day, Robert charged up the granite steps of St. Brigid, bullhorn in hand. The parishioners were scheduled to march to

St. Mary's Cathedral, next to the home of Archbishop Quinn. They wielded signs and leaflets, rosaries and candles. A thick fog had descended over the church.

Robert took in the tall lights of the television cameras. For the St. Brigid flock, it was a chance to pray. For him, it was time for a press conference to publicize his belief that good churches like St. Brigid were being shuttered for reasons other than those stated. He wasted no time, yelling out to the crowd: "Parishioners should not be paying for the mistakes of our leaders. Especially with the closing of our churches."

His southern drawl heavy with anger, he went on: "The archdiocese has rationalized this closure of St. Brigid as something that is for the good of the Church, for God, for Jesus. For centuries, people have used religion to rationalize things that are not right."

As reporters held their tape recorders high, some parishioners fidgeted.

John Ross said to his wife, "Marching around and making these pronouncements is not what we should be doing."

Standing before the cameras and the sign-wielding flock, Robert declared, "It is time for the Vatican to send someone from Rome." He withdrew a letter from the pocket of his blue blazer.

Siu-Mei Wong looked on, wide-eyed. She did not like anyone to disparage a priest or the church.

Speaking with the intimate intensity of a lawyer addressing his jurors, Robert said, "You have been taught from the time you started attending church not to question the bishop or the priest. In the case of St. Brigid, we are hearing, 'Don't question the bishop or challenge the priest. They know best. They are God's representatives on earth.' The news that I am about to deliver is going to be difficult for you to hear, but sometimes these religious leaders don't know best, sometimes they don't do what's best. Sometimes these perfect men are more imperfect than you ever imagined." Pausing for effect, he raised his voice and said, "I have credible information that at least one high-ranking priest in San Francisco is soon to be arrested." He paused. "Arrested for unthinkable deeds."

Helen and Tillie Piscevich looked at each other with raised eyebrows. Siu-Mei held her clasped hands to her mouth. Ross touched his wife's elbow to signal it was time to go.

Waving his letter in the air, Robert said he was urging the Vatican to investigate what he saw as the moral and financial sins of the San Francisco archdiocese. He said that the priest—a friend of the revered archbishop's—had been accused of child molestation. The archdiocese was secretly making payments to parishioners who had been sexually abused by clergymen.

"It is my prediction that the archbishop is going to respond by saying they are being subjected to undue scrutiny. Archbishop Quinn will deny any allegations. Then, when he can deny no longer, he will say this is an exception."

Robert told the group he was in the process of contacting an attorney in Louisiana who was documenting cases of clergy sexual abuse and had eighty-six plaintiffs lined up, with more preparing to join civil lawsuits against the Catholic Church. He said he knew of other reports beginning to surface in a diocese in Oregon. "In San Francisco, the Roman Catholic Church is land rich, cash poor. It is my belief they need to sell our beautiful church," he said.

After his speech, Robert was swarmed by reporters. They wanted him to name names. He had the names of more than one priest under suspicion, but he said he needed to let the police do their job.

The parishioners huddled together. Helen and Tillie said they had heard from a niece about an abusive priest in San Bruno. The niece said the parishioners first noticed something was off when the priest began using profanity around children on the playground. Pat Anderson, who had been baptized at St. Brigid and made her first communion there, said she had been hearing rumors of a bad priest in San Francisco's Sunset District. "If this is all true," she said, visibly shaken, "how will we ever go to our priests and say, 'Father, I have sinned'? Maybe his sins are worse than mine." Bebe St. John was there with her mother, an immigrant from Mexico who had come to San Francisco in 1965 when she married Bebe's father, and she felt sick to her stomach. Her faith had been shaken by the threat to St. Brigid. Now this.

Lily Wong tried to provide comfort. Holding her walking stick in one hand and her rosary in the other, she said, "We have to hold on to our faith—now more than ever. This is something that is happening to test us."

When the march ended back at St. Brigid, Robert was approached by Louisa Stanton. She lived across the street from the church and had attended Mass there for seventy years. She handed him a check for $5,000 made out to the Committee to Save St. Brigid. "Take it," she said. "You're going to need it. This is going to be a long fight."

Robert marveled at one thing: The concern was not about an archdiocesan cover-up but about a beloved church's closing.

In the weeks that followed, Robert staged similar impromptu news conferences in front of his law office downtown on California Street, on the steps of St. Brigid, and in front of the archbishop's residence. He quickly put together a legal challenge over the closure, which he filed in the Vatican's lower court, asserting misrepresentations about St. Brigid by the San Francisco archdiocese and self-serving maneuvering by some priests. The officials had not told the truth when they said St. Brigid was a weak parish, he contended. St. Brigid had twenty-one different parish groups and nearly three-quarters of a million dollars in its account. The church had not been undermined by the 1989 Loma Prieta earthquake, as the church officials in San Francisco stated. Robert had discovered that it was the San Francisco archdiocese itself that had gone to City Hall in December 1993 to voluntarily request that St. Brigid be listed as structurally unsound. An engineer told him that it was “highly unusual” for the owner of a building to do this, as it “creates a considerable financial hardship.” Robert believed the archdiocese had done this to justify the closure it had recently announced. He also asserted that the process leading to the closure order was unfair, “since no one from the church was told that closure was a possibility.” And finally he noted that one of the important priests advising the archbishop on which churches should be suppressed was the Reverend John K. Ring, head of the nearby St. Vincent de Paul—a block up from Union Street—who would only benefit from St. Brigid’s closure.

At every turn, Robert assured the parishioners that he was not engaged in a character assassination of the archbishop but was instead carefully constructing his case. Regardless, his antics and accusations were being closely followed by church officials.

8 *Resistance*

THE HEADLINE IN the liberal *National Catholic Reporter* newspaper landed at the San Francisco archdiocese with a thud: ST. BRIGID IS ON THE VERGE OF OPEN REBELLION.

Archbishop Quinn had never seen a public relations crusade quite like it. Nor had most of the country. The order to close a dozen churches in San Francisco had prompted other protests, but none at the level of St. Brigid’s. Quinn knew of the legal challenge that Robert Bryan had filed with the Vatican. And now, even worse, this attorney—not even a Catholic yet—was hurling scandalous allegations about priestly misconduct.

In announcing the church closures, Quinn had anticipated sorrow, maybe even some initial anger. But he never expected a revolt: not from priests across the city and not from the laity. He considered the suppression of these churches difficult but necessary. Fewer Catholics in the city meant less revenue for staff and programs. Nearly every Catholic church in San Francisco was more than fifty years old and filled with memories and sentiments. All of these old, sentimental churches had old, leaky roofs, old, faulty sewers, old, cracked floors or walls or something else old needing repair. Many churches had been damaged in the 1989 earthquake, and their repairs would cost in the tens of millions of dollars—somewhere between $60 million and $100 million, Wesolek had told him. When Quinn thought of St. Brigid Church, epicenter of the protests, he thought of a fading parish in a costly building. As one of his aides said, St. Brigid was a parish "of grandmas and grandpas."

Quinn had been in the city long enough to witness the erosion of its Catholic base. There was a demographic shift, coupled with the fact that San Francisco had fewer youth than any major city in the United States. And the city's large gay population was anathema to Church teachings. In his defense of the closures, Quinn told Vatican officials that the changing demographics were a "further indication that San Francisco is not a family city."

He had written to the parishioners whose churches were slated for closure: "As at the death of a loved one, something very dear is being taken away. I feel your pain."

The parishioners at most churches responded with understanding and obedience. And in a sign of the church officials' sensitivity, one closure order had already been reversed. St. Paul's Parish in the family-friendly Noe Valley had organized so well, and in such a conciliatory manner, that Wesolek had been among those agreeing the church had a future. As he said, "There is a difference between St. Paul's and St. Brigid's in terms of how they are objecting. At St. Paul's, there is a real sense of community, of everyone being involved. At St. Brigid, you think of Robert Bryan leading the charge. You think of certain personalities. St. Paul's is more of a community rather than individual stars."

However it was described, St. Brigid was the headache that wouldn't go away. Quinn wrote to the papal courts, saying that the new Committee to Save St. Brigid was leading a "duplicitous and vicious" public relations crusade. He called it a "small but vocal group fostering division in the parish.

"Mr. Bryan has chosen to argue his case publicly by means of appealing to the news media to sensationalize the situation at St. Brigid," Quinn went on to say.

To quell Bryan's allegations of sex abuse of an esteemed priest, Quinn sent another letter to the Vatican saying that his charges were unfounded and fabricated.

"Mr. Bryan has been employing a private investigator who has been examining the personal life and history of at least one priest of the archdiocese," Quinn wrote. "Needless to say, this action on Mr. Bryan's part has exemplified total disregard for the basic rights of the priest; it is a violation of his privacy and good reputation."

The archbishop was hearing from his top lieutenants about Bryan, and he had loyalists on the committee who shared details about the group and its efforts.

Wesolek remarked: "Bob Bryan is exceedingly naïve because he is thinking in terms of American jurisprudence, not canon law. He thinks he can prove that the closure of St. Brigid can't happen. But canon law will look at what procedures were followed. Bob Bryan is going to learn that it's not about the facts, but instead about whether procedure was followed." He concluded, "I don't think he knows what he's up against, but I will concede that he knows how to organize people."

Monsignor Harry Schlitt, director of development for the archdiocese, said, "The problem with Bryan is that he thinks he can treat the archbishop the same way he treats another lawyer in court. What we're dealing with here only comes from a very disgruntled group."

* * *

The nine steps leading to the ten-foot-high main door of St. Brigid were showing their age. Their edges were chipped. Pieces of chewed gum had lodged in cracks. The wax of skateboarders who buzzed the periphery at night had started to take hold. Someone had painted two red swastikas on the side of the church, and the upper door on the Van Ness side had been defaced with five large Xs keyed into the wood.

Early one Saturday morning, hours before the first Mass, a housepainter as tall and thin as one of his ladders left his home on Union Street and walked the three blocks to St. Brigid. He carried a fifty-pound commercial pressure washer, some Brillo pads, scrub brushes, soap, and cleaners, including his own mixture of baking soda and water. Arriving at the darkened church, he set the heavy washer down and made his way around the back of the building to the school and convent. The lights were on, so he knocked quietly until a nun peered out. Taking off his baseball cap, he explained he was a parishioner and just wanted to clean the steps of the church. He said he was doing it on his own time, to "care for the church."

The nun unlocked the door. She knew how the parishioners loved this church and were trying to save it. She told him he could use the hoses in the schoolyard anytime he needed.

He focused the washer first on the slate gray steps, then on the cracks in between. The hardened gum popped out, but the wax—a swampy, brownish green—was still there. He would need something stronger, probably a professional pressure washer with a heater that could steam the wax. "You can't use cold water to remove wax," he admonished himself, adjusting his baseball cap lower on his head. Still, he kept at it, stopping to scrub parts of the steps by hand, dipping into his tried-and-true baking soda mixture. Stepping back to the sidewalk to look at the church, he noticed new graffiti on one of the smaller main doors. Even in his wildest partying days, when his favorite type of communion was with Jack Daniel's, he could not have fathomed defacing a house of worship.

He returned to the steps. Working with his hands centered him. His twelve-year-old son and namesake would be with him the following weekend. He had spent the first few years of his son's life thinking pretty much only of himself. His brief marriage to a woman he met in high school and married when they were twenty-one had ended badly, and for several years he had seen his son maybe once a month. But when he reformed himself, he returned to court to change the custody agreement. Now his son was with him almost every weekend. They slept in the same room in his small flat, talking about hiking and camping and baseball. He had stuck glow-in-the-dark stars above his son's bed, so the two often fell asleep talking about the moon and the stars and imagining life on other planets. Or they would drift off while debating the talents of the players for the San Francisco Giants, his son's favorite baseball team.

The housepainter felt the porous stone of the steps, thinking about how others were marching and making signs. He wasn't much of a joiner or a talker, but he had his skills, and the church had its needs.

St. Brigid had given him hope and faith, mostly hope. Hope about the future. Hope perhaps that some of his sins would be absolved. Hope that his son would find faith too, faith that could see him through life's tough times. He owed this church.

After putting the hose back in the schoolyard, he paused on the front steps and said a silent prayer. He touched the cool stone on the side of the church. He would be back soon to do more.

9 *Intercession*

FATHER O HELD ALOFT St. Brigid's gold monstrance and set it down in the middle of the altar. The small shrine displayed the consecrated host, the body of Christ, and was the focal point of a novena that would bring the faithful together nine nights in a row to pray for the salvation of St. Brigid.

Father O knew that the novena, a ritual of public prayer and devotion as old as the Catholic Church itself, would not be viewed favorably by the archbishop. Members of the Committee to Save St. Brigid had been warned not to gather in the sanctuary to organize or plan.

The priest was well aware of the growing tension between the archdiocese and the committee and had heard Robert Bryan's accusations. He distanced himself from the allegations; while he disagreed with the closure decision, he would do nothing to attack the church. When he first heard the rumors about high-ranking priests, he was stunned. There had been reports of problems in Ireland, but those too were being denied by respected church leaders. He would wait until the stories were substantiated to respond. For now, his focus was on a parish that had no reason to be closed. He had told his flock that he would do anything for them that was "sensible and rational." There was nothing unreasonable about gathering to pray. In becoming a priest, he had pledged to be obedient to his superiors, not to sell his soul.

That night in late January, some eighty people joined Father O in the sanctuary. The mood was solemn and purposeful. The parishioners wore white towels over their shoulders. The opening hymn was "Come, Holy Ghost, Creator Blest." Rosaries were taken out of pockets and purses. The hushed church was filled with the soft hum of the repetitive prayer. When the parishioners received the Eucharist, they closed their eyes and asked that St. Brigid never close.

Father O said, "No one knows the outcome of this struggle and of our church. But if you have hope, and you have love, you don't let go. I do not see what we are doing as disobeying. How can it be disobedient to stand up for a church?"

Unlike the rallies and marches, there was no need for instruction here. These parishioners were seasoned in prayer.

They sang a hymn, "Immaculate Mary":

We pray for the church
Our true mother on earth
And beg you to watch
Over the land of our birth.

Lily Wong was there, as was Eleanor Dignan and her son, Joe. Father O was happy to see Joe. He wasn't a regular churchgoer, but the priest knew him to be a person of character, a person who was struggling in his faith. Joe appeared to have had a gilded youth, attending elite private schools and graduating from the University of California at Berkeley. But Father O knew some of the trouble that played out behind the Dignans' closed doors.

He also noticed something subtle happening tonight: The parishioners were sitting closer together. And instead of rushing home after the novena, they lingered in the pews.

The next night, the novena drew just as many parishioners. But when Father O went to the tabernacle, the monstrance wasn't there. It wasn't in the safe or at the altar. It was gone. Holding a novena without a monstrance was like serving communion without wafers. Father O could not conduct the prayers. In his mind, there could be only one explanation: The novena had been stopped by the archdiocese. He remembered Quinn's cold stare.

Father O left the sanctuary to question Daniel Keohane, the priest brought in by Archbishop Quinn to oversee the closure of St. Brigid. (Only days before, Father Hanson had left St. Brigid, citing stress.) Father O found the tall, dark-haired priest in the rectory and asked whether he was aware that the monstrance was missing. Keohane said yes. Father O asked whether he had called the police. Keohane said no. Father O went straight to the phone to summon the police, who arrived at the rectory door. A report was filed on the missing monstrance, but no one claimed responsibility.

* * *

A few days later, Father O was called to the phone at the rectory. Archbishop Quinn wanted to see him—immediately.

Father O's first thought was, *Oh, God, here goes.* He told Quinn's secretary that he had an important meeting with a parishioner that he wouldn't change. There was a long pause. The secretary finally said, "You've got to come."

Father O replied, "I have an appointment. Give me another time." He was put on hold. When the secretary returned, it was agreed that Father O would meet with the archbishop the next morning.

Father O had known this day was coming, but for the first time since becoming a priest, he felt deeply alone. For the first time, too, he was hit with a fear of the unknown. It was not out of the question that he would be removed from the archdiocese and sent to a priestly equivalent of Siberia. He might be allowed to remain a priest and hold on to his duties, but he knew that the archdiocese was perfectly capable of making a priest wish he were no longer a priest.

He stayed up late that night, thinking about his love of his church and his calling to the priesthood. The church of his youth, St. Augustine, had made him understand the spirit of a sanctuary. Right on the main street of Cork, the church was as spare as the town, poor in everything but spirit. It was open every day, and he and his classmates would spend afternoons there, playing table tennis and other games. He started as an altar server when he was seven. On Sundays, the austere stone building was warmed by bodies and joy.

Father O had questioned his calling to the priesthood only once, during his third year of the eight-year seminary program in Ireland. The twenty-year-old awoke one morning consumed with doubts about why he wanted to be a priest. He asked himself, What am I doing here? Do I really want to be ordained? He decided to skip classes that day and seek an answer in nature, in the library, and in the wisdom of an older priest. Finally, he went to the chapel. He told God he was uncertain about his future and asked for an answer in thirty minutes. Soon he began to feel a tremendous sense of peace. He believed that God was telling him to stop worrying.

As he dozed fitfully to sleep on this night, a sense of peace eluded him.

10 *Cooperation Was Expected*

FATHER O BUTTONED his jacket as he stepped into Quinn's office and took a seat across from him at a table. The archbishop, whose eyes sloped downward into his cheeks, was in his suit and collar and wore a large silver cross on a silver chain that ended at his waist. He was flanked on each side by bishops.

There was no small talk. The man of few words and a reserved demeanor, who relaxed by playing classical piano, wanted cooperation.

"Your first allegiance is to the archbishop," one bishop said. "You are a priest. You promised obedience."

The archbishop began by talking about how the archdiocese was facing the high costs of retrofitting old buildings. The City of San Francisco had mandated the upgrades but would provide no financing. Quinn also cited a decline in Mass attendance.

"The time has come to end all official or unofficial support for campaigns which criticize or seek to reverse the closure decision," he noted, instructing that parishioners had no right to "utilize churches, schools or auditoriums to oppose the church closures."

Father O nodded and listened. He was uncomfortable and sensed Quinn was as well. To Father O, retrofitting costs and attendance problems were not reasons enough to close sanctuaries.

Quinn handed Father O a letter. The priest could see it was

from the Vatican. He knew this was not a good sign. The room felt hot and confining. He concentrated on folding the letter carefully and placing it in his suit pocket. The archbishop suggested he read the letter immediately. The priest said he would read it and respond accordingly, but not under duress.

No one spoke.

Father O thanked the men and stood up. Before he reached the door, a bishop said that if he did not support the closure of St. Brigid, there would be ramifications—serious ones. The archbishop needed his answer immediately. The priest nodded and left.

Back in his room at the rectory, Father O poured himself a glass of Scotch. He felt he had no one to turn to. The stand he had taken put him at odds with all the other priests in the diocese; they refused even to sit next to him at events. Of the forty-one men who originally signed the letter of protest, all had publicly reversed their opposition after the meeting with Quinn. He was learning that priests didn't cross authority unless there was a consensus. He pulled the letter from the Vatican out of his pocket. It restated the reasons given by the archbishop—the seismic upgrade expenses, the declining number of parishioners, fewer men entering the priesthood—and said the closures were in the best interest of the Catholic Church. He was urged once again to back the archbishop's decision.

Father O went through the letter several times. One word, an unexpected one, kept playing through his mind: ridiculous. In his heart, he believed that what was happening to the parishioners did not represent the will of God. To him, the people of St. Brigid were right and the church leaders were wrong. All his life, he had been taught that the church is untouchable, sanctified. Now officials come along and say they are closing churches and the churches are no longer sacred? St. Brigid was more than bricks and mortar.

He tucked the letter into a drawer under the few books and

musical instruments he'd brought from Ireland. He would do his job until they forced him to stop.

"St. Brigid, from our analysis of all of the data, wasn't at the bottom of parishes," George Wesolek told Archbishop Quinn during a monthly briefing in the fourth-floor archdiocesan conference room. "But they are not a growth-oriented parish. It's not the family-focused place it once was."

In the briefings on the status of the closures, Quinn typically said little but listened attentively. Wesolek wasn't surprised, for he had had some experience with the laconic leader. On one occasion, the two had been seated together on a flight back from Guatemala, where they had visited a priest from the San Francisco diocese working in a village. It was a six-hour flight, and the archbishop said all of a few words from takeoff to landing. He spent his time reading and praying.

"We want the money from St. Brigid to go to a poor church, such as St. Boniface, in the heart of the Tenderloin, which needs seismic work," Wesolek said. "This is almost like triage to save certain churches." St. Boniface served the homeless, transients, and the city's working poor. Sacred Heart was in the mostly black Western Addition neighborhood.

In his patient, counselor's way, Wesolek—who had been a successful psychotherapist after leaving the priesthood—went back over one of the original considerations for closing churches.

"One serious discussion we had early on was, 'Do we just close churches that have unreinforced masonry buildings?' Do we say, 'You have six million dollars in bills and only two hundred people attending church'? That could have been very clean. But we decided we couldn't do that. A lot of poor parishes would've gone out of business. Think of St. Boniface and Sacred Heart. These are churches that are the anchor of survival for their community."

Wesolek also shared his thoughts about Father O. "We are in a perfect storm," he said. "Everything is hitting us at once—from the allegations by Robert Bryan and his protesters to Father O'Sullivan. I must say that I don't care for what Father O'Sullivan is doing. As a former priest, I can see how he would be attracted to stand by his parish, to take the side of his people. But from a church discipline point of view, he was assigned to the church. He needs to help with the program." He paused and added, "Father O'Sullivan is an obstacle."

Monsignor Schlitt was in agreement. "St. Brigid is a fading parish. It is, as I've said before, grandmas and grandpas there. It is run-down. It is going to take five million to seven million dollars to fix it. As far as Father O'Sullivan, the question is, do you practice obedience to the archbishop and his successor? Yes, of course. His first allegiance is to the archbishop. He is a priest who said he would obey. He didn't do that. He is sowing disunity."

It was dinner hour in the rectory when Father O heard a knock at the door. He had been in his room, with its tall ceilings and spare but lovely wood furnishings, packing his books, his pullovers and wool caps, and the instruments he'd brought from Cork, including his flute.

When he opened the door on Broadway, Father O was startled to see dozens of parishioners lining the steps and sidewalk. Everyone talked at once. The parishioners held signs: DON'T SEND OUR BELOVED FR. O'SULLIVAN AWAY and FR. O'SULLIVAN — BANISHED ON FEB. 17, 1994.

Mary Baynes, an Irish immigrant with two young children, called out, "You are the only one who has been on our side. You have been our strength." Moe Frix asked what she was supposed to tell her son, Alex, an eighth-grader at St. Brigid School. He was an altar server and had learned to play soccer with Father O. He loved being Catholic, largely because of the good-natured priest from Ireland. She wondered what message it would send to the schoolchildren when a priest was sent away for disagreeing with his bishop.

Siu-Mei Wong was distraught. "What are we supposed to do now, Father O?" she asked. "What can we do for you?"

Father O had been given twenty-four hours to leave St. Brigid. He was being reassigned to a church in South San Francisco. The archdiocese had ordered him not to talk to parishioners and not to return to St. Brigid.

Peering outside, he tried to calm the parishioners, to get them to turn around and go home.

They were not going anywhere.

Finally he closed the door behind him and made his way down the rectory steps. He felt their anxiety, felt his own heavy heart. He reassured them that everything would be fine.

"The committee has a motion of its own," Father O said. "It does not depend on one person. I know you will continue for St. Brigid. You must stand up for the truth, and be ready to take the heat. What I have done is merely part of being a priest. It has nothing to do with courage."

In time, after sharing hugs and consoling tears, Father O walked back up the steps. He gazed down at all the faces. In his flock he saw the spirit of fighters, the grace of saints.

Back inside, Father O sat at his desk. He had never wanted to be a priest in Ireland, telling his family and peers: "I want to go to America—it is the most progressive society." He remembered the day he received his first assignment as a priest. All he knew of San Francisco was that "it was somewhere in America. It was vibrant and modern. And it had a reputation of being friendly to the Irish."

The next morning, Father O left St. Brigid.

The archdiocese issued a statement: "Father O'Sullivan has had some personal difficulties accepting Archbishop Quinn's decision to close St. Brigid. One of the responsibilities of a pastor is to gently guide people to their new place of worship."

Heading to his new assignment, feeling his future uncertain, Father O was clear on one thing: The battle for St. Brigid was just beginning.

11 *A Final Warning*

ROBERT BRYAN STOOD at the front of St. Brigid, delivering a weekly committee update, when he spotted one of Archbishop Quinn's top lieutenants barreling toward him. He continued speaking, smiling even, as the short, stout figure drew near.

The week before, in mid-March, the archbishop had written to the fifteen hundred St. Brigid parishioners, ordering them to stop making "Save our church" announcements after Sunday Mass. He said Robert and the others were "using the sacred liturgy itself as a means to incite and encourage factions and divisions."

Robert had continued the announcements anyway. In a letter to Quinn, he wrote: "The parishioners have met and fully discussed your concern. With all respect for you, we have decided to continue with the announcements and meetings. Your resolve to terminate and suppress this 130-year-old parish is wrong and against the spirit of the Roman Catholic Church. Informing the parishioners of what is going on is essential to the ongoing appellate process. Any effort by the Archdiocese to interfere with these functions is an attempt to obstruct the appeal."

On this Sunday, Quinn's lieutenant, Father Thomas Merson, reached the altar, walked right up to Robert—and switched off the microphone. The loquacious attorney was rendered momentarily speechless. Robert saw his four-year-old daughter, Auda Mai, giggle.

Ending the silence, Renato Gallina, a retired surgeon looking elegant in a suit, sweater vest, and tie, stood up in his pew and shook his fist, saying, "Let him speak! For the love of God, let him speak!"

Soon, others began to chant: "Let him speak! Let him speak!"

Merson, startled, retreated to the back of the church. A beaming Robert motioned to the parishioners to quiet down. Without the microphone, he told them that it was important to take a moment to pay tribute to "our courageous Father O'Sullivan—who was banished for standing up to the powers that be." He said he had visited St. Brigid School after Father O's transfer and was saddened by the children's comments and questions.

"One student asked me what had happened to Father O," Robert said, making eye contact with Merson. "I asked this young boy what he thought had happened. He said that he and his friends wondered if they had done something wrong to bring it about. They considered Father O a friend. They were blaming themselves—like children of divorce."

Many of the parishioners turned to look back at Quinn's aide. One held up a sign: WE HAVE NO POLITICAL POWER OR CHURCH CANONICAL POWER, BUT WHAT WE HAVE IS WHAT HAS STOOD FOR CENTURIES—CHRISTIAN FAITH.

When word of the microphone imbroglio got back to the archdiocese, Quinn issued a final warning, saying that "if this behavior continues," St. Brigid would close months early.

Robert knew to pick his battles. He moved the announcements to the church steps.

Wearing a white towel draped over his navy blue suit, Robert prepared to approach St. Brigid's altar. It was Holy Saturday—the first Saturday in April—and Robert Bryan, the Baptist from the South, was about to become a Catholic.

There to greet him was the Reverend Daniel Keohane, the administrator brought in by Quinn to oversee the closure of the church. Robert and Keohane had clashed before, mostly over Robert's use of the church to deliver committee news. Before he reached the altar, he removed the towel. Keohane had asked him "not to wear the towel during the reception into the Church." He didn't want any disruptions on this night.

As part of the ceremony, a sacrament begun in the early days of the Church and intended to bestow grace, Keohane extended his hand over Robert and anointed the crown of his head with oil.

He made the sign of a cross and said, "Be sealed with the gift of the Holy Spirit."

Robert's path to religion had been full of stops and starts, belief and disbelief. When he was a child, church was something the family did, like saying grace before meals. By the time he was a teenager, he felt a distance from the church. He never understood how Christian leaders could preach the Golden Rule while remaining silent on things like racism. But when his father died unexpectedly right before Christmas when Robert was fifteen, he was comforted by the faith he had begun to reject, by a feeling that the soul lived on. Something always drew him back to believing. Then something would push him away.

On this day in April, as his wife and daughter looked on, Robert was confirmed as Catholic, but he felt no joy. The struggle for St. Brigid was anything but holy.

The next morning, Robert was standing outside the church before the first Mass on Easter Sunday, a day that was supposed to be about resurrection and hope. Feeling tired and groggy, he reviewed the committee updates he planned to deliver after all five Masses. He smiled at the writing on the back of the Easter program: "Father O, thank you and God bless you and keep you always." He hoped the program would find its way to the archdiocese. As he turned to go inside, he was jolted into alertness. A few feet away stood Archbishop Quinn, making a surprise visit to the church.

It appeared to Robert that Quinn, a small man with a strong jaw, dark eyebrows, and closely cropped hair, was looking up at the massive granite walls of the church. He ventured over and said, "It's sad that this church is going to be closed."

The archbishop responded that it was for the good of the Catholic Church.

Robert replied, "No, it's for the good of your bank account. You want the money." He then added, "Incidentally, I need to introduce myself. I'm Robert Bryan, head of the Committee to Save St. Brigid."

Without a word, the archbishop turned briskly and headed into the church, his black robe with a long fuchsia sash trailing behind him.

12 *A Meeting with the Archbishop*

After five months of calls, letters, cards, petitions, protests, and appeals, the Committee to Save St. Brigid had an appointment to meet with Archbishop Quinn. Twenty-one members of the committee were ushered into the conference room of the San Francisco archdiocese at 8 A.M. on Friday, April 8. Siu-Mei Wong remained outside to pray.

The archbishop, sitting at the end of a long table, was joined by six aides, including Wesolek. While taciturn, the archbishop was seasoned in confrontation—and at much higher levels than this. In the late 1970s and early '80s, as president of the United States Catholic Bishops, Quinn had taken a strong stand against the American policy in Central America, testifying before Congress and becoming highly disliked by the State Department. After the assassination of San Salvador's Archbishop Oscar Romero on March 24, 1980, Quinn attended his funeral Mass in El Salvador. The March 30 ceremony, which drew tens of thousands of mourners, ended in mayhem and bloodshed, as people—Quinn included—were fired at in the square and forced to flee for their lives.

Seated next to Quinn was Robert, who pulled a stack of papers from his briefcase. Some parishioners placed rosaries on the table. Others anxiously set handwritten notes before them. Because the group was so large, many sat in extra chairs placed around the edges of the room. The parishioners had brought family photos of happy times at St. Brigid they hoped to share.

John Ross, who had a legal notepad in front of him, was reassured by Robert before the meeting that he would not be confrontational. Ross expected Robert to show respect, but he was apprehensive. He had come to see Robert as the type of lawyer who would do anything to win a case, whose fighting instinct was in his marrow. Ross had told him, "I feel it's inappropriate to be confrontational with an archbishop regardless of how he came to his decision."

The introductions were short. Quinn avoided eye contact. Lily Wong tried to clasp the archbishop's hand, but he withdrew it.

Robert nonchalantly set a tape recorder in the middle of the table and began presenting the parishioners as he would star witnesses. One of Quinn's aides stopped him, saying the meeting could not be taped. Reluctantly, Robert agreed.

Gina Delle Sedie, whose family had attended St. Brigid for nearly seventy years, addressed the archbishop as "Your Excellency." Demure and elegantly dressed, she thanked him for the meeting and said her prayers were with him. She said that she and her brother had graduated from St. Brigid School. "What we learned in the classroom was enriched within the walls of the church," she said, reading from her notes. "The students learned to love their church from the priests and nuns. The preparation we received for the life of Catholicism was learned in the ultimate classroom—St. Brigid Church."

Robert watched and listened. These parishioners—these so-called grandmas and grandpas—had a way of coming through, making their case now before a man who was accustomed to having his ring kissed, accustomed to being called "His Excellency."

"Personally, my family and I always believed that St. Brigid would be there for us in joy and in sorrow," Delle Sedie continued. "It is our spiritual home. My dearest father's funeral Mass was this last year at St. Brigid. Who would ever imagine that the church may not be there for my beloved mother, Lucia Vivorio, a parishioner for over sixty-six years?" Her voice trembled.

Joe Dignan introduced himself as a third-generation parishioner and said that his daughter, Mary, had recently been baptized at St. Brigid. He said he had heard of the closure order through his mother, Eleanor, a "devout Catholic if there ever was one." He said that life without St. Brigid was unthinkable—like Christmas without "Hark, the Herald Angels Sing." He shared stories that made Quinn glance at the clock.

"As a child, I really looked forward to Mass ending," Joe said, prompting laughter from committee members. "I loved watching the old priest standing out there in the parking lot in his full robe and cap, directing traffic. I remember he was furious because parishioners were so inept in trying to exit the parking lot.

"But in all seriousness," Joe went on, "St. Brigid is a part of me. It is a part of all of us."

Ciaran and Mary Baynes, recent immigrants from Ireland, said the St. Brigid community had welcomed them. Their two young children were enrolled in the parochial school, and Mary worked in the school cafeteria. Ciaran, a roofer, was the star of the church's top-ranked men's soccer team.

"Archbishop, in a little over three months, we have collected nineteen thousand signatures of support for keeping St. Brigid open," Mary said. "*Nineteen thousand.*" She talked of St. Brigid's history: the church as a refuge after the 1906 earthquake; a meeting place during World War II; a sign of something transcendent to all who passed by. And she talked of the Irish settlers who built St. Brigid from a small one-room church on sand dunes to the magnificent structure it is today.

Nelly Echavarria, the feisty seamstress, stood up, adjusted her beret, and smoothed her dress. "It is hard for me to put into words what St. Brigid means to me," she began. "I have attended Mass at St. Brigid every day for twenty-seven years. I recently lost my mother, father, and sister. The thought of losing St. Brigid is too much for an old lady to take."

Finally, after several others talked of their love for St. Brigid and its personal and historical significance, Lily spoke. She remained seated in her black slacks and a blouse, her long black hair pulled into a loose bun. Her voice was cheerful and composed. She explained that her ten brothers and sisters, as well as her mother and father, had all converted from Buddhism to Catholicism thanks to the loving Irish Catholic nuns who came to Burma to teach in her village after World War II. She said their devotion was contagious.

"The nuns who taught us were very strong in their faith," Lily said. "They were greatly admired. They had to leave their families and country and come to this wild place in the jungle where we lived. They sacrificed so much. What we are asking is that you give us a chance to prove ourselves, to show our faith."

Speaking directly to the archbishop, Lily said that she liked to attend Mass at St. Brigid every day. "My vision is going," she said. "I will not be able to see anything at all for much longer. But I know the inside of St. Brigid like I know my home. I will lose my independence if St. Brigid is closed. At St. Brigid I stay for Bible classes and ladies sodality. And being at St. Brigid gives me the energy to go home and study the Old and New Testament—not an easy thing when you read Braille with one finger."

Lily could see Quinn in silhouette. He was not looking her way. Joe also was studying Quinn. As the members of the committee took turns speaking, Joe, who had a habit of scribbling phrases, observations, and little details on scraps of paper, noticed the archbishop adjusting his ring and repositioning his cufflinks. The archbishop picked up and set down a heavy Montblanc pen. Joe wondered if he sent some sort of signal to his team with that pen. He noticed when it was raised, another bishop who was speaking would quickly finish what he was saying. Joe tuned back in. An engineer hired by the archdiocese distributed a report describing the estimated costs of seismically strengthening St. Brigid. The engineer said it might be possible to come in between $3 million and $4 million.

Ciaran Baynes said, "It appears to me you have not done a complete analysis. It seems like the figures are a guessing game. This makes no sense."

Robert, quiet until now, took this as his cue. "Archbishop," he said, standing up, "we will raise the money ourselves to pay for that. Again, we are here to work with you."

Quinn was silent. Finally, he said that allowing the committee to raise the money would give the appearance that the archdiocese favored a wealthy parish over some of the poorer ones on the closure list.

Robert smiled. He had anticipated, rehearsed, and prepared. This was his case to win. It was time to sweeten the offer.

"We also have the financial means to help save another, less endowed church," he said. "All you need to do, Archbishop, is to select a church, and we will do the rest in coordination with the archdiocese. We will rescue two churches in the process, paying for St. Brigid and adopting another church."

Quinn's expression did not change. He said his decision to close St. Brigid was final. "It's possible that even Old St. Mary's could be closed," he said, insinuating that even the city's most hallowed church was vulnerable.

Father Robert McElroy, who was working closely with the archbishop and Wesolek on the closures, added, "We can't afford to keep all of these churches open in a city with too many churches."

Quinn then added, "I am not willing to go back and reopen the work of the commission."

Wesolek, taking it all in, considered it accommodating of the archbishop to be holding this meeting, considering the animosity that had been expressed. He knew the archbishop to be a brave and honorable man, but he didn't like the confrontational way Robert was treating him. In situations like this, Wesolek felt his background as both priest and psychotherapist helped him. As a therapist, he had learned the importance of listening and being sensitive, and not getting caught up in the emotions. In the world of psychotherapy, it was called countertransference, where you take on the issues of the person you are trying to help.

At ten-twenty, the archbishop stood to signal that the meeting was over. It had taken more than two hours. He made a move toward the door—only to have Robert stop him.

"Excuse me," Robert said, finishing a note to himself that read "Will the arch change his mind?" "We normally end our meetings in prayer. Would you join us in prayer? Please join hands with us."

John Ross cringed. *This cannot be happening,* he thought. A new Catholic, a lawyer from the South, trying to lead the archbishop in prayer?

"We are here to do the work of the Lord," Robert said. Ross shook his head.

The archbishop returned to the table. When he did not initiate a prayer, Lily offered to close.

"Grant me the gift of knowledge, so that I may know the things of God," she began. "Grant me the gift of fortitude, so that I may overcome courageously all the dangers of the world which threaten the salvation of my soul." The prayer lasted for several minutes.

Outside, after the meeting, Robert put his hand on Joe Dignan's shoulder and said incredulously, "We were offering to raise ten million to fifteen million dollars! What sane person rejects this? I really thought it would be impossible for Quinn to say no. Boy, was I wrong."

Joe nodded, but before he could respond, Robert went on, "I mean, it was a two-for-one. What shocks me is there was absolutely no reflection on their part. They didn't even give it a thought."

13 *Cracks in the Committee*

John Ross decided the time had come to take matters into his own hands. The Chevron attorney had heard enough from the lawyer from the South. He felt that everyone from St. Brigid wanted the same thing, but he at least had a very different idea about how to get there. Raised an Episcopalian, Ross had converted to Catholicism in 1992 when his wife, Janet, who was Catholic, said she wanted to get back into the church. Ross was fine with Catholicism; it made his wife happy. She had gotten involved in parish life and was responsible for starting up the RCIA program for adults interested in converting. Ross adopted parts of Catholicism and was unperturbed by the parts he disagreed with. The liturgy was similar to what he'd known in the Protestant Church, but he had already found the hierarchy and dogma far stronger in the Catholic tradition. Still, he believed in playing by the rules. He had worked his way up in his own career, always mindful of manners and seniority. But now, since Robert had hired his own investigator to track priests and had called press conferences without telling committee members, he felt more than justified in taking a stand.

Ross had told Judge Figone, who had also grown weary of Robert's grandstanding, "I was appalled when Robert made his 'work of the Lord' speech to Archbishop Quinn. We had agreed before the meeting that we would listen and not be confrontational, but Robert couldn't resist taking the opportunity to preach to the archbishop. I do not agree with him from a tactical standpoint."

On April 26, with Figone in agreement, Ross wrote a letter to the cardinal at the Congregation for the Clergy, the Vatican court weighing St. Brigid's appeal. Using the committee's letterhead, he wrote: "As happens when groups of people come together to pursue a common cause, there was a difference of opinion on how to achieve the common goal. Your Eminence should not let the failure of the Committee to act in the highest Christian standards as the justification to ignore the reasons why the parish should continue to live. That some have acted in a shameful manner should not be reason to deny the appeal." He sent the letter while Robert was out of town.

By April 29, Robert got wind of Ross's letter. Furious, he drafted a letter to Ross and Figone, accusing them of trying to derail the group's effort and leading with their egos.

Ross quickly fired back at Robert: "I have to respond to your statement that Richard and I are on an ego trip. You don't know either of us when you make this statement, and I think you have identified the wrong people who are on an ego trip."

Before long, everyone knew of the mounting tension. Siu-Mei, a natural peacemaker, sent off her own letter—to all three men: "All the parishioners in St. Brigid are fortunate to have each one of you on our side. You are all successful people in your career. Probably you always have the last say in every decision in your daily life. I can imagine that it would be difficult to work with people with the similar caliber as yourself. However, we are not competing in a business world to show who is doing the best or the most. I beg of all of you, please abandon your ego, accept opinions from each other, and try to work with each other." She added, "For this reason, my Rosary every night is devoted to the committee and to the unity and the harmony of our faith community."

But Figone and Ross, two of the earliest members of the resistance, had one more letter to send. They said they would support the cause of saving St. Brigid but would no longer belong to the committee. It was all Robert's now.

14 *A Trip to Rome*

ROBERT TRAVELED TO Rome on May 2, 1994, intent on meeting with the officials at the Vatican deciding the fate of St. Brigid. The committee's legal appeal rested before the Congregation for the Clergy, a branch—or dicastery—of the Catholic Church dealing with priests, catechetical teachings, and parish matters, including suppression orders and appeals.

Robert knew he was taking a chance; he didn't even have an appointment at the Vatican. The archdiocese had refused for months now to give him copies of any pleadings and exhibits they had filed with the congregation. To him, it was contrary to due process, where all such documents had to be served on opposing counsel. In a letter to the Reverend Gregory Ingels, a nationally known canon law expert representing the San Francisco archdiocese, he wrote: "Aside from any canonical law, the withholding of responsive pleadings from an opposing party is contrary to the very essence of due process, the Second Vatican Council, and Christianity." Ingels told Robert to redirect his queries to the congregation.

In a letter Robert found patronizing and pompous, Ingels wrote: "We are currently involved as contending parties in a formal canonical process, which is presided over by the Congregation for the Clergy. Hence, any decision to make public Archbishop Quinn's response to your petition must be made by the Congregation and not by the Archdiocese."

As soon as Robert arrived at his hotel in Rome, he began working the phones. He waited for two days before finally receiving a call from a clerk from the congregation. He was told that no one would be able to meet with him.

"I've come all the way from San Francisco," he said.

The answer was still no.

He informed the clerk that Archbishop Quinn of San Francisco had been in Rome less than three weeks earlier, and he had been granted a meeting with members of the congregation to discuss St. Brigid. Robert said Quinn had made the trip to squelch the mounting furor over his plans to close St. Brigid. He knew that Quinn had asked the congregation for a quick resolution to the appeals process. Robert had a copy of the eleven-page letter

Quinn had written to the congregation before his trip. (The letter had been leaked to the media.)

"He described our petition as 'filled with many distortions and inaccuracies,'" Robert said, "which is in and of itself distorted." He said he was in Rome to present his side and to see documents from the archdiocese. "In any court of law, that is only fair," he said.

"The situation is very delicate," the clerk told Robert, suggesting he return to San Francisco and not "endanger the case."

Robert was dumbfounded. There he was, a few miles from the congregation's office on Piazza Pio, only to be told that he couldn't meet with anyone to discuss St. Brigid. Nor would he be allowed to see any of the pleadings from the San Francisco archdiocese.

In all his legal experience, he had never known anything like the Vatican courts, where many of the documents had to be submitted in Latin and a Vatican attorney would have to be hired to represent the St. Brigid committee. Dealing with the Congregation for the Clergy—established by Pius IV and instituted in 1564—felt Byzantine and mysterious. Commonly called the Sacred Congregation of the Council, it had been set up, Robert had learned, to interpret the norms issued by the Concilium Tridentinum, the sixteenth-century ecumenical council of the Catholic Church that issued decrees on everything from original sin and justification to extreme unction, cults, and indulgences.

Walking around Vatican City, Robert marveled, too, at the walled city-state of the Roman Catholic Church. It had its own currency, stamps, flag, police, and bank—complete with an ATM machine with instructions in Latin. It owned some of the world's most valuable art, from Bernini and Botticelli to Michelangelo and Raphael. Its monarch, the pope, was elected for life in a secret ceremony held in the Sistine Chapel and culminated with the burning of ballots and the release of white smoke from a chimney. And the pope was never in error—he had papal infallibility—

when issuing decrees and teachings from the throne of Saint Peter. This opponent was unlike any other.

After three more days of calling the congregation and showing up at the clerk's office, Robert left Rome, angry—and empty-handed.

Being shut out of anything was about as comfortable to the litigator as wearing a wool suit on a steamy southern day. But experience had taught him that appeals were often won or lost in the final hours and that new evidence could emerge at any time to change the fate of a case.

Back in San Francisco, word of his unsuccessful visit spread through the archdiocese. George Wesolek marveled at Bryan's energy but told a colleague: "This case is about whether we followed procedure. It's not about the facts. Bob Bryan doesn't yet understand that. He is looking at this through a different lens."

Chuckling to himself, Wesolek pictured Bryan charging the steps of the Vatican. With a billion people in the Catholic Church, the attorney from San Francisco still expected to be heard. He didn't consider that maybe the Church had bigger things to think about than one heated parish protest thousands of miles away.

On May 25, 1994, San Francisco police made an announcement: Monsignor Patrick J. O'Shea, one of the highest-ranking priests around, who once headed the diocese's altar boys program and who was well known within the archdiocese and a confidant and friend of Archbishop Quinn's, was under investigation for molesting young boys and teenagers over a period of nearly twenty years. He was alleged to have taken altar boys on weekend trips to Napa, where he let them water-ski and drive his sports car, and offered them booze and boat rides. One former altar boy told the police he had confided to Catholic officials that he had been molested, only to be told, "It's been taken care of." Not long after, the victim learned O'Shea had been named a monsignor. In addition, the police were investigating allegations that O'Shea had misappropriated funds of parishioners and church groups for his vacation home near Palm Springs.

And there was more. Yet another high-ranking priest, the Reverend Martin Greenlaw, also a member of the archbishop's inner circle, was under investigation for allegedly embezzling hundreds of thousands of dollars from Church coffers. Parishioners had tipped off the police years before to the pastor's questionable spending habits and lifestyle, only to hear archdiocesan officials insist Greenlaw had done nothing wrong. Quinn even moved him from his parish and put him in charge of the archdiocese's Propagation of the Faith Office, which raised money to support Catholic missions—a move one community member called, "Putting the fox in charge of the henhouse."

As the police conducted their probe of Greenlaw and at least two other priests, law enforcement sources were quoted as saying they were shocked by the loose accounting procedures of the archdiocese, which had taken in $32 million the previous year from parishes in San Francisco, San Mateo, and Marin counties.

For Wesolek and other officials at the archdiocese, it was the worst possible timing. Similar reports of misconduct were beginning to surface elsewhere. In Ireland, there was talk of problems at church-run residential schools. In Germany, issues were being raised at certain Catholic boarding schools. While nothing was proven and rumors were emphatically denied by respected church leaders, Wesolek felt concern for the morale of priests. He also was thinking about what all of it—church closures, alleged bad priests—would mean for people's faith. And, as a former priest, as someone who had always revered the good fathers, he simply could not believe it was true. These reports had to be anomalies, isolated cases representing problems in a few parishes.

But for Robert, the news served as validation for his decision to hire an investigator to monitor priests—including O'Shea and

Greenlaw—and confirmation of his hunch that more was at play than demographics and retrofitting in the sudden need to close churches.

15 *Not a Fading Parish*

On a Saturday in late May, the St. Brigid men's soccer team, intent on showing the archdiocese that theirs was not a fading parish, charged onto the field at the University of San Francisco's Negoesco Stadium for the Catholic league's championship game. The St. Brigid Mariners were facing their archrival in the city's competitive adult Catholic league. There was no prayer, but the determination was fierce.

St. Brigid was to be shuttered in a matter of weeks.

There to greet them on the field was their coach, Father O. The Irish priest who had been banished from St. Brigid had not gone far. His parish now was just across the bay, in Marin County, but his heart remained with St. Brigid. He had founded the men's soccer team in 1991, a year after arriving at the parish. In Ireland, as in many countries across Europe, sports were another form of ministry, and the men watched out for one another like a close-knit clan.

Father O pulled his fisherman's cap low. He stalked the sidelines, his baggy pants touching the trodden grass. He had watched as his scrappy team practiced, rain or shine, and as they went from underdogs to contenders. He didn't believe in putting time into sports to lose. And, like his players, Father O relished the idea of having the league's winning team representing a supposedly failing church.

Since his transfer from St. Brigid, Father O knew he was being watched. His mail was opened. His schedule was monitored as he came and went. Archbishop Quinn had warned him, "I direct you to have no further contact with the parishioners at St. Brigid or to involve yourself in any manner with any activities associated with the parish. Should you fail to abide by this directive, it will become necessary for me to impose a canonical censure and to suspend you from all priestly ministry."

They were serious words that Father O weighed carefully but ultimately could not live with.

His belongings were in storage in the basement of the Mission San Rafael, where he had been sent after a brief stay at the South San Francisco parish. He hadn't bothered to unpack; the new parish was not his home.

Cupping his hands around his mouth, he barked orders to his team. Here, he wasn't called Father O'Sullivan or even Father O. He was Cyril—and he was inured to the expletives and language of the field.

Siu-Mei was there, taking pictures for the team and for the scrapbook she kept, and handing out towels and words of encouragement. Dozens of St. Brigid parishioners filled the sidelines, jumping and cringing and cheering for their field warriors. Children, teachers, parents, and even the nuns from the school were there.

The St. Brigid Mariners zigzagged across the grass in their yellow and blue uniforms. The Holy Name Panthers, who had a reputation for playing hard and not always fair, wore red and white. The opening goal by St. Brigid was a dramatic diving header by Ciaran Baynes, the team captain and the roofer who served as treasurer of the Committee to Save St. Brigid.

The crowd went wild.

The Mariners pulled off a one-point victory in overtime and celebrated at an Irish pub near St. Brigid. Over pints of Guinness, one of the Mariners sat on a barstool as his teammates shaved his head bare; he had agreed to the bet before the game. The next morning the team, led by Baynes, carried the gleaming trophy into Mass.

16 *Intimate Reflections*

Joe Dignan sat quietly inside St. Brigid. It was a weekday afternoon, and he was alone in the sanctuary, with its cool air and prism light, in the pew of his youth.

When he thought back to Sundays at St. Brigid, he could sense his mother's warm hand, could feel the scratchy wool of her suit. He could hear her listening to the church organ and exclaiming, "Isn't the music just magnificent?" Sometimes she called it "marvelous" without ever pronouncing the *r*. And he could hear her admonishments: "If you don't stop fidgeting, I just don't know what I'm going to do."

His ties to the church spanned generations. His grandmother, Julia Posades, was married there. His father, Joseph John Dignan, was baptized there. His mother attended Mass weekly. He had been baptized at St. Brigid, as had Mary—by Father O. Yet he had a stronger history of distancing himself from the church, of making fun of what others took so seriously.

In catechism class as a child, he eschewed a devotional song and instead parroted a satirical ditty by Tom Lehrer called "The Vatican Rag." The nuns informed Eleanor, and Eleanor informed her husband, that little Joe had sung something blasphemous. It soon became official: Joe was flunked out of catechism class, one of the few children at St. Brigid to own that distinction.

But somehow, after all these years, the old church pulled on him, a magnet of stone and sentimentality.

As he sat in the dark wood pew on that spring day in May, his gaze was drawn out of habit to the arch above the altar inscribed with the names of saints. He remembered reading the names aloud until he was hushed by his mother. When he had learned as a boy that these saints often died horrible deaths, he was even more mesmerized. There was Joan of Arc, burned at the stake.

There was Saint Stephen, stoned to death. There was Saint James, the son of Alphaeus, beaten to death. They filled his imagination. They were his warriors, his toy soldiers.

Catholicism, with its bloody history, elaborate traditions, and loving gestures, was all Joe knew. He had been taught when to stand and when to kneel. He had been told to respect his priests, who walked like shadows in their dark clothes with drawn expressions. His mother had said these were perfect men.

Now the world was learning for the first time that these were not perfect men. Priests—these icons of the transcendent—were being charged with the evilest of deeds, with harming the most innocent among them. Over the weekend, Joe and Eleanor had watched a tape of *60 Minutes* devoted to the outright denial and apparent cover-up of sex abuse cases by the Catholic Church. In the episode, Mike Wallace reported that Archbishop Robert Sanchez of Santa Fe, New Mexico, had known about pedophile priests for years but had done nothing to stop them; in fact, he had been sexually active himself—only in his case with young women. The Catholic Church officials said the alleged victims had "made it up." Eleanor had reacted by saying the Catholic Church was right. It was simply impossible, she said.

Looking around the sanctuary, Joe wondered what would happen to the faith of his mother, to the faith of so many—including new friends like Siu-Mei Wong, surely the sweetest person he had ever met, who was fast becoming someone he turned to—if the doors were closed for good.

Joe drew back his bicycle glove to check his watch. He had a meeting with an engineer hired by the committee to do an independent analysis on the retrofitting costs, given the fluctuation in estimates cited by the archdiocese.

As a theater and lighting manager, Joe was surprised that he enjoyed working for the committee. He considered himself a hanger-on, but he was writing the weekly newsletter and overseeing the engineering report. The committee meetings gave him the comfort of routine, a sense of belonging. Not because he felt he fit in. He didn't. This was not his tribe. He belonged because there was a shared purpose. And he didn't mind a reason to be away from home. His marriage was troubled at best, and he was squarely to blame. For many years, he had hidden his true self from his family and friends. The truth was ugly: He was having affairs that he didn't understand and that filled him with shame. Any affair was bad; his, he knew, were worse.

Walking down the center aisle of the church, Joe noticed some of the ladies from the committee who came daily to pray. He envied the simplicity of their faith. They lit candles. They circled the church in prayer. They collected donations in a coffee can.

Before leaving, he stopped by the pale gray baptismal font. Made of Italian marble and purchased in 1909 for $9,000, it was the gift of Alice Phelan Sullivan, a member of one of the city's founding families. Joe turned and looked at the heavy wooden door of the confessional, which had terrified him in his youth. When forced to go to confession, he was instructed to wait for the light before beginning. When it went on, young Joe quickly mumbled, "Father, forgive me, for I have sinned." Then he began with the Nicene Creed, saying, "I believe in God, the Father Almighty . . ." He stopped. He couldn't remember the rest. The priest urged him to continue and helped him along for a few lines. Joe forgot again. Finally the priest bellowed, "You are very bad. Memorize your lines and come back." Joe fled from the booth.

These days, Joe needed to have a conversation with God more than ever. But he didn't know where to begin.

In late June, Robert Bryan faced an anxious crowd in the packed auditorium of St. Brigid School. The parishioners now had less than two weeks to save St. Brigid.

Robert took off his jacket, loosened his tie, and rolled up his sleeves. He held up a sign: GOD PUT ME ON EARTH TO ACCOMPLISH A CERTAIN NUMBER OF THINGS. RIGHT NOW I AM SO

FAR BEHIND I WILL NEVER DIE. Turning serious, he said he still hadn't heard anything from the Vatican about the committee's appeal. He had collected 1,068 signed affidavits attesting to the importance of St. Brigid. He said he planned to file a motion asking the Vatican to keep St. Brigid open while the appeal was being decided. He said it was time to gear up to fight harder, to get the Vatican to understand St. Brigid's rich past and promising future.

Robert was continuing to press his case in the media, making daily calls and sending a flurry of faxes to reporters at newspapers, magazines, and radio and television stations. He was publicly calling for Archbishop Quinn's resignation and sending unabashed letters to Rome, asserting, "The level of corruption in the San Francisco Archdiocese is astounding. There are profound and far-reaching problems in the leadership, including mismanagement, financial and moral corruption among some priests, and a callous disregard for the needs of the faithful." In a letter to His Eminence Bernardin Cardinal Gantin, prefect of the Congregation for the Bishops, Robert wrote about new revelations in the *San Francisco Examiner* of criminal wrongdoing by priests. Top-of-the-fold headlines announced: CHURCH PAYS $500,000 IN 'ALLEGED' SEX ABUSE CASES, MOLEST CHARGES AGAINST S.F. PRIEST, and MONSIGNOR CHARGED WITH MOLESTING ALTAR BOYS. He informed the cardinal of the case involving Reverend Greenlaw, now accused of stealing more than $600,000 from Catholics in a blue-collar community who had given despite their personal hardships. He wrote that Greenlaw had served as director of the San Francisco Society of the Propagation of the Faith, a position previously held by none other than Monsignor Patrick O'Shea, now jailed on multiple counts of child molestation. He noted that Archbishop Quinn's original response to allegations of problems with Greenlaw was a statement: "An internal review was made, and there was no evidence that indicated misappropriation of funds." He further informed the cardinal that nine men had filed a lawsuit against the archbishop, alleging he had done nothing to prevent priestly abuse and had tried to cover up past cases.

In his defense of O'Shea, Quinn had referred to his "good reputation." And in his own defense, he told officials at the Vatican that the allegations against him were coming from a "tabloid evening newspaper filled with lies and allegations against me and the Archdiocese. The [San Francisco] Examiner has consistently attacked the Pope and the teaching of the Church, especially the moral teaching. This paper is virulently anti-Catholic."

Robert sent letters to the Vatican in English, Latin, and Italian. In Italian, he signed off with "*Sinceramente in Cristo, Robert Bryan, Capo, Comitato Per Salvare la Chiesa di Santa Brigida.*" In many of his missives, he wrote: "The pope might want to take a look" at what's happening in San Francisco. He continued to write to Reverend Ingels, the canon lawyer for the archdiocese, who continued to deny his requests for information.

Pledges of support poured in. The actor Gregory Peck, whose mother had attended St. Brigid, lent his name, saying, "I do this in the memory of my mother." Blue and white campaign-style signs reading SAVE ST. BRIGID were posted in the windows of homes and businesses around the city. Nelly Echavarria plastered the windows of her sewing shop with pictures of the church. All-night vigils were held, beginning after Saturday night Mass and continuing until Mass on Sunday. Many of the vigils were led by the elderly—those grandmas and grandpas—who were proving more tireless than anyone could have imagined. Prayer groups were formed. Ads were placed in local papers: "Our 130-year old parish needs your help! We are on appeal to Rome. Visit our beautiful church." The parishioners prayed to all of the saints they could think of, particularly Saint Jude, patron saint of hopeless causes.

"This is the most important period in the history of this venerable parish," Robert told the crowd in the school auditorium, echoing the words written by Father Hanson in his appeal in early

January. Then, addressing something most parishioners had not had time to consider, he said, "Even though our prayers are for an early victory, we may need to continue to fight after the church is closed. We must be prepared not to give up." He talked of a similar case in Chicago, where parishioners protesting a closure lost their case before the Congregation for the Clergy but won on appeal to the Supreme Tribunal of the Apostolic Signatura—the Vatican's highest appellate avenue. "We will continue the good fight, for as long as it takes," Robert said. "We will continue to oppose the medieval way in which these closings are being handled. We have seven hundred thousand dollars in our parish bank account. At midnight on June 30, that money—our money—goes to Archbishop John Quinn."

Robert recounted a recent radio interview he had heard, in which Quinn had expressed confidence that the Vatican would uphold his closure decree. "Quinn said that the Congregation for the Clergy is familiar with parishes protesting closures. He said that seven years ago, the pope suppressed a hundred parishes in Italy in one day. Our archbishop also said that he wasn't at all moved by the level of protests in San Francisco. His words were, 'When a doctor tells a patient he has to have his leg amputated, he doesn't expect a party.'"

Lily Wong stood close to Robert. She always took her place next to him, quiet and prayerful, holding his arm. For the first time since the closure was announced, she felt something other than optimism; she couldn't escape a tinge of melancholy. She had been confident that good would prevail, but something had changed for her after Robert returned from Rome empty-handed. In her mind, it didn't bode well that the clergymen at the Vatican didn't have the courtesy even to see him. He had flown thousands of miles. He represented a group of devoted Catholics. He had spent hundreds of hours on a heartfelt, well-informed, and cogently presented legal appeal. The parishioners had collected nearly twenty thousand signatures of support. All they wanted was to save a church and, in their minds, to protect their faith. For the Vatican officials to refuse to listen reminded her of the socialism she had fled in Burma.

After the meeting, Lily made her way home. Friends offered to give her a ride. But even though her vision was dimming by the day, she insisted on walking alone. She was clinging to her independence as long as she could.

17 *Trying Times*

DRIVING FROM SONOMA to San Francisco one morning in late June, George Wesolek listened to his daughter Noelle chatting away, pausing occasionally to sing along to songs on the radio. Living in a household with four girls and his wife, he was accustomed to everyone's talking at once and all the time. His daughters were a welcome distraction from the stresses at work.

"Hey, Daddy, look!" said eight-year-old Noelle, pointing from the back seat. "Look at that bumper sticker!" They were slowed in traffic on the long span of the Golden Gate Bridge. Wesolek scanned the nearby cars.

"Where, honey?" he asked.

"There! There! The red car!"

Wesolek spotted it: a car with a SAVE ST. BRIGID sticker.

"Those are the people who are really mad at you, right?" Noelle asked in her chipper voice.

"Yep, sweetheart, they are mad at me," Wesolek said, smiling into the rearview mirror. "They think I'm a bad guy."

"You're not a bad guy!" Noelle said.

"You're right, I'm not. But in this case I look like one to some. Do you want me to explain it to you?"

"Sure," she said.

"The closing of a church is to many people a really difficult thing," he said, as cars inched toward the toll booth. "People are losing something they love. So there is sadness and anger and all of these emotions. And, you don't know this yet, but the Catholic Church and the Catholic people are not really great about change. They like their traditions, their way of doing things. To have change in the Catholic Church takes one hundred or two hundred years. So this is a tough time, and yes, people have been upset and emotional. I'm in charge of the churches being closed, so I'm being blamed. It's not that much fun for me."

Noelle seemed satisfied and returned to her chatter. She was a funny one, Wesolek thought. They could never get in the car to go anywhere without her asking if they had enough gas to reach their destination.

On their way to her school, Wesolek passed by St. Brigid. As always, there were parishioners out front toting signs and bullhorns. And as always, flowers lined the steps.

It was now only days before the churches were to be shuttered. News stories containing scandalous revelations about O'Shea and Greenlaw were appearing weekly. When Wesolek picked up the paper or turned on the television, he wondered who would be named next. One of the latest scandals involved the botched extradition in Ireland of a notorious pedophile priest, Brendan Smyth. It was clear that the public had begun to link the sex abuse and fraud scandals with the impending closures. The priests' morale was at an all-time low. He remained in disbelief about O'Shea, whom he had seen around the chancery for years, and couldn't reconcile that this same man was being charged with decades of abuse. O'Shea even looked the part of a monsignor: tall, elegant, silver-haired. Wesolek talked with clergymen who said they now feared even to venture onto a playground. They feared holding closed-door counseling sessions. Even the unflappable Archbishop Quinn appeared tense these days, his hallmark peaceful expression gone.

Pulling over briefly, Wesolek saw the nuns receiving the children in the schoolyard behind the church. He smiled at a memory. He was in sixth grade in Owosso when Sister Mary Immaculate came up to him from behind and said she wanted to speak to him. He knew she was approaching because nuns had this particular smell, clean and unperfumed. She whispered in his ear: "You ought to think about the seminary." He was surprised by her words. He'd always been a troublemaker at school, getting ignominious pink slips from the principal's office. Only a month earlier, he had been hauled into the front office after yanking the wimple off a nun's face. When his parents arrived, he was asked why he had done it. He shrugged and said, "I wanted to see what was underneath."

But over the next few years, young George began to think about Sister Mary's words. And in eighth grade, after starting a snowball fight with icy snow, he was again called to the front office and again met by his stern parents. This time he was told he was going to jeopardize his chance of getting into any seminary if his unruly behavior continued.

Pulling away from the curb, Wesolek understood. Faith was not logical, but once it settled in, it was hard to shake.

18 *Cast Out*

About a thousand parishioners, many with white towels draped over their shoulders, slowly took their seats in St. Brigid. Some clutched handkerchiefs. Some took pictures. They were all dressed for Mass, although it was a Thursday, not a Sunday.

In the back of the church, under the choir loft and stained-glass windows, uniformed police officers stood their ground—a precautionary move by the archdiocese in case the parishioners refused to leave after the Mass.

Everyone was there. Near the front was Lorraine Kelley, her fine silver hair swept into a loose bun. She held her husband's hand and looked at the altar where they had married a half-century earlier. Sitting alone in the fifth row was Cleo Donovan. It had been three years and eight days since her daughter Leslie's death. Her daughter's spirit was in this pew.

Joe Dignan and his mother, Eleanor, sat near the front. Joe's father had not attended church for years. He was another one who certainly needed to be at Mass, Joe thought. He fidgeted and looked around at the windows depicting the life of Jesus, Mary, and Saint Brigid, patroness of the church and the greatest of Ireland's women saints. He looked at the fourteen stations of the cross, representing the final hours of Jesus. He looked up at the soaring ceiling and back at the choir loft. He caught the eye of parishioners he had gotten to know and nodded at his friend Siu-Mei.

Nearby, Lily was filled with questions—not about her faith but about the Catholic Church. Priests were supposed to embody God, to comfort, heal, and inspire. Yet all she felt, for the first time since she had fallen for Catholicism, was disappointment. The priests seemed to be ignoring parishioners and defending their own. Even Pope John Paul was dismissing allegations of pedophilia as an attack on the Church by its enemies.

Robert was in his customary pew on the left side of the church, about halfway to the altar. Despite a months-long barrage of motions, letters, and vigils, there had been only silence from the Vatican. In June alone, he had filed four pleadings. He had been certain that he would at least get a response to his most recent request—for a last-minute stay. But still no word. Nothing.

St. Brigid Church was scheduled to close in a matter of hours—at midnight on June 30, 1994—after more than a century of service.

From the pulpit, his expression serious, his tone somber, Father Keohane said, "Although tonight we may disperse in sadness and go home in suffering and pain, we know inside there is a sense of God. There is a sense of faith. There is a sense of believing. It must be those sentiments that rise to the surface of our lives, that rise to become our strength and courage. Despite all the challenges of this world, despite all the things that seem to take us away from God, we somehow remain a people of faith."

Cameras flashed. There was the sound of crying.

Keohane continued: "Though this may be a time for us to say good-bye and we may not meet here again in this place, it may also be a time to carry forth the good faith and courage that is the people of St. Brigid."

After the Eucharist, Keohane left the sanctuary through a door behind the marble altar. His altar servers trailed behind.

In the pews, the parishioners remained seated. They were not about to leave. They had until midnight.

Robert smoothed his tie as he approached the altar. He gestured toward Louisa Stanton, wearing her trademark robin's-egg-blue hat and matching jacket. "She is eighty-eight years old and first came to St. Brigid seventy years ago," he said. "She lives across the street. She coined a phrase, one I'd never heard, that we are treated by the archdiocese as 'throwaway Catholics.'" His voice rising, he thundered, "Louisa, you are not a throwaway Catholic. No one here is a throwaway Catholic."

He removed the white towel draped over the shoulder of his navy blue suit and held it high, as Father O had done in the same place seven months earlier. "The closing of this church is a sin against the good men and women who are here tonight," he said. "The archdiocese tells us that this is our last Mass. I do not believe that. I will not believe that. We will prevail. We will be returned to this church, one day, somehow."

A man playing highland bagpipes walked up and down the aisles. At Robert's urging, the parishioners approached the altar to share their memories. They talked of baptisms, burials, and weddings. They spoke of finding joy and solace at St. Brigid. They talked of moments that soothed the soul.

Guido and Mary Alacia, both eighty, talked about how all the Italian families in the neighborhood would gather at the corner of Union Street and Van Ness and walk to St. Brigid together. They said their children were baptized at St. Brigid. Mary's sister, who was eighty-eight, was the last person to be buried from St. Brigid.

"Children from the neighborhood would sit in rows one through five, boys on one side, girls on another," Mary said, holding a gold charm of the guardian for the Genoese. "If you didn't go to Mass, you'd have to have a note for your priest explaining why. It would be the grand inquisition." Smiling, she continued, "It seemed like I grew up with this church. As it changed, I changed. I seemed to add to my life as the church grew and expanded."

Her husband, holding a rosary blessed by Pope Pius XII at Christmas in 1944, added, "We'd get all dressed up for Mass. Women wore dresses, hats, and gloves, and men wore suits and hats. Of course, during the Depression, you were lucky if you had a suit."

Before leaving, Mary looked at the many familiar faces. "We socialized here. St. Brigid was always our lives. It was the home of our faith. We just felt this church belonged to us."

Shortly after 11 P.M., the crowd filed out of the church. Robert joined them. Many parishioners paused in the tall, arched doorway to look back one more time, to inhale the memories, like a family forced to leave a cherished home. They lined the church steps, lighting dozens of small white candles.

Helen and Tillie Piscevich remained inside. They wanted to pray one more time to their saints, Helen to Saint Anthony and Tillie to the Virgin Mother. When Tillie approached her statue, she noticed something different. Stepping back, she studied it until she realized that the long string of rosary beads around the Virgin Mother's neck was turned around. Tillie had never seen the cross facing inward. She motioned to Helen, pointing to the statue.

"It's a sign," she said. "I'm going to take it and keep it safe." She told her sister she had been thinking about this for weeks now. When St. Brigid reopened, she would return the rosary. She would simply be safeguarding the necklace. Helen looked around the church. She knew what the statue and rosary meant to her sister; it was her talisman and confidant. But she told Tillie, "We can't take church property—even if it's what parishioners paid for. It is not right."

Tillie looked at the statue. Reluctantly, she conceded to her sister. The two walked slowly out of their church and down the steps. Tillie shook her head. "I think I should have taken it," she said.

Nearby, the parishioners were using white chalk to scrawl messages on the sidewalk: "Archbishop Quinn, we are your people. Why have you abandoned us?" "Save this part of San Francisco history." "Is this what Catholicism is all about?"

Robert Head, the pipe fitter and welder, rhapsodized about the artistry of the church, particularly the woodworking of the pews and the pulpit.

Lorraine Dietz, a lifelong Catholic, had decided that she would begin attending Grace Cathedral, an Episcopal church on Nob Hill. She didn't know whether she would call herself a Catholic again.

Glenn Corino, the athletic director at the school, announced that he had stopped putting money into the collection basket, but he promised that when St. Brigid reopened, he would compute the number of Masses missed and make a large contribution.

Louisa Stanton said, "When I came to St. Brigid, I felt like the weight of the world was lifted off of my shoulders. Now, I fear I am finished."

Father Keohane had ventured outside several times to watch the parishioners. He was touched by what he saw, by how they simply wanted to be with their church until the last possible moment. His assignment at St. Brigid had been difficult, and it was about to get tougher. Soon he would be closing—and locking—the doors. As the clock approached midnight, he could feel the parishioners' conviction that this was not the end for St. Brigid. He listened to them sing a dozen songs, concluding with the civil rights anthem:

> We shall overcome,
> We shall overcome,
> We shall overcome some day.
> Oh, deep in my heart,
> I do believe,
> We shall overcome some day.

As the singing ended, another sound began. To everyone's astonishment, after decades of silence, St. Brigid's enormous, weighty bell high in the tower began to ring. It started slowly, screeching through years of rust. Then it picked up speed and power until it rang with the force of a baritone. To those below, it sounded part death knell, part call to arms.

The parishioners held their candles up to the midnight sky. They couldn't make out the figure in the dark tower. For tonight it would remain a mystery.

Across the San Francisco bay, Father O sat on his bed in the rectory. He had not attended the final Mass, but it was all he thought about. It was now well past midnight, and he was alone, a candle lit. He had watched the clock, feeling the parishioners' hope and grief. He had pictured the closing of the heavy doors. He blew out the candle and said a prayer for St. Brigid and its people.

PART II

SUFFERING

Evil brings men together.

— ARISTOTLE

19 *Out in the Cold*

IT WAS EARLY EVENING in late August 1994. The summer fog had arrived, cold and dense, settling in like a shadow over the buildings, softening in color and texture as it reached the sky. Underfoot, the slate gray steps of St. Brigid Church felt slippery, both from the moisture and from the wax of the skateboarders who circled the dark building at night.

Blankets were handed out. The parishioners huddled together. It was the weekly meeting of the Committee to Save St. Brigid. The church had been closed for two months, and the parishioners without a parish had nowhere to meet except the front steps. A padlock hung on the door.

On this typical San Francisco summer night, Robert Bryan struggled to be heard above the diesel buses, motorcycles, and commuter traffic barreling along busy Van Ness Avenue. His pale, freckled skin pink from the cold air, he withdrew papers from his briefcase. As everyone had surely heard, he said, the committee had lost its appeal to the Congregation for the Clergy in Rome. In July it had ruled that the closure was warranted: Archbishop John Quinn had followed canon law and had provided parishioners with alternative places of worship.

Robert told the group he had learned of the decision, not from the Vatican, but from their opponent, the San Francisco archdiocese. He had received a press release fax from Quinn's office on July 11. It did not even include a copy of the ruling. For that, he was told by Reverend Ingels, he would have to request it in writing *from the archdiocese.* Finally, he received a copy of the decree, which covered one page and was scant on details.

"The ruling makes no sense, and the way it was delivered has me outraged," Robert said. "The case we presented for keeping St. Brigid open was powerful. It's as if we weren't heard."

He read from the fax issued by Archbishop Quinn after the ruling: "I am grateful for the Congregation's decision. And I pray that God will bring comfort and healing to our people and that we will move forward to make the gospel message a lived reality in our revitalized communities." Holding up the fax, he told the shivering parishioners, "Our so-called church fathers are clearly wrong. We are not *moving forward.* We are staying right here. And our community, the one right here, is certainly revitalized."

There were cheers of support.

Robert scanned the faces of the faithful. They no longer looked like the reluctant group he'd first met, who seemed most at home with the Beatitude "The meek shall inherit the Earth." It had been a rough seven months, and their resolve had not diminished. They had moved from lambs to lions.

Lily Wong, standing nearby, raised her white cane. "Church officials seem to think we are in a cult," she began, "and that we will just follow wherever they go, do whatever they do, and say whatever they say. They tell us we are doing the wrong thing. I think we are doing the right thing. The church is supposed to be for its people. It needs to be open so more people can serve God, can love God, can praise God." Raising her voice, she said, "I am beginning to think they are more materialistic than spiritual." Lily's sister, Janie, listened in wonder. Janie had never heard Lily say a critical word about the Catholic Church until now.

Eleanor Croke, a parishioner since 1957, said her letters to Archbishop Quinn garnered no response. "I have sent him a birthday card every year since he arrived, fifteen or sixteen years ago," she said. "And not a single response."

Joe Dignan stood at the bottom of the steps, leaning on his bicycle. He smiled at the sweetness, and tenacity, of people like

Eleanor. His own Eleanor—his mother—wasn't able to make it to the meetings but always asked about them. The meetings were one of the many things his father found inappropriate for his wife. Eleanor Dignan was not to be an agitator. She was not to be a leader. She was to do her painting and cooking and gardening. Those things were acceptable. Joe listened and took an occasional note. He had still not come clean to his wife, friends, or family. He had not stopped his affairs. He loved his wife, but to a degree; something had always been missing. He didn't love Polly as a husband should love a wife.

His thoughts were interrupted by Moe Frix, who suggested that the committee call on Catholics throughout the city to stop putting money in collection baskets. Another person said they should consider raising money for the retrofitting costs by holding a farmers' market in the parking lot of St. Brigid. Other ideas were floated, from hosting dinners and raffles to calling on city officials. Names were taken for who would attend vigils, who would man the phone trees, and who would picket in front of the church at rush hour.

Glancing at his watch, Robert jumped back into the discussion. These meetings had a way of dragging late into the night, and he could see that people were freezing. He told the group that their prospect for success through litigation remained excellent. They had a great case and—as he saw it—an unraveling archdiocese.

"Our case is about injustice," he said. "It is about the archdiocese abusing their power. It is about a process that was never democratic. It is your classic David versus Goliath tale, and we are going up against the all-powerful. But we have uncovered a great deal of abuse. More is coming out now." He said they would appeal to the Supreme Tribunal of the Apostolic Signatura, the Vatican's highest court. "It is the equivalent of the U.S. Supreme Court," he said, "except that with our courts, the justices set law. With the Vatican court, the pope is absolute—with executive power, legislative power, and judicial power." He said they would need to hire a Vatican lawyer to represent them. Having done his research, he suggested they employ the Vatican court's only female lawyer. He liked the idea of a woman going up against the "old boys' network," as he called it.

Robert then read from a letter he had sent to Cardinal Bernardin Gantin at the Vatican. He had written it to "enlighten" the prelate on the "most sad and troubling leadership crisis involving our archbishop." He wrote: "For many years, the archdiocese has chosen to remain ignorant about the terrible tales of sexual abuse against kids by priests. I again ask for an independent investigation and an audit of all its financial matters, and a resolution of the problem with effective leadership. The lack of moral and financial accountability is most disturbing. Finally, I request that consideration be given to the removal and replacement of Archbishop John Quinn."

There was applause.

As the wind picked up and people clustered closer together on the steps, Robert saw in them something as rare as a miracle: a group whose actions were devoid of ego. They gathered almost nightly, candles and rosaries in hand, to walk repeatedly around the church they loved, praying for its survival. They were silent but constant. He was constant but rarely silent. He was learning about faith from those who followed.

He knew that they would hold a vigil after the meeting. Then they would walk one another home, sharing stories of spouses, children, and friends, gossiping like schoolchildren. Most had met before but were only now beginning to share their lives.

And after everyone went home, Siu-Mei, who kept track of the mailings and minutes from meetings and called herself the housekeeper of the committee, would perform a task that she vowed to continue until the church reopened. She would walk up to the top step and light a small white candle.

Lily Wong took the wrong bus and was let out on a corner blocks from her destination. Finally, aided by a woman walking in her direction in the city's Italian neighborhood, Lily made it across

Washington Square Park to the steps of Saints Peter and Paul Church. The bells of the beautiful white church in the heart of North Beach pealed out across the square.

Entering a church, Lily liked to go first to the baptismal font. At St. Brigid, it was to the right of the front door. At Saints Peter and Paul, she didn't know where to go. Next, she liked to light a candle and say a special prayer. At St. Brigid, the red candles were at the front and back. But she didn't know the layout of this church. Everything felt different. She hated relying on other people for her every move.

Finally seated, Lily quieted her mind. It was December 1994 and Christmas was approaching. She felt the beads of her rosary and listened to the opening hymns. The routine of Mass comforted her, with its wafts of incense and dramatic organ music. But then the priest began speaking—in Italian. She sighed and put her rosary away. This was not her home.

Across the city, other exiles from St. Brigid were trying out churches in the Sunset District, Nob Hill, the Marina, and the Haight-Ashbury. Helen and Tillie Piscevich went from church to church, eventually calling themselves "the roaming Catholics." Robert Bryan and his wife and daughter on occasion attended Notre Dame des Victoires, where Mass was said in French. Cleo Donovan didn't have the strength to forge an alliance with another church. She went to a church in the Sunset District but felt a distance. She found the sanctuary of Saints Peter and Paul beautiful but thought the priests were elderly and the message outdated. Only one place gave her peace, brought her close to her departed daughter, Leslie: St. Brigid.

Joe Dignan and his mother attended Mass at a small, stucco chapel in the Presidio, San Francisco's former military base which was being converted into a national park. The nondenominational interfaith church, not far from St. Brigid, held services for Protestants at 8 A.M. and Mass for Catholics at 11 A.M. The priest had to bring his own sacraments.

Joe, his mother, and a number of other parishioners from St.

Brigid—including Siu-Mei—delighted in knowing that the military church was not a part of the San Francisco archdiocese. The St. Brigid faithful had made a pact that they would not join any other parish. They would go to Mass but say they were just visiting.

Joe found himself fidgeting less at the army chapel, where there were no memories, no reminders. Military insignias were inlaid in the wood. Murals depicted wartime heroes. Here, he could sit back and look at the stained-glass windows, free of religious themes, and not be reminded of his own shortcomings.

20 *The Painful Truth Erupts*

Joe returned home from a committee meeting, exhausted. He was not sleeping well, not working well, not feeling like he was doing much well. At least the committee was constructive. The parishioners seemed to genuinely appreciate what he brought to the table. They listened attentively when he presented a report concluding that the archdiocese had overstated the church's seismic repair costs by millions of dollars. Their own independent analysis stated it would cost around $700,000 to retrofit St. Brigid.

The parishioners took him at his word, something that only reminded him that he needed to come to terms with the truth in his personal life.

That day came soon enough.

It was in the spring of 1995, in a moment Joe didn't expect and didn't want. He and Polly were sitting in her truck at the stables where she worked. The weeks before had been full of escalating fights, tension, and innuendo. Joe had taken to staying out late or, at times, not coming home at all. When a red-eyed Polly asked where he had been, Joe would reply, "I don't care to discuss it." Polly, who had had a sheltered and privileged upbringing, choosing to spend more time with horses than boys, had started to believe Joe was having affairs. He was being secretive and strange, occasionally arriving home in the middle of the night jumpy and sweating profusely. Polly began to have a certain inkling, one that terrified her.

Sitting in the truck at the stables, she turned to him. She thought of her father, who had recently died an unhappy man. She wasn't going to continue in a marriage riven with pain and distance. She looked at her husband. Then her words came out: "Are you gay?"

The two had been married for ten years. Their daughter was now toddling around. He loved the little life that she was, tantrums, sweetness, sleepless nights and all. Joe closed his eyes. When he would go away, even for a day to Los Angeles, Polly would tell him she didn't want him to leave. She would cry at the airport. He thought of his mother and father. He thought of his faith.

Being gay was not possible.

Polly deserved the truth, and he deserved the truth. He had been living a lie that affected every part of his life. His eyes still closed, he said that he wished it were otherwise. He hated himself, and he felt shame.

"Yes, I am gay," he said softly.

The days and weeks that followed blurred together for Joe. Polly moved out and took Mary with her. He couldn't work. He didn't answer calls. He spent hours sitting on the worn leather sofa in his living room, crying out in anguish: What have I done?

His and his wife's lives had been woven together, starting with his proposal of marriage on bended knee and taking them to this terrible moment. All he had wanted was a traditional family life. He was twenty-eight when he met Polly, who was visiting from England with her father. He was taken by her practicality and efficiency. She was a country girl, straightforward and uncomplicated. She was able to get ready—showered, dressed, and out the door—in no time. Within months of their meeting, she had moved in with him and he had proposed. The two had a lavish wedding at the Metropolitan Club in San Francisco, where his mother was a member, and again in Polly's hometown, a farming community in Yorkshire, in the north of England.

The truth of his sexual orientation was complicated. He was capable of loving a woman—as he had his wife. But it wasn't complete. It wasn't entirely right. He believed that sexuality could change over time, as the researcher Alfred Kinsey had asserted, that he could be incidentally heterosexual as he slowly became more homosexual.

Days later, after Polly told Joe's father that his son was gay, Joseph Dignan Sr., an attorney, summoned Joe and said bluntly, "Go back in the closet." Not doing so would "get him in a lot of trouble," Dignan said, and he would face discrimination. Eleanor said she had suspected he was gay since his college days, but she never said anything because she didn't want to "encourage" him.

Eleanor Dignan's attitude was shaped by her religion, which looked at homosexuality as a disorder and a sin. She knew of the passage from Leviticus: "*Thou shalt not lie with mankind, as with womankind: it is abomination.*" And as hard as Joe had tried as a youth to block out the teachings—babbling through Mass, evading classes, fleeing confessionals—the dogma and ritual had become a part of him.

Now he wandered around his house, looking despairingly at photographs and Mary's toys. He couldn't put anything away. He set about repairing whatever appeared damaged: a rocking chair no longer used, a stuffed animal with a hole in its ear. He needed to fix things.

21 *Holding On*

At 6 p.m. on June 30, 1995, hundreds of parishioners gathered at St. Brigid for the first anniversary of the church's closure. They decided it was better to hold Mass on the sidewalk near the rectory, where traffic wasn't as deafening.

Father O was with them. The threat of canonical censure remained in place, but Father O would not stay away. His altar was a folding card table, borrowed from the school's cafeteria. Pews were created from school benches. Standing in front of the rectory he had been banished from, Father O wore a long white robe and alb. A gold cross hung around his neck.

After a welcome and hymns, he talked of the Old Testament's Book of Job, saying that Job had suffered greatly but had always refused to blame or curse God's name. He talked of perseverance as a theme in Scripture, and of Saint Paul's urging, "Run the race so as to win." "There has been a breach of trust in the church leadership toward its people," Father O said. "But I am not here to put down personalities or people or even the institution of the Church. I am here, with all of you, to say that I will not stop supporting the cause, which is the validity of St. Brigid and the community of St. Brigid."

He looked from face to face. He knew their stories, disappointments, and dreams. "We were all blindsided by the news that our church would close," Father O said. "I know that the hope of the archdiocese was that the committee would not gather momentum. But that has not happened. In fact, we have gathered strength in exile."

The wind whipped the paper tablecloth around and extinguished the tall candles on the makeshift altar. Father O returned to Job, saying in Latin, "*Post tenebras spero lucem,*" and then in English, "After the darkness, I hope for light."

When it came time for the Eucharist, the parishioners formed a line that stretched to the end of the block. A prayer was offered by Lily Wong, who had been homebound of late, taking care of her mother. Jan Robinson played the harp. Father O joined her on the tin whistle he'd brought from Ireland.

After Mass, the group walked the two blocks to Holy Trinity, a Russian Orthodox church that had become their haven in recent months. Its priest, Father Victor Sokolov, was a dissident who knew what it meant to be in exile, and he had offered the basement of his church as a place to meet. He had told them, "We are neighbors. We are two blocks away. If your diocese doesn't want you, join us." He could not comprehend how any church would turn away such devoted believers. The parishioners were grateful that committee meetings no longer had to be held on the freezing front steps of St. Brigid.

Tonight, the potluck at Holy Trinity was abundant. There was barbecued ribs, cornbread, chocolate chip cookies, fruit salad, sandwiches, and sushi. The wine flowed into plastic cups, refilled by their energetic server, Father O.

Robert Bryan arrived late, having appeared on a television talk show as a commentator on the O. J. Simpson murder trial. He wanted to deliver a pep talk on the prospects of the ongoing litigation and on his relentless campaign against the administration of Archbishop Quinn. He began by praising the members of the committee for their hard work. They had hosted luncheons and dinners and summer picnic Masses in San Francisco parks, participated in the St. Patrick's Day parade, and held food and clothing drives for the poor. At Christmas, they ran a program to help the homeless, calling it "the homeless helping the homeless." Every weekend for a month, from 10 A.M. to 4 P.M., they took turns standing in front of St. Brigid, seeking donations of clothing and blankets. They regularly volunteered in a nearby soup kitchen, all wearing matching St. Brigid aprons—made for them by their fellow committee member Nelly Echavarria.

Robert reported the results of a recent survey in which St. Brigid's parishioners were asked if they had joined other churches. "Of the nearly fifteen hundred parishioners sampled, nearly all stated that they have not registered with another church," he said. "Most also said they were not contributing to archdiocesan coffers."

After dinner, the parishioners headed back to St. Brigid. As they turned the corner in view of the church, they were stopped by the spectacle before them. The building glowed with light. Nearing the steps, they saw that white floodlights had been placed around the massive building, illuminating it from the base to the tower. Smaller lights framed the sides of the church in hues of pink and rose. Standing on the steps, smiling sheepishly, was Joe. The theater set designer had piled the lights, cables, and generator into his small car and, while others were at dinner, had scrambled around the building setting his stage.

The bright building lifted their spirits. Their dark church was suffused with life. The steps were blanketed with bouquets of fresh flowers. Dozens of candles created a flickering sea. A large sign was posted on the front door: VANQUISHED, VANQUISHED, ALL OF THAT RAVISHED, BY THE GREEDY, WITH NO NEED. Only Siu-Mei knew who had come up with the slogans and made the signs: Father O.

The parishioners remained until midnight, as they had done a year earlier, singing songs, praying, and looking forward to the day they would be returned to the pews of their church. Their final song was the civil rights anthem sung the year before, "We Shall Overcome," selected by their man from the South—Robert Bryan.

22 *Secret Plans*

A NEW SIGN WENT UP on the front door of St. Brigid under a graying bas-relief frieze of Jesus: SOLD FOR THIRTY PIECES OF SILVER.

One month after the first anniversary of St. Brigid's closure, a secret report from the San Francisco archdiocese—one of three existing copies—made its way into the press. The archdiocese was livid, claiming the report had been stolen from the chancery. Marked "Confidential," it outlined the market value of various church properties and the "highest and best use" for each. St. Brigid was on the list.

To the parishioners, the news was, at best, a steely-eyed assessment of something they held sacred. At worst, it seemed to answer the question they had been asking since the closure was announced: What did the archdiocese plan to do with their church?

The 160-page report was dated November 1993—the same month the archdiocese announced that up to a dozen churches would be suppressed the following June. The stated best use for St. Brigid, whose land was valued at nearly $17 million, was to be replaced with "maximum density" residential housing. The report factored in certain expenses, including one that caught everyone's attention: The cost of bulldozing St. Brigid was placed at about $800,000, with "demolition @ $20/sq.ft."

Their historic church could be replaced with a high-rise.

Lily Wong had the story read to her by her sister, Janie Yee. She listened closely. When Janie was done, Lily said, "So, they did not target weak parishes for closure, but rather those with money in the bank and situated on valuable land." She thought back to the group's meeting with Archbishop Quinn in the spring of 1994. Denise Nicco had asked about the plans for the building if the closure went forward. George Wesolek and the others said there were no plans. Denise had asked, "Then why close it?" She got no reply.

A spokesman for the archdiocese responded to the report by saying that it was in fact changing demographics, a decline in Mass attendance, and the high cost of mandatory seismic retrofitting, not a desire to make money from church properties, that dictated the choices for closure.

Robert Bryan, who had received a copy of the report from a source before it made its way into the public eye, said to his wife, "This is the straw that broke the camel's back. It's clear the archbishop and his staff lied to parishioners about the reasons for closing the churches. Their plan was to shut down houses of God to reap financial profit. They are no better than common thieves."

He told the committee that he didn't know who leaked the report, but he considered the person "a real hero. I get calls all the time from people inside the archdiocese who are tired of the fraud going on there, who are troubled by what they are seeing."

The same day the news broke of the report, Robert wrote another letter to Cardinal Bernardin Gantin at the Vatican, making sure to "cc" the pope. He said, "A number of local Catholics have again asked me to seek your intervention concerning our archbishop, who is causing great hardship to the Roman Catholic Church in San Francisco. This request is unique, but the problems are extraordinary. There is nowhere else to turn. A San Francisco newspaper has just uncovered a confidential report that establishes that Quinn and his staff made material misrepresentations and lied about his reasons for closing a number of viable parishes including St. Brigid."

He enclosed a copy of an editorial in the *San Francisco Examiner,* which stated: "The archdiocese continues to dodge ever-increasing allegations of fiscal mismanagement as well as charges of sexual misconduct and pedophilia on the part of its clergy." Robert wrote: "We were appalled by the report. With its $17 million worth of prime property, St. Brigid's parish must have whetted appetites in the inner sanctums of the archdiocese's real estate department."

The letter closed: "Your intervention is humbly sought for the purpose of putting an end to the ongoing financial and moral catastrophe in the Archdiocese of San Francisco."

Robert then turned his pen on Quinn, writing: "Many Roman Catholics have contacted me regarding the enormous problems plaguing our Archdiocese due to your morally corrupt leadership. We ask that you and your staff resign before the Catholic Church here is damaged beyond repair."

On August 16, 1995, Archbishop John Raphael Quinn, appointed San Francisco's sixth archbishop in 1977 by Pope Paul VI, announced his resignation.

A priest close to him said the archbishop was "tired of all the negativity and assaults on his character." The archdiocese had been rocked by the parish protests, Robert's accusations, and a burgeoning scandal involving some of his most trusted priests.

George Wesolek was surprised and saddened by the early resignation. He knew Quinn didn't care for the administrative side of being an archbishop; he had always been more of a natural academic and in-depth theologian than a CEO. He also knew the closures, attacks, and revelations about the abuse by priests had taken a toll. At least Quinn could now do what he loved, Wesolek thought, which was to read, write, play music, and lead retreats.

Robert learned of Quinn's resignation late in the day, having spent the afternoon meeting with clients on death row at San Quentin. He was juggling a dozen cases, serving as a television commentator, acting as head of a national coalition to abolish the death penalty, and working daily on St. Brigid's behalf. The news thrilled him; he wanted to pop open a bottle of champagne.

In his mind, he had outlasted his nemesis. Surely this would improve the chances of reopening St. Brigid.

23 *A Discovery*

ROBERT SAT IN THE resplendent St. Peter's Basilica, surrounded by sculptures by Bernini and Michelangelo. It was March 5, 1996, and he had reservations for a papal audience, a once-a-week Mass celebrated by the pope himself. He looked around the basilica, consecrated in 1626 and said to be "the greatest church in Christendom" and the burial site of Saint Peter. He had studied Bernini's *Cathedra Petri* and *Gloria* and thought of the hundred or more tombs below. He could have gazed at Michelangelo's *Pietà* for hours.

But he became consumed with two thoughts: how weak Pope John Paul II looked, and how the powerful and wealthy government of the Vatican, this mystical entity, this bride of Christ, was trying to kill his client, St. Brigid. Soon, he would have to file his last brief to save the church, its case now before the Supreme Tribunal of the Apostolic Signatura.

After the Mass in St. Peter's, Robert let himself enjoy one of the world's most glorious cities. For the afternoon, at least, he would have a rare family getaway. With the work of the committee and his expanding law practice, Robert had limited time with his wife, Nicole, and their daughter, Auda Mai, who by now had attended almost as many committee meetings as he had. There were weeks when he felt like a stranger with Nicole. The two had met in December 1988, when she was visiting San Francisco from France. She spoke little English; he spoke little French. They were married on April 22, 1989, and two of their ushers had served time on death row.

The Bryans took in the sights of Rome, with its blend of beauty and barbarity, its glorious churches and its coliseums, where early Christians were slaughtered by lions as a form of entertainment, where early Etruscans worshiped a triad of gods. Auda Mai was enchanted by the statues, especially the horses. She drew pictures in a book and carried her trusted teddy bear, Fufu, worn and brown with a Burberry plaid bow tie, everywhere they went.

The next day, Robert was back at work. With Nicole, Auda Mai, Fufu, and an overloaded stroller in tow, he went to the home of Dr. Martha Wegan, the Vatican attorney the committee had hired. She lived on Via di Monserrato, a charming residential area with narrow streets and old stone buildings, with Vespas parked on one side and improbably small cars on the other. While Dr. Wegan worked in the next room, Robert and Nicole sat on a sofa in the tidy, book-filled den and went through files. Seeing some of the papers for the first time, Robert couldn't believe any court of law could operate this way. To his disgust, he had been getting only periodic briefings on the case. The officials at the San Francisco archdiocese had continued to refuse to send him pleadings pertaining to St. Brigid, saying he would have to get them from the Vatican. The congregation had been of no help, even when he'd flown to Rome two years earlier.

Flipping through file after file, it was Nicole who came across a manila folder with a letter on Vatican stationery. As she began to read, her eyes widened. Urgently and quietly, she handed the letter to her husband.

Robert saw his name, and he saw the incendiary language. He scanned the rest before making a split-second decision. With the Vatican attorney working just steps away, he tucked the letters into his battered briefcase. He motioned to Nicole to scoop up Auda Mai, who had been working on her drawings. It was time to go. After a quick good-bye to the lawyer, the Bryans hustled out the door, spiriting the "Confidential" documents with them.

On the street, they piled into the back seat of a taxi. Robert's briefcase, a gift from the committee, was wedged between his knees. Amid the ancient stone buildings of Rome, Robert searched for something thoroughly modern: a Kinko's, somewhere he could make copies. He took the papers out of his briefcase. He read the first letter, from *Congregatio Pro Clericis* to "Your Excellency, the Most Reverend John Quinn." Two years earlier, the letter revealed, the Vatican had granted his last-minute appeal to keep St. Brigid open. The fifteen-day stay, according to the letter from His Eminence, Cardinal Jose Sanchez, prefect at the Congregation for the Clergy, was granted on June 28, 1994, just two days before the doors of St. Brigid were to close. The prefect said that more time was needed, given the "deluge" of faxes and letters from San Francisco. St. Brigid had been thrown a possible lifeline—but word never got back to San Francisco. Robert had never heard of the victory, despite his barrage of appeals.

As the taxi driver honked and yelled at a truck blocking the narrow road, all he could think was, *We won. We had won.* How is it possible, he asked himself, that no one was told? It was like not telling a death row inmate awaiting execution that the state had granted a last-minute reprieve.

Also in the folder was a letter from Archbishop Quinn, marked "Urgent" and written on June 28, 1994, the same day the congregation informed him of the reprieve. In his "very frank" letter, Quinn asked the congregation to withdraw its stay immediately. "Once your decision becomes public that I am to delay the closing of St. Brigid's," he wrote, "Robert Bryan will assume a new importance. The decision will appear to legitimize him and his tactics." He said that a stay would also give the impression that "Rome favors the wealthy parish and has been intimidated by Bryan and by the volume of protests received in Rome." He further cautioned the prefect: "Once the media pick up that I have been ordered to delay in the case of St. Brigid, they will begin to relate this to the scurrilous reports in the [San Francisco] Examiner. Allegations and half-truths, together with the delay order, will become an object of national media interest. What were scandalous stories and allegations in one tabloid newspaper here, will then be raised to a national scandal and will be reported everywhere."

The archbishop's letter called Bryan a "demagogue who deals in falsehoods and half-truths" and said "he has been a Catholic only since April." Quinn concluded: "I cannot stress how harmful I believe it will be if the Congregation does not withdraw this order to delay the closing of St. Brigid."

This, Robert thought wryly, was coming from the man who was supposed to be a pillar of goodness and kindness and peacefulness, the epitome of a generous and forgiving spirit. Back at the hotel, a wound-up Robert paced the room. Nicole, who reverted to speaking French when angry, was also wound up, but for other reasons. The letter was an attack on her husband. Robert was many things—long-winded, passionate, and stubborn, to name a few. But he was not a liar. He was not a demagogue. Robert told Nicole they needed a plan. They had to come up with an excuse to return to the attorney's apartment to slip the letters back into her files.

On the day of their return to San Francisco, the three made

their way to the attorney's home. Dr. Wegan seemed slightly perplexed to see them. Robert said he wanted to look over the pleadings one more time. Auda Mai, with her curls, engaging chatter, and teddy bear Fufu, proved an excellent distraction for the attorney, and the papers were slipped back into their folders.

Robert went ahead and filed the last appeal. Though he had sparred with powerful opponents before, he felt he had never met more formidable foes than Quinn and the Catholic Church. Formidable, he thought—and arrogant. How could their own attorney, Dr. Wegan, hired with money donated by the parishioners, have withheld the information from him? The news would have sent cheers across San Francisco.

On the flight home, he went over the letters again. He was appalled at Quinn but felt oddly validated. The stay proved that the St. Brigid churchgoers had a viable claim. It also made him feel that he was trying his case before the ultimate biased jury.

Two days after arriving from Rome, Robert and the Committee to Save St. Brigid met for the first time with William Levada, the city's new archbishop. A fourth-generation Californian, Levada had come to San Francisco from Oregon, where he had served for nine years as archbishop of Portland. He was regarded as a savvy leader, comfortable as both an administrator and a theologian. In Catholic circles, he was considered someone to watch.

The meeting was held on March 14, 1996, Robert's fifty-third birthday. Despite his simmering anger, Robert had decided not to bring up the subject of the Vatican letters, as it would surely make the archbishop uncomfortable. And Levada had nothing to do with them. What's more, the revelations in Rome had made it increasingly clear that the battle to save St. Brigid was going to have to be won in San Francisco, not at the Vatican. He remembered something George Wesolek had tried to impart: The case was not about the facts but about whether the correct process was followed. Robert, relieved to have a new archbishop, hoped they could resolve things amicably rather than legally.

Where Quinn had come across to the committee as formal and cold, Levada seemed warm and engaging. He asked questions, made eye contact, and took copious notes on a yellow legal pad. He used a Bic pen rather than the expensive Montblanc of his predecessor—something members of the committee took as a good sign.

Joe Dignan made it a point to welcome the new archbishop and to convey the committee's willingness to help the archdiocese. He had a positive feeling about Levada, who was rumored to be a major movie buff, foodie, and baseball fan.

Robert began grandiloquently and optimistically, as if he were in court: "St. Brigid is a jewel in the crown of the archdiocese of San Francisco, and should be saved." He presented Levada with the committee's engineering study, which concluded that St. Brigid would require minimal seismic work at an estimated cost of $700,000. He noted that this was nearly 80 percent less than the figure cited by Archbishop Quinn when he closed St. Brigid.

He reiterated the group's willingness to raise the money needed, saying that "the parishioners want to raise a minimum of $1.5 million to ensure that the church is completely upgraded to present-day standards and that the beautiful interior finishes of the sanctuary are correctly restored after structural work is complete." Pausing for effect, he went on, "It will cost the archdiocese nothing to save this wonderful church."

Levada said he would consider the group's plea. When Robert asked whether they could settle their differences outside the ongoing litigation, Levada said they needed to "let it take its course." The meeting was adjourned. The committee members were giddy to be dealing with someone other than Quinn, and they looked forward to the next session with the archbishop.

On March 31, a front-page story appeared in the *San Francisco Examiner* under the headline SAN FRANCISCO ARCHBISHOP BLOCKED PARISH'S VATICAN REPRIEVE: LETTERS SHOW QUINN URGED ROME NOT TO DELAY THE CLOSING OF ST.

BRIGID. The story had been leaked by Robert. He had decided not to share the confidential documents with parishioners because he wanted them to have "maximum impact."

Quinn declined to comment on the story, but a spokesman for the archdiocese noted that, ultimately, Rome supported Quinn's closure decisions. Excerpts from the letter revealed Quinn's derision of parishioners who wore white towels during "Don't throw in the towel" demonstrations at Mass. In the urgent letter to Cardinal Sanchez, Quinn had also addressed his reassignment of Father O'Sullivan, saying the priest had "publicly criticized my decisions regarding St. Brigid." And he described what he saw as a "calculated campaign" against the archdiocese by this group of disgruntled Catholics to "uncover incidents of scandal within the San Francisco Archdiocese."

Robert Bryan was quoted as saying he was "astonished" and "angry" to learn of the correspondence. "It was concealed from the people," he said. "None of us, the faithful, had any idea that the message we had been trying to convey to Rome had worked."

24 *Dark and Light*

THE HOUSEPAINTER SET his ladder against the door of St. Brigid. He unfurled his heavy drop cloth and searched his canvas satchel for just the right tools. First, he removed a large piece of sandpaper from the bag. He carefully cut it in half and folded it into thirds, so it would fit in his back pockets and neatly in his hand. Then he set to work on the old, mottled finish of the wooden door closest to Broadway.

He sanded in small and fast movements. Parts of the door were bleached by the sun, and other parts were dark and pitted. He felt along the beautiful black cast-iron hinges, coming toward the center like vines, four on each side of the six-inch-thick door.

He would need a special solvent for them and small tools to get around the edges, since he wouldn't be able to remove them for a proper cleaning.

It was just after 6 A.M., and the housepainter's new project was the three doors of St. Brigid—the two wooden doors with the gorgeous hinges and the massive front door. His weeding of the periphery and power-washing of the steps had been a prelude. The doors meant something to him. When they were open, he was drawing closer to his son, and his son was drawing closer to God. Now that they were closed, he felt a distance from his son, who still asked questions about why St. Brigid had been shuttered.

The housepainter, thin and elongated like a Giacometti figure, looked up Van Ness at the ornate wrought-iron main door and at the wooden door he would tackle next. He would give himself time to complete all three. He was lulled by the repetitive motion and hushing sound of his sanding. It was tedious, and it was therapeutic.

The church needed his care. Thousands of cars streamed by the closed church daily. The air that extinguished the small white candle on the front steps brought dirt and detritus that darkened the silvery granite walls. Weeds popped through cracks in the pavement. Homeless people sought shelter in side stairwells.

He had never understood why such a beautiful church was closed and was unable to explain it to his son, who was eight when he began attending and twelve when St. Brigid was closed. Father and son had then attended Mass at the Fort Mason Chapel with a number of other parishioners from St. Brigid. But soon, it too was closed—the victim of a reorganization of the Presidio. Not long after, his son started drifting away from his religion. Now, in his crucial teenage years, he no longer wanted to attend church. The housepainter shook his head. His son was almost to that place where faith could settle in.

Returning to work, he tackled section after section until his hand was numb. His already woeful fingernails were worn to the nub. He alternated between the sandpaper and steel wool, working methodically from bottom to top, side to side. To clean the hinges, he used a harsh etching solvent with his smallest scrapers and tools that could get into the sharpest angles. He used a dark stain on the thick wood of the door. Next to the door was a weathered sign: ST. BRIGID CATHOLIC CHURCH.

As he worked, he felt the cracks in the wood and the damage that came with time. Fissures and stains were beginning to appear in the bigger church—stains that were unlikely to be as easily repaired. Standing back to look at St. Brigid, he thought of all that had been given to this place. He would do what he could to give back. He likened it to the way a family keeps vigil over a comatose loved one.

25 *Yet Another Defeat*

ROBERT BRYAN ASSEMBLED the piles of St. Brigid materials on his dining room table so he could send an overnight package to Rome. He also had a briefing to prepare for a death row inmate at San Quentin whose case was in its final appeal. There were a number of scenarios for how the courts could rule on the inmate, but the case of St. Brigid could have but two outcomes. Either the doors would open or they wouldn't. There were no other courts to hear the case, and there was no possibility that a new trial would be granted.

An hour later, Robert sent the package off to Rome. It included 740 individually signed affidavits attesting to the importance of St. Brigid. He had included new materials showing that the church had not been given due process in being closed.

The parishioners were also doing their part. By early 1997—nearly three years after the doors had closed—they had built up a mailing list of more than eighteen thousand names. They were working even harder to raise funds, rally in front of the church, and help the needy. In recent months, volunteers had collected more than $1,000 in cash donations and nine hundred pounds of clothing and gifts for the homeless. They hung banners emblazoned with SAVE ST. BRIGID around the city. They held sidewalk sales.

Despite all the setbacks and hurt, the parishioners still believed the Catholic Church would not let them down again, that the Vatican's highest court would return a verdict in their favor. All signs on the home front looked good, too. The new archbishop, Levada, had heard their pleas. And under his leadership, three of the nine churches closed by Archbishop Quinn in 1994 had been quietly reopened.

As Robert said to the parishioners after meeting with Levada on March 14, "I felt a door has been opened, and sunlight is coming into San Francisco under the new archbishop."

The parishioners sent a steady stream of handwritten cards and heartfelt gifts to the archbishop, including a SAVE ST. BRIGID sweatshirt. Levada, known to take long walks around the city in layman's clothing and a baseball cap, responded, "The sweatshirt, no doubt, will be most helpful on cold San Francisco mornings."

Jan Robinson wrote to Levada about the St. Brigid men's soccer team's winning the league championship again. Levada responded, "Let me extend my congratulations through you to the members of the team for their outstanding accomplishments." Jan's letter did not mention that Father O was the coach of their team.

Robert wrote to the archbishop every week with committee updates, invitations, and fundraising ideas. He invited the archbishop to attend a committee dinner called "A Night in Italy"; a St. Patrick's Day dinner; St. Brigid School choir night; a church-sponsored tour of St. Francis of Assisi, an old church in North Beach that had been turned into a shrine; and numerous outdoor picnics and Masses.

"Our annual spring dinner for St. Brigid Church will be held at the Fort Mason Officers' Club," Robert wrote in February 1997. "On behalf of parishioners, I extend an invitation for you to attend." Levada responded promptly and politely, citing "previously scheduled engagements."

Robert wrote additional letters asking for a second meeting with the archbishop. Levada again responded promptly and politely: "I regret that it will not be possible to schedule an appointment because of my schedule for the next several months."

Robert followed up, saying that the parishioners remained in limbo—it had been nearly three years since St. Brigid had been closed. Levada responded: "You and the other parishioners of the former St. Brigid parish can be assured that I will take your views into account in my review of the multiple factors which need to be considered in arriving at a decision regarding its future."

Robert believed that if he kept asking, eventually he would get a yes. Besides, he wanted to give the busy archbishop the benefit of the doubt. Levada had stepped into an archdiocese roiled by the church closures and hit by a widening sex abuse scandal, among other challenges. The year before, in 1996, the archdiocese had paid more than $2.5 million to fifteen men who said they had been molested as boys by Monsignor Patrick O'Shea and two other priests.

In mid-May 1997, a year after Levada had met with the committee, Robert wrote his weekly letter, asking the archbishop yet again for a meeting. The critical decision by the Vatican's highest court was due in June. After Robert's experience with the Vatican, he did not share the parishioners' optimism that the robed men in Rome would do the right thing.

Levada replied on May 27: "My schedule for June and most of July is already fully booked. I regret I will not be able to meet with you until some time later this summer. In any event, I ask you to contact my assistant, after the decision has been made by the Signatura, to schedule an appointment."

At the end of June, Robert got the news.

The committee's final appeal to the Signatura had been denied—on a technicality. The news was delivered to him again by the archdiocese. (Their own attorney at the Vatican had said nothing.) The letter arrived with an unofficial translation of the Latin document from the Supremum Signaturae Apostolicae Tribunal. As Robert read the translated order, DEFINITIVE DECREE IN THE NAME OF THE LORD. AMEN, he grew angrier with each word. "With Pope John Paul II happily reigning, in the 19th year of his Pontificate, the Supreme Tribunal, in the presence of the Most Eminent and Most Excellent Cardinals . . . Prefects and Ponens . . ."

The decree recounted the entire saga of St. Brigid, from the first legal filing in February 1994 to the appeal before the high court. The tribunal determined that Robert had sought recourse as an attorney, not as an individual parishioner representing the committee, as required. The Vatican left the future of St. Brigid to San Francisco's archbishop. The order stated: "Nothing prevents the Most Reverend Archbishop of San Francisco from subjecting the matter to an examination, but only as a favor—that is, there is nothing in law urging this."

Robert was incredulous. In every correspondence, in every pleading, he had represented himself as an attorney and a parishioner elected by the committee to represent them, and not once had the Vatican courts questioned his standing. After all the years and all the work, the Vatican did not consider the merits of their case. The decision, "Given at Rome at the See of the Supreme Tribunal," came down on June 21. Robert looked at the date of the letter from the San Francisco archdiocese. He shook his head. It couldn't be a coincidence.

It was June 30, 1997, the third anniversary of the closing of St. Brigid.

Lily Wong and her sister, Janie Yee, sat with their mother in Lily's apartment. "This feels like we are in Burma, not in America,"

Janie said. "This is happening in the so-called land of freedom? Our own bishops can deny us without hearing us?"

Lily, Janie, and most of the others from St. Brigid had believed from the day their first appeal was filed that Rome was on their side, that the Vatican would see through the archdiocese's unjust business motivations for closing the church.

Lily said, "Remember how we have always said, 'When the Vatican hears our case they will understand that all we are trying to do is save souls and save our church for the community'? Well, every step of the way we have been told no. At every turn, we—who are faithful Catholics—are called troublemakers."

Janie sat back on the sofa. After all of Robert Bryan's work, after all of the filings, addendums, affidavits, and testimonials, after all the strategy sessions, money raised, and conferences with canon law experts, the Vatican had discarded their case *on a technicality, without considering the words of parishioners?*

Janie looked toward her elderly mother, whose face seemed to grow more lovely with age. "You know," she said, "I feel like we have gone to our parents—not to our brothers and sisters, but to our parents—to ask them to please, please, save us. We are their children. But they tell us they will not save us." Speaking to herself, to Lily, to no one in particular, Janie asked, "If your own bishops can do this to you, if your own church can do this to you, where do you have left to go? Who do we turn to now?"

Miriam Gray, a longtime parishioner who had raised and donated money while St. Brigid was open to rebuild the school gymnasium in the basement of the church, gathered with friends in the elegant living room of her Pacific Heights home. The verdict by the Supreme Tribunal was on everyone's mind.

With her pearl necklace and bracelet, suit, and soft dome of silver curls, Miriam talked with friends about the tumultuous spring of 1994, when the division had erupted within the committee over who was in charge. She reminded them of the secret letter sent to the Congregation for the Clergy by John Ross and Richard Figone.

"The men said that Robert Bryan was being too aggressive and was not acting in the *highest Christian standard,*" Miriam marveled. "They did not approve of Robert's use of detectives to try to find misconduct of priests—which proved true. They said it was important to *rehabilitate* the committee and try to show that we are responsible people."

Miriam disappeared into her den and brought back another letter, the one she had written to Ross and Figone at the time. It began with a wallop: "Gentlemen, I am appalled, sickened and disgusted that you would have the audacity to write a letter for the committee on behalf of parishioners. How dare you. You sent it without the approval of the recognized chairman. What an ego trip!" Holding nothing back, she went on: "You, Judge Figone, tried to worm your way out of any responsibility for this by saying you had only written one paragraph, but you signed the letter. . . . Our chairman Robert Bryan has dedicated countless hours to the work of the committee, *with the approval of the committee.* For you to try to undermine his work is unconscionable and most reprehensible."

Her letter ended: "If St. Brigid closes you will bear the guilt!"

Robert gazed at the committee members gathered in the basement of Holy Trinity Cathedral, trying futilely to conduct business. He was accustomed to drawn-out battles, to cases that dragged on for years. And he wasn't ready to give up on this one. Yet he was worried about the faith and endurance of his fellow parishioners. Even Siu-Mei, still girlish and smiling at forty, appeared worn down, saying little and on this night not even taking notes, as was her custom.

Unable to handle the grim mood any longer, Tom Curtin, a ruddy-faced Irishman, stood up at the long cafeteria table and announced that there was something that needed to be said. It was clear to *all* that spirits had reached a new low. The Vatican hadn't ruled on the content of their case. The feeling of optimism over Archbishop Levada was fading or gone. As an usher at St. Brigid for more than two decades, Curtin shared the pain of being locked out of their church.

Speaking slowly and making eye contact with those in the room, he said, "Just because St. Brigid is closed doesn't mean we are not a parish. We are a parish. We are doing everything a parish does—helping one another, helping the needy, praying, taking care of our souls. We are doing all of this without being asked, without being inside a church, without hearing the call of any priest. We are doing it because we are fighting for something bigger than ourselves, something eternal. There is a purity to what is happening here, and a sense of love and community we never had before our church was closed." As he talked, the parishioners sat up straighter. Some began to nod. Janie Yee began to applaud and was joined by others.

Robert's daughter, Auda Mai, smiled at her honorary godfather. Mr. Curtin showed up at all of her piano recitals and always surprised her afterward with a new charm for her bracelet.

After a few moments, the parishioners returned to the night's agenda. There was work to be done, prayers to be said.

26 *Carrying On*

JOE DIGNAN WHEELED his bicycle into the Holy Trinity basement. His gloves came off to the rip of Velcro. He removed his helmet and found his seat at the end of the long table. He dug into his Timbuk2 bag for a notepad and pen and set his ubiquitous coffee cup on the table. Removing a chocolate chip cookie from a bag that crinkled loudly, he mumbled to himself until one of the ladies shot him a look. The others were praying the rosary. He sat admonished but didn't join in prayer.

A view of Van Ness Avenue in 1926, with St. Brigid on the left.
(San Francisco History Center, San Francisco Public Library)

St. Brigid as seen from the street, 1994. (Courtesy of Maria Esain)

The sanctuary of St. Brigid, 1994. (Courtesy of Maria Esain)

A rally held in early 1994 in front of St. Brigid. Robert Bryan, center, is surrounded by parishioners and reporters. (Courtesy of Siu-Mei Wong)

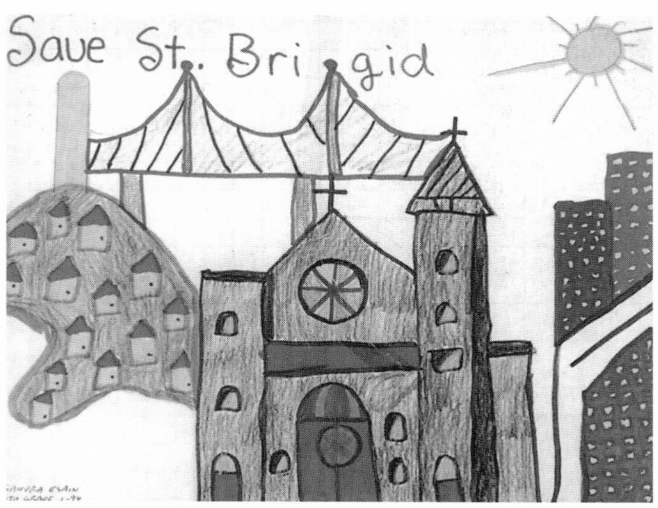

In the spring of 1994, the children at St. Brigid School tried to keep their beloved church from closing. They picketed at rush hour, attended rallies, and sent their pictures of St. Brigid to the Vatican. (Courtesy of Glenn Corino)

Archbishop John Quinn pays a surprise visit to St. Brigid on Easter 1994. Behind him is Father Daniel Keohane, who was installed to close St. Brigid. Bebe St. John (facing the camera) watches Quinn. Robert Bryan, standing on the left with a towel over his right shoulder, eyes the archbishop. (Courtesy of Siu-Mei Wong)

The first picnic Mass for the exiled parishioners of St. Brigid, held in Lafayette Park in the summer of 1994. Father O officiates. Jan Robinson has brought her harp. (Courtesy of Siu-Mei Wong)

Joe Dignan and his mother, Eleanor, at a St. Brigid dinner in 1999. (Courtesy of Siu-Mei Wong)

Lily Wong (on the right in dark glasses), the committee's spiritual leader, prays the rosary in front of St. Brigid, 1999. (Courtesy of Siu-Mei Wong)

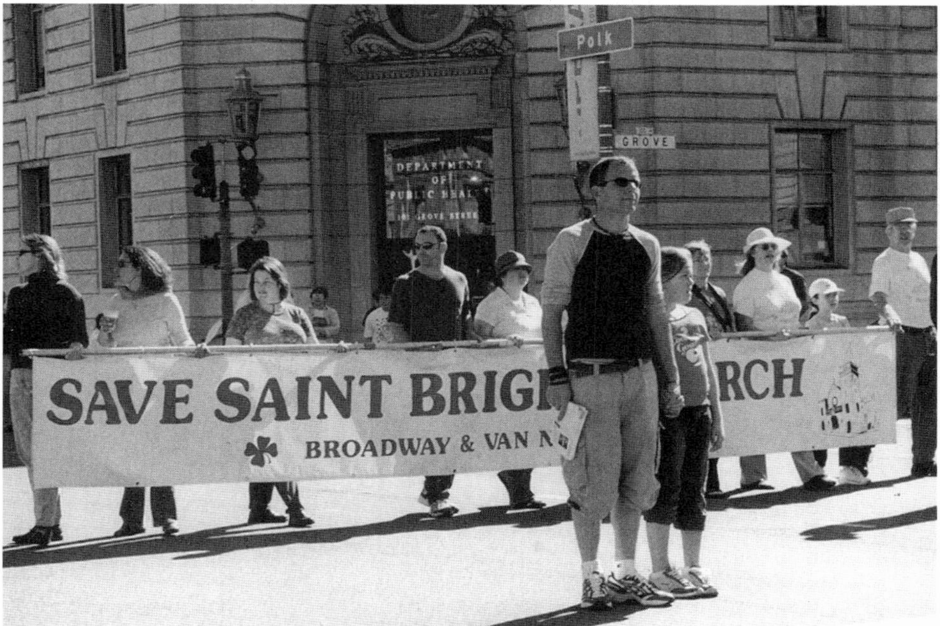

Joe Dignan and his daughter, Mary, lead the St. Brigid contingent in the annual St. Patrick's Day parade. (Courtesy of Siu-Mei Wong)

Lorraine Kelley hands out leaflets, trying to gain support for St. Brigid at San Francisco's Gay Pride parade in 2005. (Lance Iverson/Courtesy of *San Francisco Chronicle*)

Housepainter and parishioner David Hansell works on the massive front door of St. Brigid, having brought his ladder and equipment from home to the steps of the church. (Courtesy of Siu-Mei Wong)

Father O with members of his St. Brigid soccer team, which he continues to coach in exile. (Lance Iverson/Courtesy of *San Francisco Chronicle*)

Joe Dignan breaks down in the living room of his mother's home.
(Lance Iverson/Courtesy of *San Francisco Chronicle*)

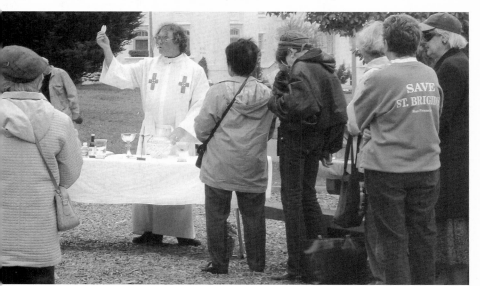

On a cold summer day in Lafayette Park, Father O officiates at the emotional last picnic Mass of the exiled parishioners. Tillie Piscevish is at the right, in a Save St. Brigid sweatshirt. (Courtesy of Siu-Mei Wong)

Maggie Zuniga, a parishioner at St. Brigid, gives Archbishop William Levada an earful about the church. (Lance Iverson/Courtesy of *San Francisco Chronicle*)

Carmen Esteva, Marilyn Aspesi, and Clementina Garcia take time after a committee meeting to celebrate birthdays. (Lance Iverson/Courtesy of *San Francisco Chronicle*)

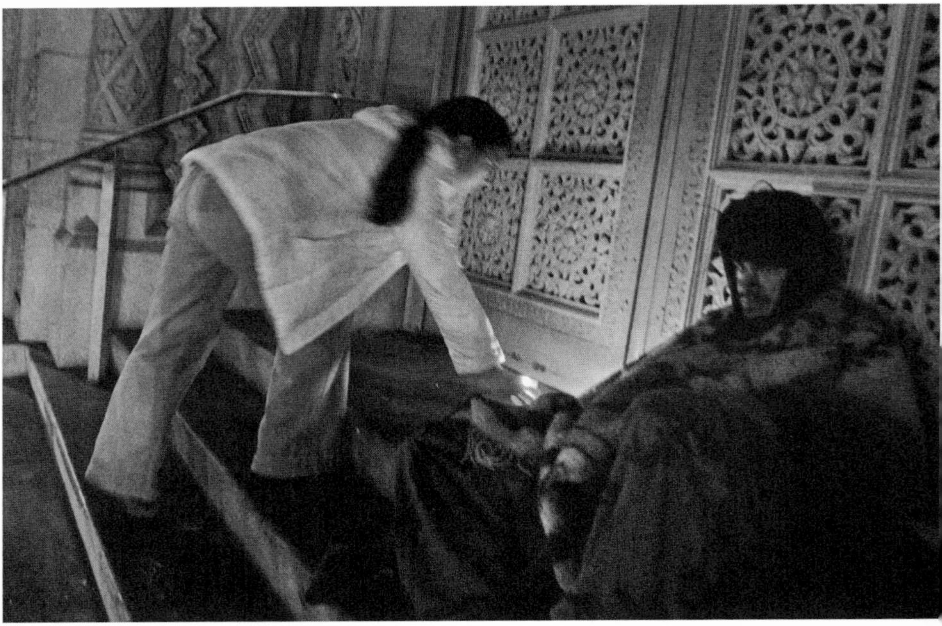

Siu-Mei Wong places a candle on the steps of St. Brigid, near a homeless person camped out there for the night. Siu-Mei and other parishioners kept a candle burning there for more than a decade. (Lance Iverson/Courtesy of *San Francisco Chronicle*)

Joe frowned. His weekend had been awful, and things had hardly improved since. His daughter, Mary, had learned over the weekend that he was gay. She was playing with the daughters of her mother's boyfriend when they got into a fight and the girls blurted out, "Well, *your* dad is gay!" Mary cried and ran downstairs, arriving just as Joe walked in to pick her up.

In the car on the way to San Francisco, Mary asked him what it meant to be gay. "It's something bad, isn't it?" she asked.

Joe had wanted his daughter to have what every child wanted: a normal home life with parents who were together. He told Mary that he had wanted her to be much older before he talked with her about it. He wanted her to understand love before she tried to understand the different kinds of love. She was only five, a darling girl consumed with dolls and princesses and sparkly shoes. Mary told him that she didn't mind having divorced parents, as that was "normal," she said. But having a gay parent was not.

Now, sitting at the table at Holy Trinity, Joe exhaled. He turned his focus back to the room, to the business of the meeting. It was the winter of 1998, and the members of the committee had settled into their usual seats at the cafeteria tables under the stylish blue light fixtures surrounded by pale yellow walls lined with dark oil paintings of Russian Orthodox priests.

Outside, the evening light waned. The parishioners had begun to mark the change in seasons by the amount of daylight at the start of their meetings. They had begun to create a new routine in exile.

Each person settled in differently, in a way now familiar to the others. Marilyn Aspesi, who could come across as sharp and impatient but had a kind heart and a sweet smile, had grown up at St. Brigid and spent all of her adult life there. She always brought a copy of the *San Francisco Chronicle.* Her glasses low on the bridge of her nose, she folded the pages methodically and vertically and began to look for people she knew—in the obituary section. Bill Van Way, an attorney and another lifelong parishioner, with glasses and a thick head of salt-and-pepper hair, kept his briefcase on his lap and inevitably shared a few jokes he'd heard at the office. Margaret Sanderson, who had a fondness for pale blue clothing and eye shadow to match and who had belonged to the St. Brigid choir, took to offering coffee and cookies. Eleanor Croke carried her own distinctive sounds: the rustling of plastic bags punctuated by a cheerful, high-pitched hello. Once seated, she searched in one of her many sacks for a snack—a part of a cookie, brownie, or piece of chocolate. Helen and Tillie Piscevich, who perched like eagles with watchful eyes on the table, tried to keep the meetings moving.

The committee returned on this night to the business at hand. Ciaran Baynes, the soccer player and roofer who served as treasurer, reported that there had been $650 in donations in the prior two weeks, bringing the operating account balance to $1,880.62. Tillie said that a cable car replica with an engine had been rented for the St. Patrick's Day parade and that committee members needed to work on improving their standing from last year, when they won third place for best decorations. Gina Delle Sedie offered to reserve the Fort Mason Officers' Club for their spring dinner and said that she and her husband, Max, would work on the invitations.

The mailbox report was given: The committee had received two mailings from Bank of America, a statement from Washington Mutual, $150 in cash from an anonymous donor, a See's Candy catalogue, and solicitations from a copy store and a company that made lapel pins.

Joe offered to write thank-you notes for the donations that had come in. Siu-Mei said, "But Joe, no one can read your writing, and your notes always have cookie smudges on them." Several people laughed. Joe stuck his tongue out and said, "Well, it's sure a lot more legible than your writing." More laughter followed. The two had grown to be close friends but bickered like brother and sister. Most of their phone conversations ended with one hanging up on the other.

Margaret Sanderson reported that she had seen Archbishop Levada at a Mass and approached him about St. Brigid. When he turned away, she followed and again asked what his plans were for the church. "He said no decision has been made," she reported. "And then he hightailed it out of there." There was some laughter, some rolling of eyes. He had still not granted them another meeting.

New business was addressed. Everyone wanted to contribute something. As Janie Yee told the group, "We have all been hurt. We have all been rejected by the religion we love. But with the help of God, we have to see what we can do. We have to rely now on our own small abilities."

Helen and Tillie had become known as the committee's "back office girls." As soon as letters or flyers were ready for mailing, Siu-Mei would pick them up from the printer and deliver them to the Pisceviches. Their small den and kitchen were turned into an assembly line.

Jan Robinson put together a database of notables who had attended St. Brigid from the turn of the century. She wrote short biographies of Lawrence Mario Giannini, from the founding San Francisco family that owned the Bank of Italy, which became the Bank of America. She wrote about James Phelan, who was born into a farming family in Ireland and became a wealthy industrialist in California, establishing the First National Bank of San Francisco. And she wrote about George Moscone, the mayor whose life was cut short in 1978 when he was shot and killed by a former city supervisor, Dan White.

With Siu-Mei's help, Jan kept a list of the parishioners who had passed away. Marilyn, the habitual reader of obituaries, proved a great source for this. The deceased were always honored at committee Masses, their names read aloud. Siu-Mei built the Committee to Save St. Brigid website, with pictures, history, timelines, and news stories.

Joe wrote the weekly newsletters and continued to talk with engineers about the specific seismic strengthening work St. Brigid needed. Robert kept up the pressure on the archdiocese, dashing off letter after letter asking for another meeting, updating church officials on the committee's work, and inviting an array of priests and bishops to dinners and other events.

Eleanor wrote to neighborhood groups asking for their support. Others brought in photos to be made into Christmas cards or posters. Some offered to attach St. Brigid posters to their cars. A list of names was taken of those who would stand in front of busy stores or at intersections and simply talk to passersby about their love for St. Brigid and their efforts to see it reopened. This was the business of the committee: the humdrum, a family settling into an everyday routine.

Before the meeting adjourned, Marilyn said she had begun putting together a yearly calendar of events for the committee. So far she had: March 11, St. Patrick's Day parade; March 25, mailing date for dinner invitation and a possible newsletter; April 28, spring dinner; June 30, anniversary vigil; July, picnic Mass; August, picnic Mass; September, picnic Mass; early October, dinner invitation and possible newsletter; late October, fall dinner; November, Thanksgiving outreach project; December, Christmas potluck and Christmas card and ornament sale.

They went over their tasks for the week, and prayed for those committee members who were sick and for those who had passed away. Get-well cards were distributed for a parishioner who had suffered a stroke and for a woman who was not feeling well. They prayed for Janie and Lily's mother. They prayed for new people to join them, to strengthen their cause by bringing their own special talents. Finally, they stood to sing "Happy Birthday" to a parishioner who couldn't make it to the meeting but was there in spirit, Louisa Stanton, who was turning ninety-two.

The meeting ended after 9 P.M. with a closing prayer. In no hurry, the parishioners collected their belongings and made their way out of the warm basement into the mild night. They took the

SAVE ST. BRIGID CHURCH sign off the entry gate. It would be put back up the following week.

A few blocks away, another parishioner was working for St. Brigid. He was alone, in the dark of night, focused on the task at hand.

The housepainter had returned to work on the church's upper wooden door on Van Ness. It was evening instead of his preferred time of early morning, as he had been busy with painting jobs.

The housepainter had come to St. Brigid in 1986, after going through a divorce and moving back to the city from Marin. He loved that he could walk to church from his home. And, once inside, he liked to look at the stained-glass windows, which he called Easter eggs. He had attended church irregularly as a child. His father was Catholic but went to church about three times a year. Still, his dad was a good man and the church had rubbed off on him. The housepainter studied the door. Toward the bottom were dark splotches that looked and felt like resin glue. At eye level, someone had keyed Xs deep into the wood all the way across. He would sand until the door was light and bare. Then he would apply a coat of stain, followed by three coats of satin varnish, as he had done with the door closer to Broadway.

He turned on his transistor radio, hoping for some good country music. Much of the genre had gotten too "sissy" for him, although he was a fan of Toby Keith. When he didn't find any songs he liked, he searched the dial for a talk show. He was a Republican in a town of Democrats, a pragmatist in a town of activists. He didn't mind. He was comfortable with who he was and grateful for how his life had straightened up. The church reminded him in his darkest days that he should play it straight. He told friends that when he was low, there was only one place to look—and that was up. And he told his son, "I forgot my teachings for a while, but then I got to the point where I guess I was receptive. It was buried for a while, but the faith was always there."

About an hour into his work, he saw someone dart up the front steps of the church. He stepped back on the sidewalk to take a look. A small figure was hunched over, lighting a white candle on the top step. The housepainter surprised himself by calling out, "Hi there."

A young-looking woman in jeans and a gray hooded sweatshirt ventured over.

"Hi," she said. "I'm Siu-Mei. I'm with the Committee to Save St. Brigid. What is your name?"

"Oh, I'm just here doing some work on the doors," he replied. Sizing her up, he finally let himself smile and said, "My name is David Hansell. I'm a parishioner here."

"That's wonderful," Siu-Mei said, her ponytail spilling out as her hood came off. "Did you do the door below? I noticed how nice it looks."

David nodded.

"All on your own?"

"All on my own."

"What are you doing now?"

"Working on this upper door, doing the same thing. Then I'll do the main door, and maybe these decorative window grates."

"Can I help you?" Siu-Mei asked.

David looked her over again. She had such a bright and happy smile. There was a childlike innocence to her.

"Sure, why not?" he said. "But a warning: I'm not much for talking."

Siu-Mei smiled. She didn't mind working in silence. So much had been said already. She liked the passage from the Book of James: *"So with faith, if it does not lead to action, it is in itself a lifeless thing."*

As she worked on a lower section of the door, she stole a glance at David, illuminated by the streetlights. His white coveralls were splattered in paint, his long fingers covered in dust.

27 *New Recruits*

WALKING TO HER NEIGHBORHOOD Starbucks, Carmen Esteva concentrated on making each step a kind of prayer. She focused on positive thoughts, on meditations for others. But then her mind wandered to the mocha Frappuccino she wanted to have but shouldn't because she was trying to get back into one of her favorite summer skirts.

Ever since St. Brigid closed, she feared for the safety of her soul. In the Philippines, where she grew up, she was taught that attending Mass daily would save her soul and secure a spot for her in heaven. Her husband, Jesus "Jess" Esteva, had worked all of his life to afford a condominium a half-block from St. Brigid. He wanted his wife to be able to walk to church every day. "I want your soul to be safe," he told her. With St. Brigid closed, she could no longer attend Mass daily.

She arrived at Starbucks and went ahead and ordered the mocha Frappuccino. Walking out into the early evening, she thought of her best friend, another Filipina. Even in their sixties, the two had competed over who was thinner. Since her friend had passed away, Carmen sometimes found herself praying to her for strength—to avoid the brownie or Frappuccino. When she got no answer, she figured her friend was telling her to go for it.

She sipped her drink as she walked the last few blocks, searching for a Russian church named Holy Trinity. She had heard that many of the people who used to attend St. Brigid were still getting together for meetings, still working to get the church reopened. She thought she would give it a try.

In the spring of 1994, when St. Brigid was being shuttered, she and Jess had worn the white towels to Mass. That was the extent of their protest, for they believed they had to accept the decision of the archbishop. They always walked to church hand in hand for the 4:30 P.M. Saturday Mass. They spent Sundays with her mother and father.

Then in May, a month before St. Brigid was closed, her seventy-eight-year-old mother, Primitiva Falcon, suffered a stroke and landed in intensive care at Seton Medical Center. Carmen spent even more time at St. Brigid, arriving early to kneel before the statue of the Virgin Mother and pray for her mother. Her husband then drove her to the hospital.

She and Jess were at the last Mass of St. Brigid the night of June 30. She wandered about the sanctuary taking pictures, feeling for all those who were grieving, and questioning why the church had to be closed. But she was consumed by losses even closer to home. Two months later, her mother passed away. It wasn't long before her father, Ananias Falcon, joined her. Then her dear Jess became ill, eventually dying in his sleep at home in 1997.

Since Jess had left her, she would bundle and unbundle his letters to her, love notes that had begun in their courtship and continued until the day he died. She kept them beside her bed, next to her rosary. She told herself that death was not the end but the beginning for the departed. She focused on her prayers, novenas, lighting of candles, and positive thoughts. The days passed, bringing a mixture of solace and sadness. It had been a year since her husband's death.

Rounding the corner, Carmen saw a lovely white jewel box of a church. She was surprised that she had never noticed it before. She looked around for the entrance and peered in a window. She saw a group of people gathered in the basement and recognized a few of the faces. Then she saw a SAVE ST. BRIGID CHURCH sign on the iron gate. She walked in tentatively but was greeted warmly and offered a seat at the center of the table. That was where Lily Wong sat when she could attend. Carmen, with her handsome unlined face and clean, pressed shirt, settled in. She took her rosary out of the plastic bag she kept inside her purse. She had never attended meetings before, let alone led one. But on this night she offered a prayer. She listened to the ideas and the banter and looked over the agenda and the minutes from the previous week's meeting.

It felt good to be out. The nights were hard, bringing silence, bringing the reality of her husband's empty chair.

She listened and took notes in her tidy handwriting. The committee had won first place for the best decorated cable car in the St. Patrick's Day parade. They had received $100 in prize money and a plaque, which was passed around the table.

About an hour into the meeting, several parishioners conspiratorially dashed into the kitchen, closing the door. With the lights dimmed, they emerged, carrying a birthday cake and singing. They set the cake in front of Mary Dignan, seated next to her dad. It was her sixth birthday.

Carmen seldom smiled broadly or unselfconsciously. The nuns at her school in Manila had cautioned the girls not to smile too much and never to show their teeth in pictures. But tonight she smiled easily, as she had when Jess would tell her stories or surprise her with love notes and boxes of chocolate.

At the end of the meeting, she offered a closing prayer. When it came time to leave, Helen, Tillie, and Marilyn said they would walk her home. As they walked along, the Pisceviches began to fill her in on who was who—on Robert and his relentless legal efforts and his ability to give a speech that went on for an hour; on Lily, who was nearly blind and had a calm and patience that were a kind of foil to Robert's indignation; on Joe, dear Joe, who was so much like a lovable errant child, tardy and noisy but full of surprises; and on Father O, who risked his collar to support what they were doing.

Carmen walked in the front door of her condominium and set her handbag down. Looking in the mirror in the hallway, she saw faint smile lines around her eyes.

28 *New Allies*

JOE DIGNAN STUFFED envelopes at an office in the Castro District, the heart of San Francisco's gay community. It was the early summer of 2000, and he had begun volunteering for the reelection of Mark Leno, an openly gay city supervisor. Part of it was for Leno. Part of it was for St. Brigid.

At the campaign office, Joe talked with other volunteers and with the supervisor himself. He shared his personal story and talked about the struggles for St. Brigid. He did whatever was needed, from calling registered voters to walking the precincts. He watched and listened, studying how Leno and his aides managed to be both openly gay and assertively political. He told another volunteer, "Until now, most of the gay people I've known were in bars. It's encouraging to see gay people sober and functioning."

Months earlier, members of the committee had sent letters to all of the candidates for supervisor, asking whether they supported the reopening of St. Brigid, favored keeping it closed, or felt it was best left in the hands of the archdiocese. Leno, a rabbinical school dropout, responded at length. The answers came over Joe's home fax machine late one night. They were handwritten and expressed absolute support for reopening St. Brigid.

In recent times, Joe had watched the committee hit a wall of silence with the archdiocese. He had begun to believe that at some point, the battle for St. Brigid would need to move from the religious to the political. The committee members had been honored by the Board of Supervisors for their years of "service and efforts to preserve the architectural and cultural history of St. Brigid" and for continuing while exiled from their church to help the poor and improve the neighborhood. They had succeeded in having St. Brigid listed on the National Register of Historic Places. But Joe knew they needed to move beyond commendations—to connections.

Late in the summer, buoyed by his experience in the campaign, Joe mustered the nerve to do something he had wanted to do for years, but he had felt constricted by the expectations of others. He applied for a job with a small newspaper that covered the gay community. When he got no response, he asked Leno for a letter of recommendation. He applied again with Leno's letter. This time, he got a response.

It wasn't long before Joe landed his first assignment with the *Bay Area Reporter*. The story, about a crisis hotline for gay youth, wasn't splashy or particularly consequential, but Siu-Mei had it framed. Within months, Joe had angled his way into becoming the paper's City Hall reporter. He spent endless hours at meetings, taking notes on absolutely everything out of fear that he was going to miss something. He knew the meetings would put some people to sleep, but he was rapt. He had a sense that every contact he made would pay off later, possibly for St. Brigid.

He proudly showed his stories to his mother. He would visit her at home, sometimes sitting with her as she rested in her dimly lit bedroom on her narrow twin bed with its quilted headboard and matching duvet. On other days, the two would pass hours in the backyard, tending her rosebushes, dahlias, avocado tree, and wildflowers. Eleanor had long marveled at the avocado tree, planted when Joe was born. "It grew faster than you did," she said, smiling. From the garden, they listened to the bells of Saints Peter and Paul Church in North Beach. His mother lamented not hearing the bells of St. Brigid. She had loved the sound, which had not been heard since the night of the closure, when the bell in the tower rang unexpectedly.

On these visits, Eleanor asked Joe to read aloud the stories he had written. He knew she boasted to friends in painting class that her son was writing front-page stories. Omitting the name of the paper, she would say that her favorite line in the story was the first: his byline, "By Joe Dignan."

In the kitchen, Eleanor asked him about the committee and its work. Joe updated her on Robert, whom she knew, and Siu-Mei and Helen and Tillie and many of the others. She listened closely, peppering him with breathless questions about who was getting along, who was bickering, about the latest ideas and dramas. It was her favorite cause and soap opera—all rolled into one.

As she began to express doubt that the church was ever going to reopen, Joe would tell her otherwise.

"What we're working to do now is to start changing the minds of the diocese and make contacts around the city that will help us," he said. "We need to raise money and change minds—in that order. We need a shift."

Leaving his mother's house one afternoon, he thought of his father, who was always either at the office or holed up in his room, his door closed. Joe knew all too well of his mother's foiled dreams. She had worked briefly during World War II as a nurse and longed to return to work in a hospital. She had considered establishing herself as an artist, for she was a talented painter; many of her oils were reminiscent of Bonnard. But there were only so many things her husband considered appropriate for her, a housewife with a genius IQ. With St. Brigid, Joe felt he was being sent on a mission by his mother because it was a battle she was not allowed to wage.

Joe had learned as he grew older that his mother put up with all she did because of him. She wanted him to grow up in a home that was peaceful—or appeared that way. He now understood, as he too had wanted his only child to have a normal family life: mother, father, home, peace. As he got ready for the committee's weekly meeting, he knew that, like his mother, he was caught somewhere between being himself and living the life others expected of him. He knew the people on the committee appreciated him and probably even genuinely liked him. But they knew the Joe who showed up at meetings and rallies—the one who was tardy and noisy but ultimately reliable. They knew he'd gone to all the right schools and was brought up in a Catholic family. They knew he had been married and had a daughter who could always make him smile.

But they didn't really know him. They didn't know he was gay, and he was not ready to tell them. In his mind, they would never be able to accept him for who he really was.

29 *Quiet Defiance*

When Father O arrived back at the rectory at St. Isabella's at close to midnight, the light under the door of the elder priest's room was still on. That's how it always was when he returned from a night out.

It was the fall of 2000 and St. Brigid had been closed for six years. Yet Father O's comings and goings at the Marin County church were still being tracked by the other priests. At St. Isabella's, where Father O had been for over a year now, the Reverend Michael Keane made it clear that his involvement with St. Brigid was anathema to church teachings and an insult to the archdiocese. There were occasions when Father O found his mail opened and learned that phone messages for him were not passed on. And there were occasions when Father O would make a point of returning extra late, just to keep his minders up.

The next morning, Keane asked Father O where he had been in his predictably nonchalant way, without looking up from the morning paper. The gregarious Father O would have loved to have said that he'd gone to see the parishioners from St. Brigid, who had a surprise birthday party for one of their own. He had caught up with Robert, who had been away in the south of France with his wife and daughter. He had talked with Joe about his new job as a reporter and said he was proud of him for having the courage to pursue his dreams. He had listened to Helen and Tillie talk about their two-year-old niece, who had stayed at their house for the weekend and created general mayhem.

But Father O replied that he had been administering to parishioners. He left it at that. He knew that Keane was asking only so he could call the archdiocese with any nugget of information. Father O smiled to himself. He didn't mind, really. It was all a part of his education as a priest. There were politics everywhere—why not the priesthood? He had learned to trust his instincts and impressions, even when they were at odds with those around him. He remembered visiting the Sistine Chapel in Rome when he was in his early twenties. It was a hot summer day. He waited in line for more than two hours to see the interior by Michelangelo. When he was finally admitted to the chapel, it was crammed with people standing elbow to elbow. He looked at the ceiling. He looked at the walls. He said, "Is that all?" and walked out.

When he first entered St. Brigid in September 1990—incredibly, now ten years earlier—he could see that it was a gorgeous, impressive church, with spectacular windows, marble, statuary, and carpets. But what got him was that scent. And that silence.

No matter how far he was from St. Brigid, the church and its parishioners were a part of him, like his unruly hair, his quick laugh, his love of storytelling. He continued to bless parishioners' homes. He presided over Masses. He attended their luncheons and dinners and rode on cable cars in parades with them. He coached the men's soccer team, baptized babies, and performed last rites. They supported him, too, making quiet appearances at Mass at St. Isabella's. They prayed for him and for his family. They sent cards and celebrated his birthday. Whenever he needed them, they were there—no questions asked.

He wrote letters urging them not to give up the fight, never to throw in the towel. In a letter to Robert, Father O expressed his appreciation for the attorney's "untiring effort" for St. Brigid. "You have done a superb job, Robert, that few could ever have undertaken," he wrote. He signed off with: "It has always been my belief that St. Brigid will be reopened as long as people are willing to sacrifice and fight for her."

Back in his room, as he got ready for the day, Father O looked at the wall calendar. Time was passing so quickly. Before long, it would be the seventh anniversary of the closing of St. Brigid. For all of these years, the Irish priest had enjoyed coming up with the slogans to be made into banners and hung on the front door of the church. For the first few years, the archdiocese would send someone to tear down the signs, but the parishioners would put up new ones. Eventually—especially after Archbishop Quinn resigned—the signs remained up for longer periods.

Every few weeks Father O wrote a new line for a banner. Most he thought up himself. A few were passages from the Bible, including SOLD FOR 30 PIECES OF SILVER and NO ROOM AT THE INN. For the seventh anniversary, Father O already had an idea.

30 *Divisions*

On November 1, 2000, Robert Bryan circled Russian Hill in search of a parking place. It was 7:40 P.M., and he was forty minutes late for the committee's weekly meeting. He circled again and again, clenching the wheel. He was trying to pack too much into a day.

He had just agreed to take over the case of Miguel Bacigalupo, who was on death row at San Quentin for having killed two people in San Jose on the orders of the Medellín cartel, a Colombian drug trafficking ring. He was representing the country's only Iranian on death row, a young man named Hooman Panah, who had been convicted of raping and killing an eight-year-old girl. He had another client, William Noguera, charged with killing his girlfriend's mother. And he remained involved with a former client, Bob Massie, who was scheduled for execution at San Quentin within three months. He liked Massie, and the looming execution weighed on him. Robert was also serving as an adviser on a handful of other death row cases across the country, and he regularly turned down worthy requests from inmates seeking representation. Between calls with clients on death row, meetings with associates, and the arrival of more than a hundred boxes of files on the Bacigalupo case, he'd made it that day to a meeting at the San Francisco Conservatory of Music, where Auda Mai, now eleven, was training in classical piano. He was exhausted. Finally, he found a parking space and carefully wedged his Mercedes sedan into the tight spot.

When he walked into the basement of Holy Trinity, Robert saw that Ken Epley, a Realtor who had recently been elected as a committee vice president, was presiding. He settled in, pulling papers out of his attaché case and looking over the night's agenda. He waited until Ken finished before greeting everyone and apologizing for being late. Putting his glasses on, Robert then started in with new business, but he was stopped by Ken, who said *he* was leading the meeting.

Ken, with his dark hair and preppy good looks, was known as a nice guy and an earnest Catholic, but he had not been a regular at committee meetings. He showed up like a few of the others when it came time to elect new officers. Robert spoke up again, saying he could now take over, but Ken continued talking.

Helen and Tillie gave Robert a puzzled look. After a few more minutes with Ken presiding, Robert stuffed his papers back into his case, grabbed his jacket, stood up, and left the room without saying a word. He didn't have the time or patience for games. He was fighting for the life of clients, including the old church just up the street. He was not about to get involved in a petty power struggle.

Back home that night, Robert slumped into his worn wingback leather chair, Halley the cat at his feet. The small living room was filled with books and photos and mementos from the family's trips to Europe. On top of the Steinway piano next to the window was a picture of his daughter with Michael Tilson Thomas, the city's symphony director.

In recent months, small and inconsequential differences of

opinion had created cracks in the committee. He supposed it was like any good family that bickered but still loved one another. What he was feeling, though, was deeper than that. He picked up his daily planner, where he logged his thoughts, and began to write. The conviction of his words took him by surprise.

"I have totally lost faith in the Catholic Church and what it stands for," he wrote. "Priests are frequently arrested for sexually molesting children and stealing from parishioners. The leadership across the U.S. is corrupt and in many cases does not care for the people."

A half-hour later, he reread his words. He was tired of supplicating before bishops and cardinals who expected deference because they wore a collar. He was tired of the naysayers on the committee who thought he was too aggressive. The archbishop had closed their church and taken three-quarters of a million dollars that belonged to them. *They wanted to be nice?* He was tired of being outmaneuvered by the Vatican because they were a closed boys' club. This was the same group that handled nascent sex abuse claims by holding secret canonical trials rather than involving police and sent pedophiles for psychiatric counseling before returning them to the ministry when they should have been tossed in jail. Their own archbishop would not meet with them, despite *four years* of requests. Maybe it was because Levada was dealing with a new headache. His former diocese in Portland was facing an avalanche of sex abuse litigation, much of which took place under his watch.

Robert had seen glimmers of beauty in houses of worship. Now he saw beauty in those who somehow continued to believe. Turning off the light, he thought that perhaps it was time to leave Catholicism. And maybe it was time to leave the committee.

At 10 P.M. on March 27, 2001, Robert Bryan stood outside San Quentin Prison in Marin County. His former client, Robert Lee Massie, was scheduled to die at 12:01 A.M.

Robert had been asked to speak. He looked out at the large crowd gathered in front of the prison gates. Behind him were the old stone buildings of San Quentin. Before him were protesters holding signs, candles, and flowers. Images of St. Brigid ran through his mind. He picked up a bullhorn and began to speak, as he had done so many times before.

He told the crowd that he had known Massie for more than a decade.

"He was a model prisoner who wasn't able to function on the outside," Robert said, adjusting to the bright lights of the television cameras. "He had a horrendous childhood in Virginia. He was sexually abused. He was put in a state mental hospital when he was a child, where he was surrounded by adults. He went through some real bad things."

He said he had visited Massie days earlier, and that Massie had dropped all his appeals. He wanted to die. "He felt by dying he was making a statement."

Massie had already faced four dates for execution, coming within thirty-six hours of the death chamber the last time. Robert said that he had filed a declaration, against Massie's wishes, saying the inmate was mentally ill. He also believed Massie had been incompetently represented.

He read from a book in which Massie was quoted as saying: "I have grown bitter and contemptuous of American justice. It was like a cat playing with a mouse the way it dragged on. The law is clear and I have every right to demand an immediate execution."

Robert told the crowd that society should not be in the business of killing fellow human beings. "My opposition to the death penalty is about the right to a fair trial. I don't want to know about guilt or innocence. Someone can do horrendous things and they still have a right to a fair trial. I don't think it accomplishes anything to kill someone. People are executed because they don't have good representation. As has been said before, the death penalty is a privilege reserved for the poor."

When he drove back across the Golden Gate Bridge at 1:30

A.M., he had the majestic span to himself. The air was cool, and the lights of the city sparkled from the Financial District to the Marina and out to Sea Cliff. Massie would have loved the sight. The burnished red of the bridge was streaked in bronze. Robert nodded at the toll taker. He couldn't get his client out of his mind. Massie had been a smart guy. Had he been given opportunities in life, he would've done something good. Now he had been strapped into a chair and put to death—at the age of fifty-nine.

Instead of heading straight home, Robert took a detour. There on the steps of St. Brigid was a small if forlorn-looking altar, with candles and flowers—like the flowers and signs placed that night at the gate of San Quentin. And Massie's words fit how the Vatican had handled St. Brigid's case: *It was like a cat playing with a mouse the way it dragged on.*

Robert still had doubts about staying on the Committee to Save St. Brigid—he had given more than six years to the cause—yet it was moments like this when he remembered why he had gotten involved in the first place. St. Brigid was that rare thing that was about the eternal, when so much of life was ephemeral. It was right versus wrong, spirit versus material. It was what his father, Russell Duval Bryan, a structural engineer who had read *War and Peace* a dozen times, had urged him to do as a youth: "Bobby, do something that makes a difference in the lives of others, that makes the world a better place."

He knew his father was right. He had to keep fighting. Yet he also knew the day would come when he would have to step away.

31 *Hope Fades*

ON JUNE 27, 2001, only a handful of people showed up for the committee's regular meeting. The group had received a $1 donation. The St. Brigid Mariners soccer team had been defeated. Archbishop Levada had declined another dinner invitation. The spring dinner had been canceled, but apparently not everyone knew; they had just learned to their embarrassment that two city supervisors had showed up to find no one else there.

The archdiocese had recently released a statement, saying it had "spent millions of dollars saving other Catholic churches, and unfortunately St. Brigid did not have the numbers demographically to make us save it." In the same statement, a spokesman said, "The archbishop has not said what he will do with the church. He sympathizes with the parishioners of St. Brigid for their loss."

Some on the committee maintained that Robert's passionate denunciations and eye-opening investigations had done more harm than good and that a new group from the committee should try to meet with the archbishop. While Robert acknowledged he had been "aggressive and strong," he said, "I served a necessary purpose for six and a half years. The archbishop may not have liked some of the things I have done in the past because it embarrassed the church, but it was the truth." A subcommittee to deal with the archbishop was formed and then disbanded after Robert discovered that they were trying to go around him in ways reminiscent of John Ross and Richard Figone.

There had always been squabbling on the committee, and even some serious divisions, but these days it was different. Committee members were assigning blame to themselves more than to the archdiocese. It didn't help matters that the news on the personal front was even grimmer.

Marilyn Sanderson reported at the meeting that her friend Claire Winter had died. Another friend, Claire Buckley, had suffered three cracked ribs. Helen Piscevich said Jo Brightwell broke her toe. Siu-Mei Wong reported that Miriam Gray had been hit in the eye by a baseball at a Giants game and required stitches. She also said that Nelly Echavarria was closing her sewing shop because her rent had tripled.

Then there was Gina Delle Sedie, a committee member since

its inception. She had been there during the spring of 1994, when hundreds of people fought for St. Brigid. She had seen the battle escalate against Archbishop Quinn and had cheered his exodus. And she had heralded the arrival of Archbishop Levada, believing in a new era of hope. But now she saw nothing coming to fruition, and she decided to leave the committee. There was only so much a person could take.

Three nights later, the parishioners made their way to St. Brigid. Father O, clad in his white robe and standing behind his regular makeshift altar, welcomed everyone: "This is our seventh occasion to gather here." Holding a microphone, he looked at the group, sitting on benches, their hands tucked under blankets. For this vigil, they had chosen a place in the parking lot that brought them as close as they could get to the altar of St. Brigid. They were separated only by the thick granite wall, by the locked doors.

Many parishioners, including Joe, stood against the back fence facing their church, facing the reality of another year's passage. Seven years was a long time.

Father O's voice boomed: "You are told, again and again, year after year, that it's time to move on. I don't believe it. I will never accept it as a priest. We will simply not move on from St. Brigid." After a talk that touched on the parishioners' long, wandering journey, a smile finally returned to the priest's face. "You know," he said, "Moses and his people spent forty years in the desert. You're heading toward a quarter of the way through!"

Communion was offered. Jan Robinson played the harp as a line formed in front of Father O. The group quietly sang the Lord's Prayer and "Lamb of God, you take away the sins of the world—have mercy on us."

After Mass, the group walked together to Holy Trinity for a potluck dinner. This year, the vigil drew about eighty parishioners; hundreds had gathered in earlier years. The evening ended back on the front steps of St. Brigid for candle lighting and quiet reflection. Hanging on the door was Father O's latest banner: GOD IS WELCOME EVERYWHERE EXCEPT VAN NESS AND BROADWAY.

Helen and Tillie stood together, their heads bowed more out of sadness than prayer. Tillie longed to kneel before the statue of the Virgin Mother, just inside the padlocked door, about twenty feet from where she stood. She now regretted not taking the rosary off the statue on that final night, June 30, 1994. Helen wondered whether the Saint Anthony statue remained inside. They were losing friends and relatives. Louisa Stanton had just died. She lived across the street and wanted nothing more than to be buried from the church. She was ninety-five and had held on in hopes that the doors would reopen.

Siu-Mei tried to brighten the mood. "Did you notice the doors?" she asked the group. "Aren't they beautiful?" She explained that a former parishioner, a housepainter, had worked on them by himself late at night and early in the mornings. He didn't want any recognition. He wanted to give something back. Siu-Mei said she happened to see him one night when she was checking on the church. "He started this all on his own," she said. "He saw that the doors and steps were all beaten up, both by humans—homeless and skateboarders—and by the forces of nature. He decided regardless of what happens to the church, he is going to make it look respectable again. He has also cleaned the steps, removed graffiti, and even pulled weeds that grow around the church."

Not far away, Carmen Esteva was struck by the still-long faces. Gone were the smiles and words of encouragement. The years were wearing on the group, as they were on the building. Catholicism itself felt less fresh. Each day brought a new revelation of misdeeds. In San Francisco, the archdiocese was now being forced by the city's district attorney to turn over records related to possible sex abuse by its priests going back seventy-five years. A directive by Cardinal Joseph Ratzinger, head of the Congregation for the Doctrine of the Faith—the office dealing with clergy abuse cases—had instructed all bishops to keep abuse cases secret. He also accused the news media of having a "desire to discredit the church." Carmen had seen good Catholics like Gina Delle Sedie come and go, apologizing as they went for giving up on St. Brigid. Many said it was damaging their faith to be ignored for so long.

"We are all a little bit discouraged with the news we get every day," Carmen said, as people joined hands in prayer. "We do not know why our prayers aren't being answered. But we must continue to pray. We must ask for a miracle." Carmen, like those who remained a part of the committee, focused on the good that was around them, on their friends and their faith. They told themselves that the evil deeds of a few reflected an institution in trouble. Where life wore them down, faith built them back up.

She said that Saint Joan of Arc had encouraged her troops to fight bravely, regardless of the odds, and had told them: "If we fight, God will give us victory."

32 *A New Spiritual Leader*

THE REQUEST CAME casually, without much discussion. It seemed like a natural progression—to all but Carmen.

At an otherwise uneventful committee meeting in the fall of 2001, Carmen was asked to serve as spiritual leader. She did not see herself as a leader, and she had come to the committee only recently, compared to many others. She looked to Helen and Tillie, Jan, and Siu-Mei as better suited than she. But she said yes; she was comfortable being a source of prayer. Others could picket and protest and work the political angles. Praying was what she did. At home, she prayed three times a day; she had different rosaries for different needs, prayer cards for every occasion, and knew what each saint represented.

Carmen had watched with admiration as Lily Wong led the

prayers at the meetings. When others talked and gossiped, Lily prayed. She prayed for those in attendance. She prayed for success in what was being attempted. She prayed for St. Brigid. Carmen had heard that whenever Robert had stood before the altar of St. Brigid delivering his weekly committee updates, blustery and full of outward conviction, Lily was at his side, strong and silent.

Lily could not go to that night's committee meeting. She needed to stay home to watch over her ailing mother, Dymphna, who had suffered a stroke. Piece by piece, time was continuing to chip away at her independence. She had had to leave her job at San Francisco General Hospital, which had always been so much more than a job: She rode the bus by herself across town, her colleagues relied on her, and her world was expanded. She didn't even mind when she rode the bus to work and, having forgotten to wear her dark glasses, would hear someone say, "Lady, why are you staring at me?"

Now, as her mother's health grew fragile, she realized she would no longer be able to attend committee meetings. Being chosen as prayer leader had introduced her to this new group: Robert, a convert to Catholicism, who could have walked away during this battle; Father O, who was driven by principle, not politics; Joe, who was full of energy and self-deprecating humor. The others were lovely, devoted Catholics.

Planning for the meetings made her dig deeper for prayers. She prayed daily for committee members and for St. Brigid, and the unanswered prayers strengthened her.

Before St. Brigid was closed, Lily had trusted religious leaders completely, never once thinking to question. Then came the betrayals and letdowns: the archdiocese's confidential property report, with valuations ascribed to St. Brigid and other churches; the Vatican's last-minute reprieve, which was kept secret; their legal appeal, denied on a technicality. Now, the Church she loved had a sickness within.

Lily told others who had grown disillusioned and felt disenfranchised from the Catholic Church: "It's not God at work here. It's human beings who are making mistakes."

She understood that her new role was at home with her mother, who had helped her all these years, worrying and trying to protect her. Now it was her turn. She told God that she carried no bitterness and that she would do her best to accept life's changes, as her mother had taught her. "I feel more attached to God because I have lost my sight," she said. "It is like a child who depends on his mother. I live from day to day. I listen to my Catholic radio."

Thinking of the faithful from St. Brigid, it seemed to Lily that she had spent her life surrounded by believers, first Buddhist, then Catholic. She was struck by an irony: The strongest believers she knew were those she'd met after their church was closed. And time outside St. Brigid was doing something interesting. While the circle of believers was getting smaller by the week, hands were ever more tightly clasped in prayer.

Carmen searched her books for just the right verses and sayings. Lily had said her prayers from memory. Carmen chose as the meeting's opening passage a preparatory prayer in which she asked God to quiet their hearts and be present with the group. The closing prayer would be a goodnight prayer she cherished: "My God, we adore you and we love you. We thank you for having created us and having made us your children and for watching over us this day. Please accept the good we may have done. May your presence and grace be with us."

Unable to attend Mass daily, the sixty-eight-year-old Filipina was learning new ways of being Catholic. She told herself that if she did a good job with whatever she was doing, if she were present in the moment, this would be its own prayer.

She knew by now to embrace life's surprises. She had been fifty and living happily with her parents when she met the man who would become her husband. She wasn't looking for anyone, telling friends, "At this age, who cares?" Jess Esteva was thirty years her senior. But then the sweet notes and small boxes of chocolates began arriving in her mailbox. Their courtship lasted for nearly ten years.

When St. Brigid was open, she and Jess would sit at the back of the sanctuary by the confessionals. Jess had back problems and found it taxing to sit, stand, and kneel, which he felt obligated to do if surrounded by parishioners. Sometimes they sat across from a woman named Maggie Zuniga, who brought her dog to church in a basket and also sat near the confessionals. Maggie was the one person Carmen knew when she joined the committee. For months, Carmen struggled to remember the names of the committee members, and she was embarrassed that she couldn't distinguish between the Piscevich sisters. She made notes to herself that Tillie's hair was darker than Helen's.

But through the weekly meetings, luncheons and dinners, the leisurely walks home together, friendships were taking hold. After all of the losses in recent years, after all of the devastating subtractions to her life, Carmen was now adding on. She knew how her friends were struggling with the silence of their own archdiocese. She prayed to her mother, and to others who had departed, to please reopen St. Brigid and help her new friends on the committee. Whenever she went to a funeral and there was an open casket, she paused to ask the departed for help with their cause. When she took communion, it was one of her prayers that the church be returned to the faithful.

Until now, Carmen had never considered challenging a priest —on anything. In the Philippines, priests could do no wrong. Churches were built first and neighborhoods followed. Everything went for one's redemption. But now she was watching others be obedient while challenging and asking questions. For the first time, she was thinking about her rights as a Catholic.

Over coffee with friends from the committee, Carmen had

asked, "Did you hear about the new Catholic lay movement called Voice of the Faithful?" Tillie responded, "It's time the Catholic Church gets the message it needs to listen to its people." Her sister, Helen, added, "I read that there are more problems starting to surface in Boston. Remember how their Cardinal Law outright denied the allegations? Now they're back. We'll see how he does this time."

Carmen shook her head. She believed the words of Corinthians 10:13: *"God will not let you be tested beyond your strength. He will also provide the way out."*

33 *Drawing Closer*

IT WAS THE SUMMER of 2002, and Siu-Mei smiled as she watched her friend Joe taste and retaste the dressing for the salad and the sauce for the prime rib. She had been the first to arrive at his home in the Potrero Hill neighborhood. It was nice to see him happy. Joe seemed different on these nights when a small group from St. Brigid descended on his home for a dinner party. He was less antsy. He slowed down. He gave the nicotine gum a break.

Tonight, Joe stood practically in place, sipping his favorite drink—a Cosmopolitan with extra lime—as he cooked, directing her on what went where, and thinking aloud about the menu and libations. He would have Scotch for Father O, white wine for his mother and Helen, and Mountain Dew for his daughter, Mary, who was off in her room. He had some great bottles of red wine for dinner. Appetizers of toast points with salmon were ready, along with the cheese platter.

Eleanor arrived first, sweeping in with her trademark oversized glasses with the brightly colored frames, slacks and a striped silk blouse, and her big and bold costume jewelry that clanked as she moved. She was followed by Father O, wearing dark pants and a polo shirt and, as usual, bounding more than walking. Helen and Tillie arrived and were courteous as always, asking what they could do to help. Phil Bailey, Joe's friend from childhood, sauntered in, big and bearlike. Joe and Phil had attended grammar school and graduated from the University of California at Berkeley together. Siu-Mei scurried around taking pictures and trying to help Joe until he shooed her from the kitchen.

The dining room table was set: lace tablecloth, china, silver candleholders, silver napkin holders, lit candles. The centerpiece was a bouquet of dahlias and blue bachelor's buttons from Eleanor's garden. Mary emerged, prompting welcoming cheers from the group. They had known her since she was a baby, celebrated every birthday, and adored the precocious ten-year-old who insisted on rolling her jeans up just so and wearing only a certain brand of sneakers.

Mary's mother, Polly, had recently moved to a town of fewer than a thousand people about four hours north of San Francisco, which made it tougher for Mary to visit her dad on weekends. She loved her visits—and her bedroom. It was decorated in shades of yellow with white trim. She had Pierre Deux sheets, a cherry armoire, a desk and chair that had belonged to her father when he was a child, and a Winnie-the-Pooh lamp.

Mary climbed into a chair next to Father O, who regaled the group with a story of his last trip home to Ireland. Siu-Mei noticed that his hair was cut unusually short—the only person who could get away with making Father O cut his locks was his mother.

The dinners were Father O's idea. He believed that parties boosted spirits like little else. In Ireland, hundreds of people showed up for even the unimportant celebrations. He told the group how the town of Cork had nearly shut down when his parents, Evelyn and Timothy O'Sullivan, announced the arrival of twin boys. As was the O'Sullivan tradition for generations, family and friends gathered in a room to collectively pick the names for the newborns. Oliver was easy, but the next boy's name was not. No one could agree. Finally, after five hours of alcohol-enlivened debate, Timothy announced that he alone would choose his other son's name. It was Cyril, he said. A near riot followed, for Cyril was an English name. But Timothy O'Sullivan had made up his mind.

The tacit rule of the St. Brigid dinner parties was that there would be no talk of the committee's work—not the latest fund-raising drive or letter-writing campaign or the continued silence from the almighty archbishop. This night was about gossiping, staying a little too late, drinking a little too much wine, and sharing.

Eleanor came into the kitchen. Joe remarked that she looked thin and pale, but his mother waved off his concern with a bejeweled hand.

"Julia?" she asked of the recipe on the counter, sipping from a glass of water. Joe knew she was referring to her patron saint of cooking, Julia Child. She religiously tuned in to Child's television show, *Dinner at Julia's,* pen and note cards in hand. The next morning, she and several friends would be at the door of their favorite Union Square cooking store when it opened to get that special pot or gadget required by Julia's recipe.

"Of course it's Julia," Joe said of the recipe. "I don't want to cross the line with you."

She laughed. Looking at her son, it was her turn to worry. He looked so thin.

"I'm working out," he replied.

At this, Jan Robinson walked into the kitchen. "Joe, all of the photos I saw of you as a kid, you were always in a little suit and tie or blazer and slacks," she said. "What happened?"

Dressed in flip-flops, shorts down to his knees, a tight T-shirt, and his trademark black bracelets, Joe replied, "When I was an adolescent, I dressed in Brooks Brothers. Now that I'm old, I dress like an adolescent."

Everyone laughed. Eleanor was proud of her son. This kid who had pulled every trick in the book to evade Mass, whose altar was the television set and whose Bible may as well have been his Batman comic books was making dinner for some of the nicest Catholics she had ever known. And, eight years after the closure of St. Brigid, Joe was still working to get her beloved church reopened.

Joe's attention was diverted by the incessant ringing of his phone. "I don't even know what song that damn phone is set to or who it's by," he said. "Mary is the only one who knows how to program it." From the other room, his daughter yelled out: "Britney Spears." He rolled his eyes. "Great, I have a Britney Spears song on my phone."

Joe seated Mary at the head of the table. He watched her talk with Father O. Most priests made Mary feel nervous, but not Father O. He was her friend. "The building is just sitting there," Mary said of St. Brigid. "It's so pretty. Why don't they let people go there? If they reopen it, I promise I would go to church." A toast was made to Mary.

Eleanor talked with Siu-Mei, who had become a friend through Joe, about her golden retriever, Lucy. Eleanor had somehow inherited Lucy after Joe's divorce. "She barks at everyone and has had a bit of a biting problem, but the problem really comes in handy," she said. "I am positive that she has saved me many times from having my home vandalized."

Helen and Tillie praised Joe for the food and urged him to eat. The two had talked earlier, somewhat conspiratorially, about trying to get him to gain weight. When they had first met him, he had full, chubby cheeks and a bushy head of hair. The cheekbones were now defined, like the rest of his body, and his hair was closely cropped and possibly highlighted. They had decided they would make him cookies and cakes to try to fatten him up. The back office girls were adopting him as their next big project.

Later in the evening, Joe saw his mother and Father O buckled over in laughter. Father O was telling another story, this one about a recent gathering of the O'Sullivan clan in Ireland. "There were a couple hundred of the Irish there," he began. "Family, friends, and strangers showed up. Remember, this is a very nationalistic group. These are freedom fighters. These are the Irish who give their lives to have England out of our country. So I stood up and told everyone to raise a toast. Pints of ale were raised. Then I said in a booming voice: 'God save the Queen!' There was silence. Absolute silence. So I said it again, 'God save the Queen!'" Father O collected himself before continuing. His face red with laughter, he said, "Anyone else who dared to say this would have been mobbed and stoned right then and there. I made sure that I was wearing the collar that day!"

The laughter continued when Mary got up from the table to perform dance moves she had learned in school. Siu-Mei found her camera and began taking pictures, until Joe grabbed it from her and said he wasn't giving it back.

Siu-Mei talked with Phil about when she first met Joe. It was around January 1994, and the Committee to Save St. Brigid was just forming. A group of parishioners staged a candlelit procession from the steps of St. Brigid to St. Mary's Cathedral, stopping in front of the residence of Archbishop Quinn. She happened to be walking next to Joe, who introduced himself.

"He was holding this Ebenezer Scrooge type of lantern, an old-fashioned lantern with a candle," Siu-Mei said. "We started talking, and he said that Father O had baptized his young daughter. We just started becoming friends around committee happenings. For many years now, Joe's mother has invited me to their house for Christmas dinner."

Phil smiled. He saw Siu-Mei and Joe as opposites. Siu-Mei was relentlessly kind. Joe could be verbally dismissive—or worse. Siu-Mei was sweet and devout. Joe was audacious, sometimes outrageous, and always questioning.

"At this point, Joe and I call each other every day," Siu-Mei said. "I know we are an odd couple as friends, but we just have this relationship. We talk every day; half the time he hangs up on me. But when I don't hear from Joe, I get nervous that something has happened."

Phil said that he and Joe had frequent conversations about religion—especially now, as revelations of sex abuse by clergymen filled the news—and about Joe's involvement with the committee. Phil, an atheist, had told Joe, "Of all the things you can choose to put hundreds of hours into, this seems like an odd cause." But he respected his friend's commitment. Also, as he and Joe had worked together in theater and stage design, they talked of the similarities between church and theater, of the spectacle and ritual in both.

"Once Joe sets his mind to something, that's kind of it," Phil told Siu-Mei. "When Polly was trying to win the license to operate the stables in Golden Gate Park, it was Joe who was writing the letters to the supervisors and working all of the political angles."

Siu-Mei looked over at Joe. Since his divorce, she hadn't seen him with anyone else. She worried that he was spending too much time alone. She closed her eyes, wanting to freeze the image of the smiling Joe in her mind.

For dessert, Joe served a fresh fruit compote with thick cream. Father O made sure the wineglasses were refilled. Jan and Tillie, who didn't drink, exchanged knowing glances. The evening was just beginning. Mary was giddy, as she was getting to stay up late. Joe was entertaining and had eaten well. The dining room window offered a spectacular view of the city's skyline. If they had tried, they could have pinpointed the location of St. Brigid, its gold cross jutting into the night sky.

Not long afterward, Joe invited Jan and Siu-Mei to join him and a friend on a weeknight for sushi followed by bowling in Japantown. When the women arrived at the restaurant, Joe introduced them to a man named Chris, who was about twenty-one. Siu-Mei didn't know what to think. Earlier in the week, she had called Joe's house and gotten the answering machine. Instead of Joe's terse "Leave a message" greeting, she heard: "You've reached Joe and Chris."

She had told Jan about it, saying she didn't know Joe had a friend named Chris, and she didn't know whether it was a man or woman.

Over sushi, Jan and Siu-Mei began to notice certain looks pass between Joe and Chris. The looks were not those of buddies, like those between Joe and Phil Bailey. These looks were *affectionate.* The women traded glances, trying to remain nonchalant, to focus on the sushi, which passed by their table on small boats circling the counter like a moat. Both knew of Joe's failed marriage. Siu-Mei had heard stories of the problems he and Polly had been through. But she had absolutely no idea about this aspect of his life.

By the end of the night, there was no mistaking it: Joe was *with* Chris.

Siu-Mei and Jan left in silence. They agreed not to share the information with anyone else. Joe, in his own way, had decided to open up to them alone. That night, Siu-Mei tossed and turned, unable to sleep. She remembered years earlier thinking that Joe and Polly's separation had something to do with St. Brigid and all of the time Joe spent with the committee. Joe had even joked once that the committee's Homeless Helping the Homeless program was going to cause his divorce. As she tried to sleep, Siu-Mei replayed one night not long before when Joe had arrived for dinner, parking his bike by the curb. Noticing the rainbow elastic band around the bike's handlebars, Jan and Siu-Mei both teased Joe about being gay. Siu-Mei remembered the look in his eyes and the way he adamantly denied it, saying he'd had the rainbow band since he was a teenager.

34 *A Last Hurrah*

Eleanor Dignan was not about to accept a substandard hotel room. It was December 2002, and she had arrived at the legendary "Pink Palace" in Hawaii with her son, Joe, and granddaughter, Mary.

Eleanor sat in a wheelchair in the lobby of the Royal Hawaiian Hotel on Oahu and refused to budge. The space offered was not to her liking. She had requested rooms high up with expansive views. She wanted to be able to open sliding glass doors, sit on the terrace, watch for the island's small and colorful birds, and smell the salt water.

The receptionist repeated that the hotel was booked. Slowly, Eleanor rose from her wheelchair and approached the desk. Joe could see his mother's determination. He took a step back. Mary was mortified by anything that caused a scene.

"I am dying," Eleanor said without pause or emotion. "This is a farewell trip for me, my son, and my granddaughter. We need the rooms we need."

Within minutes, rooms with postcard views of palm trees and turquoise water materialized. Joe smiled for the first time in weeks. His mother, who had been getting paler and thinner, had been diagnosed with terminal lung cancer two months earlier. But here she was, rising from her wheelchair, feisty as ever. It was a gusto that people mentioned when they told him, "I just love your mother."

As soon as they were in their rooms, Eleanor apologized that she needed to rest. Later, she would sit on the terrace and enjoy the view. Joe and Mary tucked her into bed, surrounding her with fluffy pillows. Sitting beside her for a moment, Joe remembered how, when he was all of eight or nine, he would bring her breakfast in bed. Later, inspired by her *W* magazine, he had started putting flowers on the tray.

Before leaving, Joe said that he and Mary would return with the most beautiful bouquet of flowers ever. Eleanor told them to go and swim some for her. As part of the deal for the trip, she had made Mary take swimming lessons at the Metropolitan Club in San Francisco.

In the days that followed, Eleanor barely left her room. Mary and Joe were in and out, talking of their swimming, of Mary's surfing lessons, of the people they saw at the pool, of the bits of shells—mostly small crabs—they found on the beach. They brought flowers and ordered room service. They shared family stories and nonsensical memories. Joe laughed as he recalled preparing traditional Christmas dinners for his mother and her friends.

"Remember those horribly greasy, incredibly fattening beef Wellingtons with two sauces and mushroom duxelles?" he asked. "No matter what, you would always exclaim to all of the guests, 'Dear, your pastry is just magnificent!'"

Eleanor told Mary stories of when she was a nurse's aide during World War II and of her stint working at a convalescent home in San Francisco. Her eyes lighting up, she said she had been a "pretty good by-ear pianist as a child, until my father died and my mother sold the piano." Joe reminded her of the family piano she bought when he was growing up. It was an upright, cotton-candy pink, with diaphanously draped naked ladies painted on the front, he said to Mary, reveling in the details. "Your grandmother loved to say, 'It's so racy! I just bet it was in a house of ill repute!'"

But Joe knew that it was the painting that had captivated his mother. In the early 1970s, Eleanor and a group of her friends started doing watercolors every Friday afternoon with a well-known teacher, George Post. He took them around San Francisco, from hilltop to park, from the beach to the city's famed Victorian row, and then around the world on formal trips. Eleanor still talked with excitement about a trip she and her friends had taken to Spain. She returned with a bullfighting poster signed by matadors she'd met in a hotel bar. It now hung in her art studio. "What a thrill that was," Eleanor said with a faraway look.

Joe knew that thrills had been few and far between for his mother. Over time, he had learned of her unexplained trips to the hospital—many while he was away at boarding school—and of how his father had used money, Eleanor's "allowance," as another way to control her. She had only recently divorced him.

The stories they shared in the hotel room in Hawaii were a mix of the common and the transcendent. Mary said that one of her favorite things that she and Grandma had done as part of their routine was to walk down to North Beach—"Little Italy," Eleanor called it—to get fresh focaccia. She also said she remembered how Grandma would superbly organize her lemonade sales, held at the bottom of Lombard Street, where all the tourists gathered to take pictures looking up at San Francisco's crookedest street. "I have saved all of your lemonade money," Eleanor said with a wink.

Their stories were inevitably cut short as Eleanor drifted off faster and slept more. One morning she looked at the calendar and said she hoped to make it to see the new year. Joe would sit and hold her hand, grimacing when she grimaced. He did this until she opened her eyes and caught him. Then she would sit up and brighten, as if pain were not in her vocabulary. She said she needed to rest and ordered him out into the sunshine.

On February 10, 2003, Father O went to see Eleanor. Joe had called. His mother said it was time.

It was a Monday evening, around seven-thirty, when he arrived at the hospice wing of California Pacific Medical Center in Pacific Heights. He found the right room and saw that Eleanor was in bed. Her long and lean frame, so much like her son's, was as narrow as a plank under the light hospital blankets. She greeted Father O cheerfully. Her mind was alert. She wore her trademark glasses, and a tube of lipstick was by her bed, next to a rosary with small, pale yellow beads. Bouquets of roses from her garden filled the room. It was the only thing she had requested, her Tropicana roses in brilliant red and orange and her prized Queen Elizabeths.

Father O always steeled himself for the last rites of people he called friends. He had grown to respect Eleanor, to understand that while she had lived a life of privilege, of painting classes, trading recipes, and tending her garden, she had endured more than her share of pain. This strong and smart woman had put up with an abusive husband because of her son. She'd wanted Joe to have the best life possible.

Father O's job tonight was to make sure Eleanor was at peace with herself. She was a good Catholic and a straight talker. He would listen to her concerns, absolve her of any sins. This was a part of his priestly duty, like knowing the different oils for baptism, for confirmation, for the sick and dying. The ritual, called *viaticum* in Latin, "provision for the journey," was as scripted as Mass, as routine as communion. But it was never the same. People died in fear. People died in joy. Some passed tragically. Others went smiling. They shared one thing, though: They all seemed to know their time was up.

Eleanor knew. And she appeared reconciled. It was just the two of them in the room, which was bathed in a soft light. The sacrament of the dying began with confession. Afterward, Father O turned to anointing each of Eleanor's five senses: on the eyes for sight, on the nose for smell, on the ears for hearing, on the mouth for taste and speech, on the hands for touch, on the feet for walking. The oil was to absolve sins committed with those senses.

Together, they prayed one decade of the rosary, beginning with the Lord's Prayer: *"Our Father, who art in heaven."* Father O recited Scripture, turning to one of his favorite passages with a resurrection theme. It was John 14:1–2, the words of Christ: *"Do not let your heart be troubled. In my Father's house are many mansions. . . . I go to prepare a place for you."* He spoke of death as a new beginning, not an ending. He said that Eleanor was going to another good place, "a place as beautiful and welcoming as St. Brigid," where she would be reunited with loved ones. She smiled slightly and said, "Please keep fighting for St. Brigid."

He anointed her forehead and her hand. As his hand moved, he could see that her peaceful expression had changed. Her eyes searched his. Father O was confident that this was not her time to die, that she still had days, maybe longer. He asked if there was something she needed to say.

Finally, her lips starting to tremble, she asked, "Who will take care of Joe?"

* * *

Three days later, on the night of February 13, Eleanor Dignan, born Eleanor Ann Lobrano, died at California Pacific Medical Center.

Siu-Mei came as soon as Joe called her. He said she didn't need to come, but she did anyway, just as she had almost every day. Since she and Joe first met on the Committee to Save St. Brigid, they had agreed on nothing—and everything.

Siu-Mei waited outside the room. Joe's cries echoed down the empty hall. She looked in from time to time to see her friend at the foot of his mother's bed, his arms wrapped around her thin frame. At some point, Joe's father walked out of the room. Passing Siu-Mei, he said, "Joe really loved his mother."

Hours passed. Joe finally emerged from the room and saw Siu-Mei sitting by herself, waiting for him. For a few minutes they stood, saying nothing. Then Joe asked whether she would go back in the room with him. They stayed until the lights were being turned off, until the nurses came and gently said it was time to leave. Siu-Mei held Joe's arm, to steady him. Walking out of the room together, Joe looked back at his mother, the yellow beads in her hands.

Siu-Mei told Joe she would drive him home. As they drove, Joe said that Father O had told him after delivering the last rites, "Your mother is going straight to heaven." Siu-Mei nodded and said, "That's right, Joe." But Joe said he didn't know what to believe, that everything was swirling and moving and nothing felt clear.

"My mother is gone," he said. "All I know is that I am never going to be loved like that again."

35 *No Weepy Wake*

THE BANDS WERE warming up to play her favorite music, Dixieland jazz and Irish folk songs. The backdrop was the elegant Metropolitan Club near Union Square, where Mary had taken swimming lessons, where Joe's wedding reception was held, and where Eleanor had played bridge and presided over the ladies who lunched. The buffet would have impressed Julia Child. Everyone was elegantly dressed—though not as colorfully as Eleanor would have liked. Most wore black.

At 6 P.M. on February 27, more than a hundred people gathered to celebrate the life of Eleanor Dignan. It was a party that Eleanor would have loved, and one she had carefully scripted. Before she died, Eleanor went over her wishes with Joe, directing him to take notes in his reporter's notepad. She was adamant about two things. This was not to be some weepy wake, and he had better not forget to invite the people on her list. She also made it clear that she was hurt she could not be buried from St. Brigid. Joe had assured her that the church would one day reopen.

At the memorial, Joe wore a black suit and red tie that his mother had given him. Since her death, he had rarely ventured out. Siu-Mei came to his house every day, bringing food, cleaning up after him, and doing his laundry. She refused to leave even when he yelled and cursed at her. There were days when she would just sit and watch him cry.

As he looked around the packed room, Joe was heartened to see Eleanor's friends and family. He saw the bridge players, the painting students, the neighbors, the Julia groupies. He saw his aunt Alice and her family. His daughter, Mary, looked so grown up in her black sleeveless dress and Mary Jane shoes. Then he saw his friends from St. Brigid. They stood near a display of photographs of his mother's life and a display of her oil paintings and watercolors.

Looking at the parishioners, he felt gratitude. Many had become close friends with his mother, who was nothing if not particular. She was urbane and clever and chic, and had been around the same kind of people. She had told Joe not long before she died that she was wowed by this group. She said they were so humble for being so remarkable.

Joe had asked Father O to say a few words, as he wasn't sure how he himself would hold up.

Father O shared stories of Eleanor that made everyone laugh. "I once asked her why she wore such big eyeglasses," he said. "She replied, 'If I have to wear glasses, I want everyone to see them.'" He talked of her frankness, of her humor—and of her love for her son and granddaughter.

"She was a real person," he said. "There was nothing phony about Eleanor. She made up her own mind on matters. She was able to laugh at life. And she was a strong woman."

There was a musical interlude of an Irish folk song called "Tip of the Whistle." Jan played the harp and Father O played the tin whistle. They were joined by a fiddler and keyboardist. Then Father O spoke for a few more minutes, finally urging everyone to drink, eat, dance, and celebrate the eighty-four years of Eleanor. One room held the Irish music. In the other was the Dixieland band.

As the party began to wind down, Joe could feel his mother almost pushing him to center stage, as she had tried to do all of his life. He knew he had to say a few words. He read a paragraph from her obituary, which he had written: "Her enthusiasms later in life, besides painting, included Dixieland jazz, opera, and playing bridge." Joe paused, drawing strength from the group from St. Brigid. "She was a great believer in horoscopes," he continued, "particularly those in *Town and Country* magazine, which summarized her character. She's cheerful and gregarious, popular and loves to party. She's hot-blooded, impatient, independent, and feisty, but above all, perceptive, warm and loving."

Turning serious, he said, "Father O told me after he delivered last rites that my mother was going straight to heaven. I'm a journalist, so I'm skeptical. But I know that she became more and more devout as she got older." Then, smiling sadly, he said, "I think she got more religious out of fear that I was straying more, that I needed more religion. She was right."

Reminded of Eleanor's admonition to keep the celebration from turning weepy, he quickly thanked everyone for coming.

"My mother was convinced that I was going to forget to invite all of you," he said.

The group from St. Brigid found a table and talked among themselves. Helen and Tillie had grown close to Eleanor and admired her greatly.

"It is interesting to see her friends," Helen said, looking around. "They are very much like Eleanor. They have a lot of stories to tell."

Tillie laughed, saying, "She knew we were baseball fans, so she always told us the story about dating the famous baseball player Ted Williams prior to her marriage."

Helen added, "Toward the end, though, she talked mostly about Joe, and Mary. She was concerned about their future." They looked over to the dance floor, where Joe was leading Mary in a dance.

Father O nodded. "Right before Eleanor passed," he said, "she told me that she was extremely proud of Joe for taking up the fight for St. Brigid."

A few weeks later, Siu-Mei went to Mass at Saints Peter and Paul in North Beach. It wasn't her usual place, but she had been trying out different parishes. She appreciated the grandness of the church, with its ornate white and gold altar, made of Carrara marble and fine stones, and the painting of Jesus on the domed wall behind. The Savior held the Bible in one hand, opened to the Latin verse from the Gospel of John: *"Ego Sum Via, Veritas, et Vita." "I am the Way, the Truth, and the Life."*

She was surprised when, midway through the Mass, the priest honored Eleanor Dignan. One of the other committee members must have made a donation for the remembrance. After Mass, Siu-Mei lingered to pray. When she opened her eyes, she was surprised to see Joe beside her. He had been at the back of the church and had spotted her. Neither had expected the mention of Eleanor. Siu-Mei asked Joe if he wanted to get lunch. He shook his head. He wanted to remain and pray.

* * *

Not long after, Siu-Mei got an unexpected e-mail from Joe.

"Here's a weird one," he wrote. "The funeral home that has my mother's ashes really wants me to come and get them. They're threatening to throw them away. Maybe you'd be willing to help me get them and put them somewhere this week. I just can't face it."

Siu-Mei responded: "I will need a note from you authorizing me to pick up Mrs. Dignan's ashes. I will pick it up sometime this week on or before Friday." She asked Joe if he preferred a certain type of urn. He said he trusted her to decide.

Siu-Mei was worried about her friend. She had been getting calls from Dane Devoil, whom Joe had hired to tackle his mother's overgrown garden. Tangles of thorny blackberry bushes now blocked the entrance, rosebushes were shooting straight up, and weeds had overtaken pathways. Dane was also going to take inventory of Eleanor's two-story pink home, where it appeared that nothing had ever been thrown out—whether a gas bill, Joe's baby clothes, or a decade of back issues of the *New Yorker*.

Dane told Siu-Mei that Joe stopped by the house periodically but could not make it past the front door before he broke down and abruptly turned to leave. He had instructed Dane not to enter his mother's room. It was where Siu-Mei had placed the urn with her ashes. And Joe pestered Dane incessantly about the health of a certain ficus tree that had thrived with Eleanor's care but now was little more than a twig.

Dane said that as he put things in boxes, he created a throw-away pile for the obvious discards. When Joe showed up, he would rifle through the latest pile left in front of the door, yell at Dane, and take everything back out. One old rusty roller skate. A broken shower nozzle. A cracked flowerpot. It was all for Mary, Joe would say.

Siu-Mei and others on the committee began meeting a few minutes early each week, to pray for Joe.

36 *New Beginnings*

On Tuesday, April 1, 2003, Robert Bryan flew from San Francisco to Pittsburgh, rented a car, and drove about seventy miles south to Waynesburg, where a gleaming new prison had been built amid rolling hills and lush countryside. Robert had an appointment at 8 A.M. the next day to see a new client, Mumia Abu-Jamal, whose case had generated more national and international attention than that of any other inmate on death row.

Robert had known Abu-Jamal since 1985 and had twice turned down the controversial and celebrated inmate's request for representation. But when Abu-Jamal asked him to take over as lead counsel, he couldn't say no. As he saw it, the case in which Abu-Jamal was convicted of killing a police officer in Philadelphia in 1981 had been terribly botched by the lawyers and investigators. Robert believed he could win an appeal.

In the prison on Wednesday morning, Robert and Abu-Jamal were seated across from each other, separated by a wall of glass perforated for sound. Abu-Jamal's case was on appeal in state and federal courts, and the two talked for five hours. Leaving, Robert thought of how the time had flown by. With some clients, he had to fight to stay awake.

Returning to San Francisco late that night, Robert sat in his living room and reviewed his schedule. He didn't like missing the weekly meeting of the Committee to Save St. Brigid, but he feared this was just the beginning. With each new day, he felt increasingly validated about his fight for the church. More and more had come out about cover-ups by church officials. The Roman Catholic diocese of Bridgeport, Connecticut, had twenty-three lawsuits involving accusations against seven priests. In early depositions, the bishop of Bridgeport, Edward Egan, had disbelieved the accusers and was skeptical of the reports. And in Boston, the scandal had erupted to a whole new level. Robert had exulted when Cardinal Law was forced to resign for having protected the abusers instead of the abused. As it turned out, he had known about the abusers, including Father Paul Shanley and Father John Geoghan and had shuttled them from parish to parish. "The corruption is at the top, the beauty is at the bottom," Robert said to his wife. "Where else does someone do something morally reprehensible, that should be criminal, and get rewarded for it? I mean, now, Cardinal Law, after resigning in Boston, becomes an 'archpriest' and is put in charge of the Basilica di Santa Maria Maggiore, where the pope himself goes for Mass."

He had defended men on death row whom he believed were innocent. Now it was clear that the Church was letting the guilty go free.

Robert had seen more than his share of injustice. In addition to his committee work, Robert was already juggling more than a half-dozen capital cases. Abu-Jamal's case was more complex than any of them. The files were pouring into his office—some two hundred thousand pages from different attorneys, as well as twenty-one years' worth of pleadings, reports, and correspondence. He needed to interview hundreds of people, and the case would require monthly visits to Waynesburg and regular trips to New York and Europe, where Abu-Jamal had a strong network of supporters.

It felt good to have a new cause, one where he knew the rules and believed he had a fair chance.

37 *A Bittersweet Celebration*

ON A GLORIOUSLY WARM Saturday night in October 2003, the kind that San Franciscans cherish as their Indian summer, more than a hundred people turned out for a special celebration: the hundred and fortieth birthday of St. Brigid Church, which came to life on September 10, 1863.

Joe Dignan was the master of ceremonies. Robert Bryan was on hand, as were dozens of others: Father O, Siu-Mei, Jan Robinson, Janie Wong and her husband Shubert Yee, Doris Munstermann, John Gregson, and Helen and Tillie, who served as event chairs, Margaret Sanderson, Bill Van Way, Donna Carico, Robert and Norma Head, Eleanor Croke, Denis Mulcahey, Barbara Hamann, Bebe and Rosa St. John, Jeanie McMillan, Lorraine and Donald Kelley, Josephine Brightwell, and Ken Epley. There were nuns and teachers and children from St. Brigid School. There were politicians, including Supervisor Gavin Newsom and Mark Leno, recently elected to the state assembly.

The party on October 25 drew more than 240 donors, a proclamation from the California State Assembly in honor of St. Brigid's anniversary, and a talk and slideshow by the noted architect J. Gordon Turnbull. Tillie had paid to have 250 magnets made with a picture of St. Brigid and the relevant dates, 1863–2003. Serving as dinner gifts, they were mailed to donors and friends—even to Archbishop Levada.

The only thing missing was anyone from the San Francisco archdiocese. Siu-Mei noted that there had not even been a mention of the event in the weekly archdiocesan newspaper, *Catholic San Francisco,* or in the recently published three-volume history on the San Francisco archdiocese.

"I'm here to congratulate St. Brigid on its hundred and forty years," said Assemblyman Leno, taking the podium. "I know the committee has been struggling for many years to reopen this church. It is truly such a remarkably architecturally significant building. We must honor its history. And, more importantly, we must preserve the community it represents."

John Gregson, a member of the committee who was a chemist as well as an amateur historian, spoke of the history of the archdiocese, founded in 1853 at the height of the Gold Rush, and of St. Brigid, which he called "a frontier parish."

Turnbull, the architect, was next. "Its Romanesque style came about in the southern part of Europe in the first millennium," he said of St. Brigid's architecture. "It is a style that has an elemental beauty to it. It is strong, heavy, rich, with thick walls and ornamental arches, and was of interest in America in the late 1800s.

"But the design of the church that we know today really came to life in 1904," he said. The 1904 building was designed by Harry Minton and "not only survived the 1906 earthquake but also lived through the evolution of a part of Van Ness Avenue from a boulevard of mansions to a strip of motels.

"By the late 1920s, it was Father John Cottle, St. Brigid's pastor for thirty-six years, who wanted an even grander church, to accommodate the growing neighborhood," Turnbull explained. "St. Brigid was then built up from an eight-hundred-seat church to an eleven-hundred-seat church." He noted that Father Cottle, who had arrived at St. Brigid in 1890 and was the self-appointed supervisor of the construction of the new church, was seriously injured when a workman's elevator crashed to the sanctuary floor. The injuries were said to have hastened his death.

Showing another image of St. Brigid, Turnbull noted, "The style of the interior is much more exuberant than the exterior. It can be described as Italian Renaissance. The perforated half-dome above the sanctuary is highly unusual. In the 1940s, the church continued to be ornamented with the stained glass, which softened the room, and the sculptures by Seamus Murphy on the front of the church. In 1967, the bell tower that we know today was completed, with its pyramid top and gold cross. And in 1983, the Ruffatti organ from Padua, Italy, was installed. There are three such organs in San Francisco—the biggest, of course, is at Davies Symphony Hall. The St. Brigid Ruffatti is remarkable: three manuals, fifty-four ranks."

He said that the design and craftsmanship of St. Brigid were "something we'd never be able to afford again." And he complimented it for "anchoring the city around it. You see apartment buildings around it, buildings that are even taller. But this church looks absolutely powerful in the midst of it all."

Joe took notes. He loved that he was still learning things about St. Brigid.

In conclusion, Turnbull asked people to consider: "If St. Brigid were not there, what would we get in return?"

Later, attendees lingered to share memories and memorabilia of St. Brigid. Guido and Mary Alacia, octogenarians who had attended St. Brigid since childhood, talked about the hundred-year anniversary on Sunday, May 19, 1963. There was a solemn Mass at the church at 4 P.M. that day.

Mary, seated close to Guido, shared a copy of an even earlier celebration, attended by her parents. It was the "Golden Jubilee Souvenir," marking the fiftieth birthday of St. Brigid—in 1913. Surrounded by parishioners, Mary read from the Jubilee's introduction: "This is dedicated to those good Catholic people of the old and the new St. Brigid's, whose sterling Catholic faith, openhearted generosity and loyal support of church and parish institutions have made this story of fifty years' progress a possibility."

The booklet, worn and faded, described the humble beginnings of the church, when San Francisco was a town of 56,802 people and the lot on which St. Brigid was built was purchased by the archdiocese for $5,000. It told of the first incarnation of the church as a wooden structure of forty by seventy-six feet, set amid immense sand hills thickly covered with brush and scrub oaks. It was reportedly perched on the summit of a sand dune and accessed by a flight of fifteen to twenty steps running up from the ungraded street.

"What marvelous changes have taken place," Mary continued reading. "A sweep of sand dunes has given way to a largely populated modern residence district. The little frame church, that well served the needs of generations that have passed, has yielded place to a magnificent granite structure, whose very construction spells permanency."

It was Father Cottle, the book noted, who in 1897 made the highest bid on some rough granite blocks being sold by the city. The blocks, which had been crossing stones—placed in dirt streets for people to cross, much as they would be used to ford a river—were fashioned into the church's walls.

Mary continued reading: "Its parish records, to date, tell of over 5,700 children baptized, of 1,480 young men and women joined before its altar in the sacred bonds of Christian marriage. Communion has been offered. Its bell has called the faithful to divine services. Thousands have thronged to its confessionals and knelt at its Communion rail. Thousands have been prepared and consoled on their bed of death by the priests of St. Brigid." Then she came to the last paragraph of the Jubilee: "It would be hard to forecast what the future has in store for St. Brigid. Changes come so rapidly and suddenly in the conditions of modern city life that we cannot tell today what tomorrow may bring."

David Hansell had just returned from six months in Iraq, where he was stationed with the navy to help build camps for the troops. Hearing of St. Brigid's important anniversary, he knew it was time for the project he'd put off for some time: the enormous front door.

In preparation, he'd taken a paint chip from the wrought-iron door to a store to have it matched. Two different shades of gray were mixed, one light and one charcoal. The project required his tallest ladder, which reached thirty-two feet. His drop cloth was positioned, his grip filled with the tricks of his trade: scrapers and brushes of varying sizes, steel wool, sandpaper, and solvents.

He climbed the ladder and began to sand, getting lost in the movements and in the patterns of the door. His time in Iraq had been transformative. He had traveled to Mesopotamia, the cradle of civilization, and to Babylon, in southern Iraq and along the Tigris and Euphrates rivers. While there, he carried a pocket Bible, which was given to all the troops. On occasion, he would open it and read a bit until he was stopped by the small type. Still, he found it reassuring to have with him. He also went to Catholic services on the base. But his most religious moments were out in the desert or along the riverbanks. There, his faith was something he could feel and breathe, something that was overwhelming in its strength.

He was thankful the power of the time in Iraq stayed with him even now. Returning to San Francisco, he had learned of the escalating problems with the Catholic Church and the continued inaction by the archdiocese. He looked at priests differently, viewing them more as regular men. The Catholic Church was different, too. It was all having an interesting effect, he thought, working on the door. It was making him go deeper into his faith.

He didn't hear the traffic picking up or the occasional person wandering by, stopping to notice or ask questions about his work. He loved this old church, and he could feel how every part of it meant something to the parishioners who came before him.

Sometime later, as the morning light brightened, he stepped down off his ladder and collected his things. The sanding was done. He would return to prime and paint.

38 *"What Has the Catholic Church Done for You?"*

JOE SAT IN THE living room of his mother's home on Lombard Street, the shades drawn and lights off. His head was in his hands when Dane Devoil walked in. Joe was finally able to enter the house.

Dane wasn't startled by much that Joe did. He had seen him be kind. He had seen him be cruel. He had seen the gregarious Joe. He had seen the sullen Joe. He had gotten to know Joe's charming daughter, Mary, who was strong enough to give it right back to her dad. And he had met Joe's wonderful Catholic friends from St. Brigid. He had also gotten to know Eleanor, though only after her death.

Taking inventory of her belongings and tending her home made him feel as though he had known her. He had met Eleanor's friends and neighbors, who dropped by to reminisce. He had marveled at her bright clothes and rococo furnishings. Some of it was outrageous. Some of it was beautiful.

Dane had seen the sunglasses with bright yellow and pink frames, the huge rhinestone earrings and bracelets. He didn't even have to be told her favorite flower was the dahlia: big, bold, and bright. He smiled whenever he approached Eleanor's house, painted pink and surrounded by splashy flowers. He had found the treasures Eleanor left for Mary, including a bag of coins and bills labeled "Mary's Lemonade Stash." And through the neighbors and Eleanor's friends, Dane heard stories of Joe's father.

Dane knew of a certain brown glass Limoges vase. It was a stunning piece, big and heavy. Joe's father would throw it repeatedly, but it refused to break. Dane saw the many chips in the vase, at the bottom and around the edges on top, and imagined Eleanor going, yet again, to retrieve it. Dane once told Joe, "Your mother had a rotten husband, but she seemed like a real hoot."

Dane did his best not to take Joe's moods personally, especially at the Lombard Street house. He knew the home was alive with Joe's mother's love and his father's anger. Joe's emotions bounced from one to the other.

He had met Joe in 2002, when he was a bartender at the Stud, a popular South of Market gay bar. Joe briefly dated the bar's doorman, then one night struck up a conversation with Dane, a tall and handsome blue-eyed blond who was establishing a gardening and landscaping business. Joe needed help with his small garden behind his home on Potrero Hill, where he had yellow roses and a giant hibiscus tree. Over time, the two became friends. Dane knew some of the guys Joe dated and weighed in with his opinion. Joe told Dane that Eleanor always said his dates seemed "like freeloaders." Dane agreed.

He put up with Joe's tirades—to a point. There were times that he simply walked away. He had become friends with Siu-Mei and called her when he needed advice about Joe. Siu-Mei said, "I think Joe can't help it. For me, that's another reason I feel so attached to him. I feel he had a very sad upbringing. He says mean things and he apologizes. That's the way his father brought him up: to put other people down. Somehow I seem to understand that Joe can't help what he says."

But now Dane saw something grippingly sad about Joe. He asked what was wrong.

"My mother died a year ago today," Joe said, looking up.

Dane nodded and asked whether he wanted to talk.

"No, I'll just sit here for a while," Joe said. Dane replied that he would be working out in the yard. When he first started caring for Eleanor's garden, the rosebushes were twenty feet high and the weeds and plants were so overgrown that he didn't know there were paths through the garden.

An hour later, Joe emerged on the rickety back steps and said that the parishioners were holding a clothing drive for St. Brigid. He looked at Dane.

"Oh no," Dane said. "You're not getting me to do that."

Dane was constantly hearing about St. Brigid—about the committee, about the cause, about the parishioners, about the archdiocese, about the marches and vigils and parades, about the years that had gone by, about new developments, new approaches, and new hopes.

"Come on," Joe said, his mood warming. "We need extra help."

Dane took off his gardening gloves. He and Joe had gotten into their share of heated discussions over the Catholic Church. Dane had been raised in a "hard-core Pentecostal" family, attending church six days a week. He'd had it with organized religion and was gravitating toward Buddhism. He believed in living well in the moment, and considered the concept of heaven and hell a bogus bargaining chip. When a wealthy client asked him to cut hydrangeas just as they were about to bloom because she thought they looked too tall, he refused. He explained they were about to produce beautiful flowers for the next six months. She ordered him to cut them or be fired. He quit.

"Joe, at some point, you are going to have to wake up from your dream," Dane said that day, standing in the lush garden, with its fruit trees—pears, apples, quince, and avocado—and its fragrant rosebushes. Overhead flew the wild parrots, which delighted tourists, made a ruckus, and nested nearby, dividing their time between the garden and Telegraph Hill.

"Your church is closed," Dane said, waiting to speak until the parrots were no longer overhead. "What are you doing? Is it because this church is historical? What is it about this church?"

Joe looked at him, the smile leaving his face. He didn't answer. But he was still standing there. Sometimes when Dane challenged Joe about religion or St. Brigid, Joe would tell him he didn't know what he was talking about or he would just leave.

Dane went on, "Besides, there is an even bigger issue than St. Brigid. You are probably going to scream at me for saying this, but I think you need to hear it. Your mother's room was filled with crosses and pictures of saints and the Virgin Mary and rosaries. But she lived in a marriage where she was afraid of her husband, where she had to hide pictures of you, of her own son. I found pictures of you, hidden behind her furniture, behind her clothes. How did the church protect her from your father?"

Joe sat down on the steps.

"You talk about St. Brigid endlessly," Dane continued. "Well, St. Brigid is no more. The bigger Catholic Church is a mess. Bishops covered up pedophiles and moved them from place to place. I just heard something about a horrible cover-up in Ireland, or was it Germany? Anyway, it is a global failure. The Vatican was more concerned with controlling the scandal than dealing with the crimes and victims. You stayed closeted for most of your life—largely because of your religion. The Catholic Church has made your life miserable. It tells you: As a gay man you're not acceptable. It's taken your family's money but never given any of you peace of mind. You curse like a sailor. You definitely don't always act like a Christian. You keep pushing for St. Brigid to be saved. You keep asking me, Dane, will you help collect signatures? Dane, will you do this and that? I listen to you constantly. You want to save your mother's church. You talk about caring for something your mother loved. But really, Joe, tell me, what has the Catholic Church done for you?"

Joe looked at him. Finally, standing up to leave, Joe said softly, "I don't have the answers to those questions."

Then, turning, he said calmly, "I reflexively cross myself when entering a church. I give up sugar or smoking—smoking for the umpteenth time—for Lent. I know when it is All Souls' Day, Candlemas, Ash Wednesday, and Holy Week. I know the seven penitential psalms and the seven sacraments, from baptism to the anointing of the sick. I guess you could say that this thing called Catholicism permeated my skin. It is the good part of the church that I can still feel, despite my best efforts to ignore it. And, on a more superficial level, I have to admit something else—I have a burning ambition to leave a mark."

39 *Another Good-bye*

ROBERT ARRIVED AT THE committee meeting at his usual time—7:20 P.M. He hated walking in while the rosary was being said; he would have to sit quietly, which was not his way. He liked to take a seat and get down to business. Besides, he didn't even own a rosary. Since the first committee meetings in January

1994, he had made it a point not to sit at the head of the table, as he found it pretentious. He preferred to sit on one of the sides, with the others.

Up for discussion was the work of a new archdiocesan liaison subcommittee, composed of Joe, Bebe St. John, and Bill Van Way. It had been suggested for years that someone on the committee other than Robert should try to meet with Archbishop Levada. Robert knew the time was right to start shifting responsibilities. At the meeting, he said, "What we may be missing is someone able and willing to work closely with the archdiocese in an effort to alleviate the negativism toward us. There is smoldering resentment among the power brokers [in the archdiocese] concerning my legal work fighting the closure decision and the investigation I initiated for the removal of Quinn as archbishop. He is gone from that position, but his influence remains quite powerful." Levada, he noted, was surrounded by the same people who had worked under Quinn. He said that maybe someone else would be able to "move on in a different and positive direction" and not be such a lightning rod.

Returning to the agenda at hand, Robert said he had a positive development to report. He read from a letter sent by Gavin Newsom, a city supervisor, to Levada requesting that St. Brigid be reopened. Newsom wrote: "Please accept this as my request for you to open St. Brigid Church. The building is of great historical importance to San Francisco, and its active use would greatly enhance the well-being of our community and city." He further noted that the San Francisco Board of Supervisors unanimously passed resolutions supporting the opening of St. Brigid on August 23, 1999, and November 5, 2001.

These days, the committee embraced any encouraging news. Newsom was still a junior politician, but he was generating buzz and respect as someone to watch.

Robert listened to updates while rummaging through his briefcase. Then he spoke up, saying he wanted to share a news story in case anyone had missed it. It was about a certain prominent canon lawyer, a favorite of Archbishop Levada's who also had been a favorite of Quinn's, a priest who had helped write the Catholic Church's policies on dealing with clergy sex abuse. Robert said he was talking about the archdiocese's own Father Gregory Ingels, one of only four experts chosen by the Canon Law Society of America to advise U.S. bishops on abusive clerics. Early on, before St. Brigid was closed, John Ross and Richard Figone had both said they should consult with Ingels—and defer to him.

"I have corresponded with Ingels for years," Robert said, noting that Ingels was the archdiocese's lawyer during the committee's appeal. "He wrote me these pompous, arrogant, and condescending letters." Robert had several of the letters with him. "I was trying to get Ingels to send copies of responsive pleadings and all supportive documentation filed on behalf of the archdiocese," he explained. "Ingels would reply and tell me about policy and procedure and say it was not possible to provide any such documents. He always signed his letters 'Sincerely yours in Christ.'

"Anyway," Robert continued, "I had heard early on from my private investigator, way back when, that Ingels was a pedophile. My experience with him in the St. Brigid litigation was that he lacked a basic sense of ethics. He was the ultimate hypocrite."

Robert proceeded to read from a *San Francisco Chronicle* news story: "A Catholic priest facing child molestation charges in Marin County is the co-author of new church guidelines on dealing with priests who sexually abuse children. The Rev. Gregory Ingels, who also is a church lawyer, is scheduled to appear Wednesday in Marin County Superior Court. According to the criminal complaint filed in late May, Ingels engaged in 'substantial sexual conduct' with a child under age 16."

Robert saw Carmen jotting down notes. Others bowed their heads. In everything they did, everything that hit them, they turned to prayer. But theirs was no longer a private piety, where parishioners genuflected in silence, where they sat side by side in church but kept to themselves. Now their piety was public. It was messy. And it was intertwined.

Later in the meeting, Robert listened to the committee members. He remained charmed by their innocence. They talked of contacting Mel Gibson, whose movie *The Passion of the Christ* had opened on Ash Wednesday. They talked of getting in touch with Dan Brown, author of *The Da Vinci Code,* to try to sell him their background information for a small percentage of the book's profits.

"Our present-day story could become the background for a Catholic novel, full of nineteenth- and twentieth-century intrigue," Ken Epley said at the meeting in late February 2004. "This will be about modern-day bureaucratic stoniness and ultimate salvation for the common folk."

Bebe shared news stories of church vigils in Boston, where the archdiocese had announced that eighty-four parishes would need to be closed to pay the victims of clergy sexual abuse. She reported that a half-dozen churches were being occupied around the clock by parishioners who refused to leave. And she reported that the U.S. Conference on Catholic Bishops had unanimously approved a "charter for the protection of children and youth" and had adopted a "zero tolerance" policy for sexual abuse.

"The parishioners around Boston are just beginning their battle," Bebe said. "We were the first and we're *still* going."

Siu-Mei asked, "I wonder if we can offer any help."

Robert saw how these parishioners hadn't stopped believing, but he felt different. He wanted out. Not because of those on the committee but because of the opponent. The church leaders who wouldn't grant them another meeting. The ones who denied their legal appeal on something other than the merits. The ones who lied about why St. Brigid was closed. The ones who signed off with "Sincerely yours in Christ."

He had dedicated ten years to this cause. His once strawberry blond hair was now a milky gray. His curly-haired Auda Mai was now wearing makeup and asking when she could drive. She had been to their parades, meetings, and public events. She had listened to her father speak so many times—Robert could talk and talk—that one time she snuck up to the podium and pulled the plug on him.

Robert had recently gone through the files in his office. He had written literally hundreds of letters as committee chair—to Quinn, to Levada, to the pope, to theologians, to politicians, to parishioners. He had written thank-you notes to every single person who ever donated to their cause, saying, "Please accept our gratitude for your recent contribution to the campaign to save St. Brigid." In his office were copies of *Code of Canon Law—A Text and Commentary* and volumes of *Vatican II*, which he used in the appeals to the Vatican. There was also the growing pile of news clippings of abuse cases.

Robert questioned the point of attending another St. Brigid annual spring dinner at the Fort Mason Officers' Club, another luncheon at the Italian Athletic Club, another picnic at Lafayette Park, another St. Patrick's Day march up Market Street. He questioned the point of attending another meeting of the committee. Over the past decade, he figured he had attended nearly five hundred committee meetings, and by now only a dozen or so people were still showing up. He knew that these loyalists represented hundreds more who still wanted to return to the church, who took turns keeping a candle lit on the front steps. But Robert was feeling St. Brigid was a case he could not win, a client he could not save.

There would be no more bullhorns. No more trips to Rome. No more private investigators. No more legal briefs. No more St. Brigid protests.

Robert was thinking this during the meeting at Holy Trinity when he saw Tillie's hand shoot up. She asked the question on everyone's mind: "If there is no hope for St. Brigid reopening, why don't they just have the decency to tell us?"

Coming from a woman who had rarely missed a committee meeting in ten years, the words hit Robert hard.

Days later, he sat down to write yet another letter to the archbishop: "If you have decided not to reopen St. Brigid, that should be known. To tell the people absolutely nothing is neither good nor proper. Keeping all in absolute suspense for so long now borders on the intolerable."

Levada responded: "You may be assured that I am well aware of your concerns. When final plans for the use of St. Brigid have been determined, I will be in contact with you."

A week later, Robert wrote another letter, this time asking Levada about a recent note he had sent to a parishioner who wanted to know if she could initiate a fundraising campaign for retrofitting the church—with the support of the archdiocese.

Robert received a letter back from the Reverend Thomas Merson—the same man who a decade earlier had shut off the microphone on Robert midsentence as he tried to deliver committee news in the sanctuary of St. Brigid. Merson had worked under Quinn, and remained under Levada.

Merson wrote: "In addition to the prohibitive costs of retrofitting the St. Brigid Church building, the shortage of clergy to staff at all of the parishes of the archdiocese make it prohibitive to consider the possibility of reopening the church."

Robert read and reread the letter. Clearly, it was time for the committee to take a new direction.

Robert had rehearsed his speech before the meeting at Holy Trinity on March 10, 2004. It wasn't going to be easy, but the time was right. The item was on the agenda under new business: "Leadership of committee." He stood up and began to read from a letter, his resignation letter.

"For ten years I have served as chair," he said, his voice firm. "It is time for a change. I am confident there are exceptionally qualified people available from which to select a new chair." Looking around, he noted that while he had made halfhearted attempts to resign before—only to be met with protests and pleas—this time his decision was final. He talked about the demands of his law practice and his desire to spend more time with his family. He asked for the group's understanding and said he was willing to serve as chair emeritus or honorary chair and would be available for crucial meetings and to speak at public events.

He continued reading from his letter: "My belief is this cause has not been diminished, for the closing of St. Brigid was wrong and contrary to what the Catholic Church claims to represent. The callous disregard by the archdiocesan leadership for the people of this community is offensive. Please rest assured that the church would have been destroyed long ago had it not been for the heroic and courageous work of you on the committee."

Putting away the letter, he looked at his friends. The hard-charging lawyer from the South grew quiet. The members of the committee knew Robert well. They knew that when he rustled in his overstuffed briefcase for papers, he had the air of a disheveled academic. Tonight, as he sat down, hands clasped, the shoulders of his suit rising slightly, he had the look of a little boy. He eyed the group with gratitude.

"You have taught me more than any priest or bishop or archbishop," he said. "You taught me that, yes, this is an important cause. But even more important is the community. The Catholic leadership has lost sight of that. It has lost sight of the everyday people like you. The ones who are doing good, who are practicing their faith, who are knocked down but get back up again, and again. I look at you, and you are my heroes."

Tears mixed with applause. Robert loved the believers from St. Brigid. But this long journey had affirmed his distrust in the establishment. He was no longer proud to call himself a Catholic. He had not attended Mass in years. *Something always drew him back to believing. Then something pushed him away.* He had remained a Catholic because of the faithful from St. Brigid.

After the meeting, Robert altered his route walking home so he could pass St. Brigid. When he reached the steps, he stopped. These parishioners may have been naïve, but they were not to be underestimated.

The candle was lit.

PART III

REVELATION

The community of believers was of one heart and one mind.

— ACTS 4:32

40 *An Unlikely Leader*

BELOW A DARK OIL PAINTING of a bearded, unsmiling Russian Orthodox priest, Joe Dignan anxiously played with the small silver hoop in his left ear. It was March 24, 2004, and the long-exiled parishioners of St. Brigid were gathered in the basement of Holy Trinity to select a new leader, now that Robert Bryan had resigned. Several people had been mentioned as candidates, including Helen and Tillie Piscevich, Ken Epley, and Bebe St. John. But most of the committee, even those nominated to lead it, saw Joe as the natural choice to rekindle hopes of reopening St. Brigid. They also saw him as a wild card.

Joe had his own doubts: not whether he could lead, but whether he could be accepted by these good Catholics. Over time, he had come to see the keen minds of those who appeared disorganized, the resolve of those who seemed meek. He marveled at people like Carmen Esteva, who carried rosary beads in her purse, sent prayer cards to friends and acquaintances almost daily, and found inspiration, comfort, and even humor in her faith. Searching for a place to park, he'd once heard her say, "Hail Mary, full of grace, let us find a parking space."

He was lucky if his shirt was ironed, if his thoughts were clean. He struggled to pay his bills, all the while letting his mother's beautiful, multimillion-dollar house sit empty because he couldn't bear to move anything out. Even Eleanor's mosaic of Post-it notes—with her tall, loopy handwriting—still dotted the walls, and her Chanel No. 5 sat on the dresser. The urn with her ashes remained in her bedroom, where the shades were drawn, casting a soft mauve light. Joe was spending too much time fighting with his former wife, Polly, over their daughter. He was worrying where Mary would go to middle and high school. He wanted to see her accepted at the boarding school he had attended, and was lobbying friends and associates to write letters of recommendation for her. Mary's interest in boys was already beginning, and he wanted to do what he could to steer her from trouble. His friends told him he still acted as if he were going through his own adolescence, with his flirting and serial dating of men he would never have brought home to Eleanor. And he still kept much of his life compartmentalized. He had his journalist friends, his gay friends, his St. Brigid friends.

Few on the committee even knew he was gay. He had confided to Jan and Siu-Mei only, trusting that they knew him well enough to love him anyway. But at forty-seven years old, Joe had learned the hard way that the truth could be suppressed for only so long. When the time was right, he hoped to share all of himself, to bring the parts together. On the phone before the night's meeting, Joe had also confided in Robert, whom he considered a social liberal, asking, "Will my being gay hurt the committee? Will it affect the work to save St. Brigid?"

"No, Joe," Robert replied. "You are not the one who is out of step. It is the Catholic Church that is out of step. Be true to yourself." He added, "Anyway, what difference should one's sexual orientation have on saving a church?"

Others were having their own discussions about Joe. Carmen said she hoped Joe would try to swear less and be more punctual. She hoped that he would antagonize Siu-Mei less so that Helen wouldn't always have to step in and play referee. But in the end she decided that Joe could be late; he could swear; he could do a lot of things. The most important thing was his dedication to the church as well as his knack for making friends in high places. She welcomed the change and already felt a surge of energy on the committee. She kept a stack of index cards with the names of the people she prayed for. She had been praying for Joe, for his grief over the loss of his mother. Now she would pray for Joe as a leader.

Jan Robinson believed Joe would be a forceful chairman. She knew of his raucous sense of humor and figured there would be a period of transition as people grew accustomed to his naughty-child ways. Before the evening's vote, Jan told Siu-Mei, "Joe wants to build a bridge with the archdiocese. All of a sudden, I feel hope that we will have a dialogue with them, whereas before, we've been ignored outright." She also thought that Joe's job as a journalist would give him flexibility and put him at the center of politics at City Hall. "Plus, Joe is just extremely intelligent and well read," Jan said, "and has a commanding presence that is impossible to ignore."

Siu-Mei felt that Joe didn't need the limelight that Robert seemed to thrive in. He had a deep, booming voice, and when he stopped slouching, he stood an imposing six feet two inches tall. He could be aggressive when needed, and she knew he could inspire each person on the committee to do more. She anticipated some controversy, but she felt Joe was the trump card they had been waiting to play.

"Whenever you have a committee, you have power plays," Siu-Mei told Jan. "Remember how from day one, we had people who were criticizing Robert? I'm sure they'll criticize Joe for all sorts of things. But they can't criticize him for his ability."

Bebe had seen Joe's many sides. He bicycled noisily into the meetings, usually showing up after the important items had been discussed, thus requiring the committee to repeat them. But she understood that beneath the jokes and irreverence was someone who cared in powerful ways for St. Brigid. She told those who doubted: "Joe will grow into the role."

Robert attended the meeting to voice support for Joe and to make sure the committee was not getting stymied by indecision or infighting. He said, "Our main focus should be on moving the committee forward and not being sidetracked by such issues as election procedures, raising money, et cetera. The committee must remain focused on the goal of convincing Archbishop Levada to open the church."

Joe had always viewed himself as a sleeper on the committee, content to stand in the back, to work in Robert's shadow. He had always stood apart from everyone. And recently, after losing his mother, he had felt apart from just about everything. The committee brought out the best in him. They saw in him something he still wasn't sure he had—goodness.

Joe listened in wonder as the votes were taken. He was unanimously elected, amid cheers.

He was humbled, and he couldn't help but wish his mother were there. He could hear Eleanor's words, "Joe, dear, please go and do something to save St. Brigid," that November 1993 morning when she waltzed into his apartment. She would laugh, recalling the young boy who tugged at her sleeve during Mass and asked, "Is it over yet?" Now she would have told him it was just beginning. It was Joe Dignan's turn to lead.

41 *The Diplomat*

JOE WAS IN THE SADDLE of the stationary bike, gloves on, ready for his daily spinning class. The music began to pulsate: Madonna, Eurythmics, Prince. Eighties rock—perfect to get the sweat pouring, the mind limber. His favorite instructor, an off-duty cop, was at the front of the packed class. The small room was heating up as fast as the wheels were spinning.

An hour later, Joe left, energized. Breakfast and multiple cups of coffee would focus him even more. He needed to turn on the Dignan charm.

Back at home, he picked up the phone and began to dial. He was going to talk to anyone who would answer at the San Francisco archdiocese. It was time for the committee to repair its relations with Catholic officials, and he was the ingratiating diplomat.

Joe followed up with his calls nearly every day. The archdiocese's director of real estate, Les McDonald, was the most receptive of anyone he reached. Joe was confident they were developing a rapport. McDonald, with his gray hair, patient voice, and expository way, came across as a kindly uncle.

Monsignor Harry Schlitt, who had served as director of development under Archbishop Quinn and was head of administration for Archbishop Levada, told Joe that the archdiocese had never appreciated how Robert treated them like a defendant at trial. Joe told him and others at the archdiocese the same thing he told committee members: "In the past, we have had a strongly adversarial relationship with the organization that is the prosecutor, judge, and jury in deciding the fate of the church. At the time Archbishop Quinn locked the doors ten years ago, that *was* appropriate. But things are different now. Archbishop Levada is an evangelist and wants to expand the faith in San Francisco. So do we."

Joe, who could be wry and deadpan, also had the charm befitting his elite education. He had attended Town School for Boys in San Francisco, then Thacher, a New England–style boarding school in the lush hills north of Los Angeles, before graduating from the University of California at Berkeley. His education had been part academic, part social.

His enthusiasm was irrepressible. "I feel like a salesman for St. Brigid," he told Siu-Mei. "I am selling this church every day. Of course, I wish the church could save itself."

With McDonald, Joe joked. Joe cajoled. Joe proposed ideas for raising money to retrofit St. Brigid. He was sure that McDonald was a good Catholic and—more important—a good guy.

Joe was trying to understand the position of the archdiocese. After ten years, he felt that the committee still didn't know exactly why St. Brigid was closed. Was it really the money? Did the archdiocese anticipate the price tag of the clergy abuse cases? Was Levada protecting the decision of his predecessor? What if the committee came up with a politically acceptable way for Levada to reopen the church without hurting Quinn?

Joe was working other avenues, including writing letters to every priest in the archdiocese, asking them to sign a petition supporting the reopening of one of San Francisco's oldest Catholic churches. He was calling the archdiocese's communications director, Maurice Healy, who early on had attended their picnic Masses and even donated money to the committee. He was trying to find a way, any way, back into St. Brigid. He pictured the faces of the faithful as they walked back into their church after years away.

Joe knew that his mood was bouncing around—"like a SuperBall," he told friends. He would hang on a few positive words from McDonald or Schlitt. Anything could give him hope, such as when someone at the archdiocese actually took his call.

Joe wanted to mend relations but to do so in an entirely different way from that of the pugilistic litigator, who waxed incandescent and had a dazzling legal mind but was ignored and outmaneuvered by the Vatican. Robert had waged a kind of tactical thuggery, exposing bad priests, calling a sitting archbishop morally bankrupt, and disputing every reason given for St. Brigid's closure.

Where Robert wore leadership with the ease of a pinstriped suit, Joe toiled in jeans and T-shirt. Where Robert toted a briefcase, Joe carried a Timbuk2 backpack. And where Robert spoke in a languid southern drawl, Joe had a cache of verbal tics, such as "idear" for "idea"—picked up from listening to John Kerry too much. And where Robert's eyes lit up with possibility, Joe's dark brown eyes still sloped with subtle sadness, even when he smiled.

But Joe was focused. He told Siu-Mei, "Every minute of this struggle, I have been sure St. Brigid would reopen soon. Every time we go to the St. Patrick's Day parade, I think, 'Thank goodness this will be our last parade.' At the core of my devotion to St. Brigid is the mystery as to why it was closed. It's like we've been thrown out of our own house. We cannot remain in ecclesiastical limbo forever. Things are going to change in our favor."

In October 2004, Joe and others on the committee began hearing disquieting rumors. Carmen Esteva heard that St. Brigid had been sold to a group of Russians. Eleanor Croke was told it had been sold to real estate developers. Joe heard it was sold to a woman from a wealthy family who planned to give the building to a group of priests from Vietnam.

The rumors were so persistent that on October 29, Joe finally wrote to Archbishop Levada and delivered the letter to the chancery in person. It began: "We have learned that you are in the process of selling St. Brigid Church. We, the neighbors, friends and parishioners of St. Brigid, are vigorously opposed to this idea, and respectfully request that you terminate this process and proceed along a path which will return the church to use as a place of worship. I am the relatively new chair of our committee, and I am determined to devise a way we can work together to make St. Brigid into a thriving center of Catholic faith."

More than a month later, Joe wrote again, dismayed that he had not received a response. He was amazed that Robert had been able to put up with being turned down and evaded by Levada for eight years.

"I am getting increasingly concerned because of what we see as the urgency of the situation," Joe wrote on December 7. Finally, he succeeded in reaching McDonald, who said that the archbishop was consumed with other issues. Joe was conciliatory, as was his way with McDonald, and said that he knew Levada had his share of problems.

The archbishop was facing depositions and mounting questions about his role as head of the Portland diocese, which had spent $53 million to settle more than 130 claims of priest abuse and was the first Catholic diocese in the nation to file for bankruptcy. And in San Francisco he was dealing with more than seventy-five lawsuits involving allegations of sexual abuse by clergymen. The archdiocese anticipated as many as ninety cases and payouts amounting to as much as $100 million—an average of $1.1 million per claim. Tens of millions of dollars were also being spent on upgrading churches seismically.

Joe returned to his own headache, asking McDonald directly: Had St. Brigid been sold?

McDonald responded that the archdiocese had received seven or eight offers on the building in the ten years it had been closed. But he said that St. Brigid was not for sale and that the archdiocese was not actively soliciting offers.

42 *The Odd Couple*

SIU-MEI STOOD at the bar, sipping a Cosmopolitan. A man in jeans and leather chaps danced in a cage nearby. Joe, who had introduced her to the drink and the bar, was across the room chatting away.

Siu-Mei and Joe were at the Stud, a popular gay bar in the South of Market neighborhood. Joe liked to bring Siu-Mei with him. Dane Devoil had long since stopped bartending, and Joe wanted a friend there. He also wanted to be free to roam. It had been almost a year since Siu-Mei had learned that Joe was gay. Slowly, he had come to trust her more and more and invite her into his private life. He knew she loved him like a sister loves her brother or a mother her son. She was protective—and forgiving.

The saloon-style bar was about as far away as Siu-Mei could get from her upbringing in a conservative Chinese family in Hong Kong. The Stud hosted transvestite cabaret nights and boasted "cheap guys and cheap drinks." In her culture, girls remained close to home and were not allowed to go to parties.

Siu-Mei was intrigued by what she saw. Gorgeous shirtless men with bulging biceps danced with other gorgeous men. She sipped her drink and smiled as Joe made his way back to the bar. With great flair and a love of gory details, he launched into an X-rated description of two men entwined in another room. Siu-Mei stopped him. "Joe, I don't want to hear it," she said, punching him gently on the shoulder. She knew he did it to irritate her.

They were the quintessential odd couple: Siu-Mei wore a thick braid and silver-rimmed glasses, Joe, tight muscle T-shirt, baggy jeans, and studded belt. Siu-Mei had her schedule calibrated to the minute. Joe had a loose-limbed spontaneity.

Minutes later, Joe was off again, leaving Siu-Mei at the bar. She didn't like the promiscuous part of what she saw, but she wasn't one to judge. She was touched that Joe trusted her with his private life.

Now that Joe was chairman of the committee, they relied on each other even more. She tried to take care of committee details so he could focus on the big picture. They exchanged e-mails or talked on the phone at least once a day. If Joe didn't send an e-mail, Siu-Mei would call: "Are you alive?" He'd do the same with her. When he yelled at her, she would let it slide. She knew that he had learned some of his behavior from his father, who communicated through intimidation. Sometimes Joe would show up at her office with a bouquet of flowers and a note, "Happy Wednesday." He did this to other friends as well: noticing something they saw in a store window and surprising them with it as a gift a day later.

Siu-Mei liked where her life had taken her. She had left home when she was seventeen to study at a university in Taiwan. There, she became close friends with a group of students from Macao, a region of China with a surprising number of Christians and

Catholics. She began attending a Catholic church and found herself drawn to the religion. She had been looking for God, trying to communicate with him. Growing up in a Buddhist family, she had watched her parents light incense and offer prayers in the morning and at night. To her, the Buddhist practice was exacting but unfulfilling. Sitting in Mass was different. It was where she began to talk with God. Many of her prayers were answered. A decade after being baptized, however, she still struggled with her faith. Because she wasn't born into a Catholic family, she felt she had to work harder than those who were. It didn't come as easy to her. At least that's how she saw it.

As she scanned the room for Joe and thought of her friends on the committee, Siu-Mei knew that each person was interpreting what was happening to St. Brigid differently. Some expected God to intervene. Others believed the closure was due to human weakness. Some had their faith crushed by the failings of the global Church. Others were finding their faith awakened.

Late that night, as the odd couple left the bar, they laughed about what they had seen and shared. As always, their talk eventually returned to St. Brigid. Siu-Mei commented, "On the committee, we are all different people. We come from different countries or areas. We look different. We think differently. We have different lifestyles. We argue on politics. We don't agree on who to vote for. But on St. Brigid, we agree: This is our home."

43 *The Legacy of "Big Joe"*

ON DECEMBER 22, 2004, Joe was working on a freelance story for the *Washington Post* when he learned that his father, Joseph John Dignan, had died. He returned to his story and filed it on time. Then he picked up the phone and called Mary. "Your grandfather died," he said, his voice a monotone.

The two had been visiting him, knowing that age and ill health were taking a toll. For Mary, the visits were dreaded. At eleven, she was aware of her grandparents' history of broken glasses, hurled vases, and Grandma's trips to the hospital. For Joe, they were a last-ditch effort to have a relationship with a man he never understood but still yearned for—he was his father.

When Mary thought of Grandpa Joe, she thought of him sitting at a table with his feet up, never particularly friendly. When Joe thought of him, he thought of his mother—and her pain. Incredibly, Joe sensed that his mother forgave his father and even continued to love him. Until she died, she called her husband "Big Joe"; her son was "Little Joe." He also believed she had only gotten the divorce, which came late in her life, to protect him. She made sure the house he grew up in was in her name so she could leave it to Little Joe.

Joe remembered that while his father owned a number of properties in San Francisco and belonged to the elite, men-only Bohemian Club, he made sure he stayed cash-poor so he could say to his wife, "I don't have it, Eleanor. I just don't have it!" It was the leash he kept her on.

Joe thought of the summer after his sophomore year in college, when he returned to San Francisco from a backpacking trip around Europe. He came home to find his mother in the hospital. As he was growing up, she had sheltered him from his father's abuse. But with her son no longer a boy, she told him, "He beat me horribly," and left it at that. Joe figured that she had needed to wait long enough so that the pain, anger, and hurt were old wounds, and she could deliver the news in a dull, general way.

His dad was the one who introduced the family to St. Brigid, but he had long boasted that he hadn't been there since he was confirmed as a child. Big Joe's mother, Julia Posades, was a devout Catholic who adored the church that hugged the corner of Broadway and Van Ness. She lived with the family in the Lombard Street house.

In his apartment, Joe stood up and wandered from room to room. He picked up the phone and called Siu-Mei, getting her answering machine. Surprising himself, he started to cry. He managed the words "My dad died."

Not all of his memories of his father were bad. Joe still owned the first bicycle that his parents had given him. He stared at family photos, lingering on one in particular: Lucy the dog, the lovable mutt who had been a part of his marriage, who had protected his mother's home, who had been cared for by Siu-Mei and others on the committee. Lucy had died a few months earlier. He and Siu-Mei had taken her to the animal hospital because she wasn't eating, only to hear that she had cancer and needed to be put to sleep—that day.

Later in the week, Joe glumly told Siu-Mei, "Now it's down to me—and Mary."

Siu-Mei helped Joe plan his father's memorial service. Sister Carmen Santiuste, the principal of St. Brigid School, said Mr. Dignan's Mass could be held in the small chapel in the convent of St. Brigid. Father O would officiate. Joe's friends would be there to support him: Carmen, Tillie, Helen, Bill Van Way, Siu-Mei, and many others.

Not long after the service, Joseph Dignan's will was read. The man of considerable wealth had left nothing to his son or granddaughter.

Joe wrote a short obituary:

> DIGNAN, Joseph John—Father of Joseph Howard Dignan; husband of Eleanor A. Dignan (dec'd.). Born in San Francisco, Mar. 19, 1917. Native San Franciscan, Stanford graduate, World War II USMC Veteran, San Francisco attorney. "He should be remembered for his great voice and his great laugh," said friend of 52 years D. D. Lopez. Mr. Dignan said he didn't want an obituary or a Funeral Service. *Oh, well.* No flowers please. Donations to the Committee to Save St. Brigid Church.

44 *A D-Day of Sorts*

IT WAS LATE MORNING on January 19, 2005, when Joe received a call from Les McDonald.

Joe started off chatty, almost gossipy. He had been talking to McDonald daily, from home, from his Italian racing bike, from his favorite coffeehouse. Of all the people Joe called at the archdiocese, it was the gray-haired McDonald who seemed the most genuine. But on this day McDonald was all business and sounded tense. Joe sat up in his chair and instinctively pulled out a reporter's notepad.

McDonald wasted no time. "St. Brigid," he said, "was sold to a developer. We met this morning with city planners to discuss options, including filing for a demolition permit."

Joe sat back in his chair. "Les, what did you say?"

McDonald, quiet and matter of fact, repeated his words.

"A demolition permit?" Joe said, incredulous. All of his recent conversations with McDonald had been friendly and sincere. Only recently, McDonald had told him, "St. Brigid is *not* for sale."

Joe barely heard the rest of the conversation. It was clear McDonald wanted to be off the phone. Hanging up, Joe was immobilized. He had the same terrible feeling he'd had years earlier when he thought he'd lost Mary. He'd taken her to a park in Oakland, and they were running happily through an Alice in Wonderland tunnel. She was five steps ahead of him when people blocked his way. Emerging into the bright sun, he couldn't see her anywhere. He ran back through the tunnel, yelling her name. He finally found Mary sitting on a bench a few feet away, smiling. It was that same sickening, pit-of-your-stomach, heart-racing feeling he had now.

He had thought when he became chair that the committee was facing a time of peace, not war, that finally, after all of Robert's saber rattling and growling, it was time to mend relations with the archdiocese. There had been ten years of stasis, of legal appeals that went nowhere, of questions that went unanswered, of meetings with church leaders that never happened. They had been writing every single week for eight years requesting a meeting that was never granted. They had been meeting once a month for more than a decade, believing good would prevail. Now this? Out of the blue?

It would not happen under his watch. He composed an e-mail to committee members, heading it: "Emergency." He was determined to come across as assured and businesslike. He wrote, "At 11 A.M. today, Les McDonald met with city planners to request a demolition permit for St. Brigid. Can we have a conference call at 8:30 tonight to plan our next actions, please?"

The muscular stone building, suffused with the everyday stirring of souls, could be reduced to rubble. Joe knew the parishioners would chain themselves to the doors before they let a bulldozer touch St. Brigid.

Joe stuffed his backpack with the papers on St. Brigid, hopped on his Italvega bike, and sped to San Francisco City Hall. He left his bike and helmet in the basement bicycle parking room and took the stairs two at a time to the second floor. Barely taking a breath, he began prowling the corridor, asking the city supervisors to help rescue St. Brigid. Where Robert had argued, Joe would charm. And where Robert had used the law, Joe would use politics. As his mother had told him, "It's not what you know, it's who you know."

Over the next week, Joe paced the long halls. His favorite targets were Michela Alioto-Pier, the supervisor who represented the district that included St. Brigid, and Aaron Peskin, the board president and a preservationist. When they saw him approaching, they knew what was coming, but they smiled nonetheless. "I know I'm the last person you want to see," he cajoled, "but we've got to save this church!" One day he trailed Alioto-Pier into the bathroom, finally realizing where he was and retreating with an "Oops, sorry."

His backpack was heavy with booklets on the history of St. Brigid, assembled by Siu-Mei, who stayed up all night to get the work done. One of the pictures was a large image of the church with a sign underneath: IF YOU OWNED THIS CHURCH, WOULD YOU TEAR IT DOWN?

As he paced back and forth, talking to himself and plotting his next move, he invariably spotted some unsuspecting official returning from a meeting. He took to running beside the politician or aide, talking up St. Brigid as he went. He soon was able to identify people out of the corner of his eye by their gait. Peskin always moved fast, his arms pumping as he walked, like a locomotive.

After meetings with supervisors, random encounters with aides, and talking to anyone who would listen and listening to anyone who talked, a plan was hatched: Have St. Brigid designated a historic landmark. That way, no one could tear it down—including the developer, which wanted to replace this beautiful church with expensive condominiums.

In early February 2005, following a whirlwind of lobbying by Joe, the San Francisco city supervisors unanimously approved a resolution urging the Landmarks Preservation Advisory Board to consider an official historic designation for St. Brigid. An aide to Alioto-Pier had told Joe, "Everyone is going to vote yes so you stop bothering us. We are sick of hearing about St. Brigid. We are sick of you chasing us through the halls."

Though the gesture was a strong show of support, it could not protect the church. California's law, which had been sponsored by the archdiocese and signed in 1994 just as parishes were being closed in San Francisco, prohibited cities from making churches historic landmarks. Nevertheless, the city's action irritated the archdiocese.

A spokesman for the archdiocese said that even if St. Brigid were to become a historic landmark, it wouldn't affect the plan to sell the building to a developer. The spokesman said that $5 million to $7 million was needed to make the building able to withstand future earthquakes and that even if members of the committee came back and said, "'We have the money to retrofit it,' I think our answer would be, 'No, the church is simply not needed now.'"

Archbishop Levada, at a meeting of the Archdiocesan Pastoral Council, said, "We do have some properties, and it has been suggested that the sale of these properties might be used to pay for settlements." One such property was St. Brigid, he allowed.

It was the first time that Levada—or anyone else—had publicly acknowledged that the sale of St. Brigid might subsidize settlements for victims of clergy abuse, an allegation made by Robert Bryan a decade earlier but summarily denied by church officials.

"We are in a time of limited priest resources and we simply have more church capacity than we need," Levada said at the pastoral meeting, adding, "A portion of the proceeds would be used for a matching grant fund to help St. Brigid School build a gymnasium."

But city officials still had another move to make. At the urging of the supervisors, state senator Carole Migden pulled a legislative fast one. She introduced a bill to exclude St. Brigid from the law and allow the city to preserve the building. St. Brigid would be the one church in California excluded from the 1994 law.

For George Wesolek, the tall Pole who had been the face of the church closures, the bill came out of nowhere and pulled him back into the St. Brigid drama. A year after St. Brigid and other churches in the city were closed, Wesolek was placed in charge of the archdiocese's Office of Public Policy and Social Concerns. He had also been involved in the creation of the original 1994 legislation that gave the Catholic Church the right to sell its buildings without being blocked by preservationists. He was stunned that the band from St. Brigid remained active—and still had an impact. While concerned and irritated by Migden's bill, he couldn't help but respect these parishioners without a parish. He marveled, "They're like the Energizer Bunny!" and "These people are really staying in there."

Still, it was not what he needed. He was consumed with a range of hot-button issues, from affordable housing for the poor and immigration reform to fighting physician-assisted suicides.

After a decade of setbacks and silence, the Committee to Save St. Brigid finally was getting somewhere. And, after eight years of asking, a meeting was scheduled with Archbishop William Levada.

45 *Not the Perfect Parent*

JOE AND SIU-MEI stood at the train station in San Francisco, waiting for Mary to arrive for her weekend visit. Joe had a surprise for his daughter, something she had pestered him for a million times and something she was sure she would never get: a basset hound named George.

"Mary always wanted a basset hound," Joe said, checking his watch. "So I go and make the mistake of typing 'basset hound' into Craigslist and up pops George. He was a rescue. I'm finding that he is a very bad dog. He is going to live with me and await Mary's arrival on weekends." George, on a leash by Joe's side, apparently flouted training. Joe kept the door to his backyard open, but George peed in the house. If he left George home alone, the dog howled incessantly. So now George waited for Joe outside his coffee shop, outside his gym, outside City Hall. While he waited, he didn't howl.

"I hope Mary appreciates this," Joe said, as George plopped down on the platform, his floppy ears out to each side.

Mary stepped off the train, saw her dad, saw the dog, and ran to them. "IlovehimIlovehimIlovehim!" she exclaimed. "He's mine? Really mine? I promise to take perfect care of him. I'll feed him and walk him and clean up after him." Joe smiled, knowing that would not be the case, and Mary hugged him at the waist.

The twelve-year-old always looked forward to their time in San Francisco. She knew her dad wasn't the perfect parent—he forgot to pay his car insurance, he was always late, he had some strange friends—but she loved that he was her dad. She knew that, deep down, he believed in the good in the world. He could yell at her. He could be exasperated by her. But he loved her more than anything.

Still, the almost-teenager gave him a hard time whenever possible. When she was younger and resented that he was gay, she would say disparagingly, "Dad, that is so gay" about a dozen times a day. Recently, she liked to antagonize him by announcing that she was an atheist. She knew he wanted her to be an independent thinker, but she also knew he wanted her to be Catholic. Every weekend visit included at least one superboring thing that had to be done for St. Brigid.

The big church had been a part of her life for as long as she could remember. Her earliest memories were of attending meetings of the Committee to Save St. Brigid. Her dad would drag her along and then send her across the street to fetch his coffee. She would ride on the cable car during the annual St. Patrick's Day parade. Mary remembered one year they borrowed a pew from Father O's church, set it on rollers, and pushed it along the entire parade route. Auda Mai Bryan, two years older than she, was always there too. She remembered the sense of calm when the ladies prayed the rosary. Sometimes when her dad was busy, Helen and Tillie would pick her up at the train station and take her home, where they would surprise her with a new Beanie Baby. She always hoped Carmen would bring her carrot cake to meetings. She remembered how nice everyone was to her.

But now St. Brigid was her dad's obsession, not diversion.

On their way home, Mary listened to their itinerary for the weekend. As she suspected, there were things to do for St. Brigid. Her dad was late in writing the committee newsletter; he had to approve the invitation for their upcoming picnic; and he needed to review and help prepare new IRS documents regarding their 501(c)(3) status.

"Dad, I have a question for you," Mary said, holding George in her lap and kissing his head. "The Catholic Church basically says that everything about you is wrong. You are divorced. You are gay. You believe in all sorts of things that the Catholic Church does not, like women as priests, like a right to abortion, like birth control."

He listened to her and smiled his sad smile. He got those questions from friends like Dane, and now from his own daughter.

"You are too smart for your own good," he said. "When I think of St. Brigid, I have powerful emotions and memories, like you do. I have images in my mind, which—for whatever reason—are now comforting. All I could see as a child was the wood of the pew in front of me. Dark brown shiny oak. Darker grain. Missal holder. I had to wear these forty percent polyester easy-care shirts and geeky pants that made me feel itchy. I think of the towering presence of your grandmother in her sixties up-do hairdo. I see myself turning around and having stern faces stare back at me. I see my mom's scolding looks. I can still sense her warm hand."

"So it's a part of your childhood and, like, your whole being?" Mary asked.

"Yes," he said. "When I got older, your grandmother started telling me that I needed to behave like a Christian. At some point as an adult, I started calling the rules I live by Catholicism. You'll learn this later. Everyone has their own story when it comes to religion. The process of being Catholic seems to have happened by osmosis, and wasn't entirely voluntary."

"But why be a part of a group that doesn't want you?" Mary

asked. "I mean, I don't want to be friends with people who don't want to be my friends. I don't want to hang out at places where I'm not wanted."

Joe laughed and said, "I am working out my relationship with God. God is real. I'm just not sure about the rest."

As a child, Joe had wanted nothing more than to evade Mass. As an adult, he struggled to articulate—even to understand—his devotion to St. Brigid. Part of it was because his mother had adored the church. Another reason was Siu-Mei. She was the one person in his life who came to comfort him after his mother died. Another part was what he said to Mary or what Mary had told him: The church was in his marrow.

But there was something else, too.

Sitting inside St. Brigid as a boy had been stultifyingly boring. Working on behalf of St. Brigid was anything but. Maybe it was the difference between words and deeds. Maybe it was what happened when faith wasn't forced.

46 *One Office at a Time*

JOE TOOK HIS LOBBYING act to Sacramento. He piled George into the front seat of his blue Miata, wedging him between posters of St. Brigid and stacks of papers on the history of the church. Joe headed first to Carole Migden's office, where he was becoming such a regular that he was given a shelf to store his materials. Standing in the reception area, he pulled his lucky red tie out of his backpack. He talked to Migden's aide while fixing his tie in the reflection of a framed Museum of Modern Art poster.

"Is my tie straight?" he asked, in his single-breasted suit and dress shoes scuffed from racing around City Hall. "It'd be the only straight thing about me."

Joe pulled a list of assembly members out of his bag. It had been prepared by Siu-Mei and included office numbers by floor as well as the legislators' political interests. He started out fast. His head was slightly ahead of his body, reflecting his pursuit of someone, anyone, to corner. He carried his Timbuk2 bag under one arm and three giant posters of St. Brigid under the other.

The day would be spent lobbying legislators to support Migden's bill to protect St. Brigid. Joe had the zeal of an evangelist and the energy of a child. From office to office, he talked about how St. Brigid was established just weeks before Lincoln gave the Gettysburg Address. He read from a San Francisco newspaper article published on December 10, 1904, about the dedication of the remodeled church. The story described the bishops and prelates and the overflowing congregation, as well as the beauty of the building: "The sanctuary, with its handsomely carved altar, brilliantly lighted, together with the domed ceiling and arched in electric lights, made a wonderfully impressive scene, especially when to it was added the magnificent solemnity of the Mass, the chanting of the celebrant and his assistants, taken up by the choir singing Schubert's Mass in G until the great structure was filled with a flood of harmony." Joe talked about St. Brigid as a place of eternal moments and vibrant souls—of Carmen Estevas, of Siu-Mei Wongs, of his mother, of all those in the laity and clergy who preceded them.

He said that this sacred place was being threatened with the wrecking ball—to make way for yet more expensive housing in the city.

In the reception room of a senator's office, the television was showing the soap opera *All My Children*. As a receptionist reluctantly pulled her gaze from the show, Joe began his speech: "I'm here to talk about this beautiful church." The woman, looking back at the TV, said the legislator was out and asked Joe to leave his card. He said he didn't have one, as he was part of a volunteer committee. He smiled and thanked her and said he would be back.

Later in the day, after another cup of black coffee, he lamented that he had missed his spinning class. Every day now was consumed with St. Brigid. He tried to compensate by taking the stairs instead of the elevator.

Every few offices, Joe managed to touch someone with his message or enthusiasm. A chief of staff would invite him to come in and talk about St. Brigid. Joe showed pictures and told funny stories. He said a small misfit band of believers had waged a crusade for more than ten years to save the church. He said their crusade had outlasted any other parish protest anywhere in America, from Boston to Seattle and all places in between.

By the end of the day, he was retrieving positive feedback on his voice mail. One important assembly person was talking to another, he was told.

"I'm getting things done!" he exclaimed, racing down the stairs to the next floor. He was winning support one office at a time.

Driving back from Sacramento, he talked to George, who was a bad dog but a good listener. Joe reported that while they were working in Sacramento, committee members were meeting to organize. Letters were being sent to thousands of people urging their support for landmarking the church.

Levada was under pressure from all sides. His tenure as archbishop of Portland, Oregon, continued to dog him. Abuse survivors there were seeking $155 million in damages, and three of the area's plaintiffs had committed suicide. In San Francisco, news stories had begun questioning his role in allowing accused priests to continue working in parishes. An article in the *Catholic World Report* stated: "The Archbishop has been roundly denounced by sex-abuse victims for what they see as his uncooperative attitude in efforts to identify and punish clerical abusers."

Levada was also facing uncomfortable and relentless questions about St. Brigid. The front-page headlines were not helping: SALE OF CHURCH LAND WOULD PAY ABUSE CLAIMS, CITY HALL RALLIES TO SAVE CHURCH FROM DEMOLITION, and POLI-

TICIANS MOVE TO PROTECT CHURCH. Concerned legislators were beginning to weigh in on what Archbishop Levada should do with his church.

47 *A Meeting—Eight Years Later*

AT 1 P.M. ON FEBRUARY 18, 2005, in the conference room at archdiocesan headquarters, Joe sat at a long table across from Archbishop Levada, who was seated next to Monsignor Schlitt and Les McDonald. With Joe were Ken Epley, Doris Munstermann, and Bebe St. John. The archbishop had asked that the meeting be kept small. They began with a prayer, led by Doris, who had been a Catholic schoolteacher for decades and served on the archdiocese's ecumenical council.

Joe was anxious, as were the others. He had rehearsed his lines, held conference calls with the committee members, lost sleep, and expected the worst. It had been eight years since the last meeting. He needed to get everything right.

The archbishop didn't waste time. Surprising everyone, he said that the deal with the condominium developer was off and that he wanted to find a solution to keep the church standing.

The deal was off? He wanted to find a solution? Joe sat forward in his chair. He had anticipated Levada's asking them to accept plans to make way for much-needed housing in the city, but he hadn't been prepared for this. He smiled. "That is incredible news," he said, quickly launching into an apology to Levada for the strained relations between the group and the archdiocese. Joe acknowledged the "difficult and combative history that at times was deeply personal and painful," and added, "We want to be your allies."

Schlitt, with the untroubled, soothing manner befitting his decades as a priest, said, "More than anyone, the archbishop doesn't want to close churches." A variety of ways had been explored to keep St. Brigid by turning it into a Catholic museum or a self-sustaining shrine. None of the ideas panned out.

Bebe watched and listened. There was something that had yet to come up. She could feel it.

Joe, sitting at the edge of his seat, offered to raise money to retrofit St. Brigid. Levada appeared receptive but said it couldn't be done in the name of the archdiocese—a caveat that Joe knew limited their possibilities. He suggested that he could find developers who would come up with plans to develop the land around the church, thereby funding the retrofitting costs. It was something he had discussed with Wesolek. Levada nodded, as if it were a fine idea.

Joe emphasized that the committee had no intention of abandoning its effort to reopen St. Brigid. The archdiocese reiterated that it had no intention of reopening St. Brigid as a church.

Joe listened as others from the committee spoke, but his mind wandered to the committee's first meeting with Quinn in 1994 and to their first meeting with Levada in 1996. He had taken it as a good sign that Levada had wielded a Bic pen at that meeting, not an expensive Montblanc. But now he noticed that Levada and his staff were holding Montblanc pens. He also couldn't stop himself from looking from Levada to his portrait, directly behind him. The portrait was massive, formal, and ancestral-looking. It was slightly intimidating: Levada sat in full vestments with a purple sash and an enormous gold cross in the middle of his breastplate. He smiled beatifically. On the third finger of his right hand was a large ring, symbolizing faith.

Joe brought his attention back to the room. It surely was a silly way to think.

Finally, Schlitt cleared his throat. Here, Bebe thought, was the moment she was waiting for.

Schlitt said that the archdiocese would indeed welcome ideas from developers and cooperate with the committee. But he needed to make one thing clear: The archdiocese was not happy with Senator Migden's bill. He suggested that the committee—in this new spirit of cooperation and conciliation—work to get the legislation withdrawn. The bill made the archdiocese feel as if there were a gun to its head, Schlitt said.

Bebe smiled. She thought to herself, *At last, a balance of power. They are forced to deal with us.*

Joe nodded and, without responding directly to Schlitt's request, said that he looked forward to working together, with common goals.

Despite their different agendas, both sides seemed intent on remaining productive and cordial. For the first time in more than a decade, there was a feeling of peace. And, more than that, for the believers accustomed to defeat, there was victory. While Levada had not given them permission to raise money in his name, he had no problem giving the committee limited access to the church to do tours for potential donors, contractors, and engineers.

In their own way, the committee members had faced down the bulldozers—and won. At least for now.

48 *A Short-Lived Peace*

THE NEXT DAY, Joe sent an e-mail to the committee headed: "Great news!"

"We met with the archbishop yesterday about St. Brigid," he wrote, "and I'm very happy to report that I can't imagine how things could have gone better. The archbishop was thoughtful and open to new possibilities. His Vicar for Administration, Msgr. Harry Schlitt, said that more than anyone, the 'archbishop doesn't want to close churches.' We believe the archbishop would like to see a workable plan that will save St. Brigid. He will appoint a liaison to work with us to examine solutions that will restore the church as a center of our neighborhood." Joe thanked all of those "too numerous to name, who helped make this step forward possible," and said, "After 11 years, we may soon be able to save St. Brigid."

On the following Tuesday, February 22, Joe received an e-mail from Les McDonald, written to "clarify a few things." McDonald wrote that although "it is true that the archbishop is most reluctant to close churches, he also made it clear that [he] did not plan to reopen St. Brigid as a parish. The archbishop does appreciate your interest in preserving the building. However, time is of the essence. The archbishop [also] made it clear that no funds should be raised in his name. I hope this sets the record straight."

Joe shared McDonald's e-mail with the other committee members.

Bebe responded: "When we left the meeting, I felt like there was progress, that something good could happen. But thinking about it, they really gave away nothing. They want us to kill Migden's legislation, but they are not willing to reopen the church. They want us to raise money, but said we can't do it in the archdiocese's name.

"We need to keep this bill moving forward," she said. "It's our bargaining chip."

Monsignor Schlitt and Archbishop Levada, who had known each other since studying together in Rome in 1961, headed out for an evening walk. Levada liked taking long strolls around the city, unrecognizable in layman's clothes and a San Francisco Giants cap. As the two rounded the corner of Van Ness and Ellis Street, they spotted an enormous billboard just across the street and came to a halt. On it was a photograph of St. Brigid and the words HELP SAVE ST. BRIGID, PROTECT OUR LANDMARKS, and SUPPORT SB169. SEN CAROLE MIGDEN. The billboard was as wide as the building under it.

Schlitt was the first to say he felt duped. He had thought Joe and the others were trying to cooperate with the diocese, that they had been open to his plea to quash Migden's bill. He had taken Joe's apologies for previous tensions seriously and recalled his words: "I want to publicly apologize for all of the things that have gone on before." Joe had presented himself as "very much the gentleman," Schlitt remarked.

He continued angrily, "Here I am, having to lay people off. We are faced with all of the problems that are happening in Catholic churches across the country. We do not have extra capital. We are having to let go of our ethnic population representative. We are having to let go of our family life ministry that trained couples for marriage."

They resumed their walk. Schlitt mused, "What we're dealing with here only comes from a very disgruntled group. They have turned around and blocked us at every corner. We have had to get a lawyer every step of the way. Why don't they just take their families and go and start over somewhere else? Why do these people not give up?"

49 *The Power of Prayer*

TILLIE PISCEVICH, now seventy-three, was at home when she received a call from her doctor, informing her that she had breast cancer.

After recovering from the initial shock of hearing the news not in person but over the phone, not in a compassionate way but as a declaration, Tillie confronted the medical path she faced.

The first call Helen and Tillie made was to Denise Nicco, a member of the committee. Denise, who lived across the street, had herself battled breast cancer. She came right over and began calling other friends from the committee.

Though the group was in the throes of a landmark legislative battle, the members didn't hesitate to make time for Tillie, who had been one of their own from the beginning. Within a week of her diagnosis, dozens of cards conveying healing and support began to arrive at her house. There were Mass cards, prayer cards, and cards with words of encouragement. They started with Carmen Esteva, who had notes for every occasion. Carmen had carefully gone through her stack and selected a card from Padre Pio, an Italian priest who had been canonized as a saint and was known as "Angel of the Sick." It was a Mass card with "A Prayer for Healing."

"Send your holy angels to watch over me," the prayer read. "O divine healer, free me from useless anxiety, and grant me a sense of serenity."

Carmen made a donation to a Padre Pio foundation for a Mass to be said in Tillie's name every week for as long as she needed it. She also signed Tillie up with a national prayer group that would send cards of healing.

Carmen understood tribulation and believed in the power of prayer. She and her mother, father, and sister had come to San Francisco from Manila in 1972 because her sister, Soledad Falcon, had heart problems, and they hoped to get the best treatment possible. But Soledad caught an infection in the hospital that was supposed to save her. It was a mistake that wasn't supposed to happen. She died at the age of thirty-three. Carmen and her family had been comforted by the prayers of family, friends, and the strangers who reached out to them.

Now Carmen prayed three times a day. Her prayer list was organized by category: sickness, general, departed. As she prayed for Tillie and organized others to do the same, she felt her faith becoming more active. She knew that Church law stated that Catholics have a "serious obligation" to attend Mass on Sundays and on the six Holy Days of Obligation—January 1 (Mary the Mother of God), Ascension Thursday (forty days after Easter), August 15 (the Assumption of Mary), November 1 (All Saints'),

December 8 (the Immaculate Conception of Mary), and December 25 (Christmas). But she had learned that Church law does not specify that these Masses must take place in a church building. Now she prayed as she walked, and she prayed when she met with friends. She tried to see Jesus in everyone she met, though she acknowledged it was easier with some than others.

She was now praying for sixty-six people daily—fifty who were living, sixteen who had departed. At every committee meeting, she began the rosary by praying for Tillie.

Soon, Tillie had a stack of cards six inches thick. She kept them neatly bound, aligned by the stamps. When she felt fearful or weak, she sat at her kitchen table and opened them again, one at a time. She couldn't even discard the envelopes. Someone sent her a card with a keychain of the Blessed Mother. She prayed Carmen's prayer, "A Prayer for Healing," every day.

Helen told Tillie—"Til," she called her—that with all of the prayers coming in from the city and from across the country, everything was going to be fine. Helen said she would go to St. Dominic's, the only church in San Francisco with a shrine to Saint Jude, and light a candle to the patron saint of lost causes.

Helen saw Tillie as the better Catholic. Tillie demurred that that wasn't true, that Helen was quieter but no less faithful. The two had lived together since 1960, the same year they began attending Mass at St. Brigid. Helen worked for Chevron for thirty-eight years. Tillie was a schoolteacher and a counselor. They came from a family of twelve children, four boys and eight girls, who grew up in a desert town in Nevada. The town had a few hundred residents, one school, and no hospital. All of the Piscevich children were born at home. They had become a close clan, now with dozens of nieces and nephews.

One of her sisters told Tillie that she should pray to Saint Peregrine, the patron saint of cancer. She began reading a daily prayer to the saint.

More than ever, she regretted not taking the rosary from the

Blessed Mother at the last Mass of St. Brigid nearly eleven years earlier. The statue remained locked in the church. Tillie wanted to hold that rosary and pray. There was something about it she couldn't explain to anyone, something she was sure would help her in the fight for her life.

50 *The Big Day Arrives*

JOE PARKED HIS CAR in front of St. Brigid at around 8:30 A.M. on May 3, 2005, and stumbled out. His unfastened backpack was stuffed with papers that threatened to spill onto Broadway. He mumbled hello to his fellow committee members and said something about a late party. The admission, coupled with his disheveled appearance and dark-rimmed eyes, did not fill the members with confidence on their big day.

Siu-Mei stood nearby, wearing her blue SAVE ST. BRIGID sweatshirt. Her long black hair was in a thick braid, and she looked exasperated.

"Joe, why are you always late?" she asked. "Today is not a good day to be late."

He shot her a look that said he didn't need reminding.

After working in obscurity and uncertainty all this time, the Committee to Save St. Brigid was about to be heard at the state capitol in the office of Governor Arnold Schwarzenegger and were to appear before a senate panel.

Robert Bryan, who had never lost touch with the committee, serving as chair emeritus, offered ideas and encouragement. The day-to-day work was Joe's. Robert had taken the St. Brigid battle to the august corridors of the Vatican. Now Joe would lobby his case in the brightly lit halls of Sacramento.

But before Joe could lead them into battle, he needed fortification.

"Can we just, maybe like, swing by Starbucks?" Joe said sheepishly as he climbed into the back of a van with seventy-five-year-old Lorraine Kelley at the wheel.

"Of course, Joe," said Lorraine, who had volunteered to drive the committee to Sacramento.

Eleanor Croke was in the front seat next to Lorraine. "I'm all fired up," she said, adjusting her elegant hat. "We've had our meetings for all of these years. We know all of the facts. We're ready." With a mischievous twinkle in her blue eyes, she looked at the back-seat passengers and said, "I have a one-track mind to save St. Brigid."

After a quick stop for coffee, Joe settled back in his seat and began to wake up. He asked Siu-Mei, "Can I use your cell phone to call Greece? Mary is there on vacation." Siu-Mei handed over her phone.

After making sure Mary was fine, Joe turned to rifling through his backpack. Flustered, he gave up and asked Siu-Mei, "Do you have Peskin's number?" He wanted to call the president of the city's Board of Supervisors.

In the front seat, Lorraine and Eleanor chatted away.

"I feel that for the first time in a long time, we really have a chance to save St. Brigid. I'm very excited," Lorraine said.

St. Brigid had been the center of her life since childhood. She was born and reared in a home a few blocks from the church, and she and her husband of fifty years lived in that same house now. She told Eleanor how she would walk to the girls school, St. Brigid Academy, which opened in 1931 and was described in a newspaper article at the time as an "elegant and substantial wooden building, conspicuous for its size, being one of the largest edifices in that part of the city." Just a few doors down from St. Brigid Church, the school had been sold by the archdiocese in 1953, demolished, and turned into an eyesore of a motel.

"The school was a beautiful old home with a circular staircase," Lorraine recalled, pulling onto the freeway. "We had to wear these uniforms, like navy uniforms with a white shirt with a mantle and a navy wool skirt.

"I was in the sixth grade when World War Two broke out," she continued. "Girls had started wearing silk stockings. When the war started we had to stop. Everything was rationed. Coffee. Butter. Gasoline. My parents sold the Packard. I remember we went into St. Brigid and put together care packages to send to soldiers."

By 11:15 A.M., as they neared Sacramento, Joe was fully awake. He combed his hair, buttoned his shirt, and smoothed his suit jacket, which was folded on his lap with his lucky tie. He said it was time to prepare for their meeting with Schwarzenegger's legislative aide, Cynthia Bryant.

"There are several points we need to make," he told the others. "The church does not belong entirely to the archdiocese. The city has given it free property taxes for a hundred and forty years. St. Brigid belongs to the community. People over the century have supported this church. The parishioners paid for the stained glass, the Italian organ, the carpets, the marble, the statuary, the font, the pulpit, the roof, the gymnasium, and just about everything else. We have to point out that no one has tried to tear down a church as historically important as this. The stained-glass windows were designed by the Harry Clarke Studios in Dublin—Clarke being one of Ireland's great glassmakers. The statues on the front of the church were made by Seamus Murphy, one of Ireland's great sculptors. This is not a matter of freedom of religion, as the archdiocese will probably argue. It's a matter of the life of an old church where important things have happened for generations."

Once inside the governor's office, Joe stood in front of a painting of Abraham Lincoln. He cheerfully told the receptionist they were trying to save a church that had come to life when Lincoln was president. He said that he hoped during the meeting to place large pictures of St. Brigid around the room.

He asked the others, "Would anyone like to tell a personal story during the meeting?"

Jerry Suich, who had not attended meetings but who had long supported the committee, said, "My grandparents were married at St. Brigid in 1910. My grandmother told me that after her wedding, she walked out the front steps of the church and saw her old boyfriend standing across the street."

"That's good," Joe said. "That's the kind of story we need. Emotional impact."

Lorraine asked, "Should we ask the aide how we can get in touch with Schwarzenegger's lovely wife, Maria Shriver? She's Catholic."

Joe suggested they work first on getting the message to the governor.

As the meeting began, Joe, sitting at the head of a table large enough to accommodate fifty, gave an overview of the senate bill that would allow St. Brigid to be preserved as a historic landmark. He also talked about the enormous effort the committee had made to save St. Brigid from sale or destruction and see it reopened as a house of worship. They had met once a week, sometimes more, week after week, year after year.

Several parishioners shared stories. Eleanor talked about her grandparents in Ireland and their devotion to their own Catholic church. She said that when she came to San Francisco from New York in August 1957, she was grateful for a city that welcomed her. She had lost her mother to Lou Gehrig's disease when she was sixteen and her father to pneumonia two years later. She put herself through college and nursing school before heading west. Shortly after arriving in San Francisco, she met a priest who invited her to St. Brigid. "From that first day, I just fell in love with the church," Eleanor said. "I felt so at home."

Joe could see that Eleanor was charming Bryant, a woman paid to listen dispassionately before making a recommendation to her boss. When Joe first joined the committee, he'd discounted the

Eleanors. Now here she was, her white hair askew, her lipstick drawn a bit beyond her lips, her story enchanting.

As the meeting ended, Bryant continued talking with Eleanor, laughing and peppering her with questions, including her take on the new pope, the former Cardinal Joseph Ratzinger. Eleanor said that she had hoped for someone more progressive and less conservative—and certainly someone with a better track record handling abuse cases. As if adding a juicy twist, Eleanor then said she had heard that San Francisco's archbishop, William Levada, was "buddies" with Ratzinger—the same cardinal who as head of the Congregation for the Doctrine of the Faith had issued the edict telling bishops to keep cases of clergy abuse secret.

After the meeting, Joe embarrassed Eleanor by giving her a big hug. "I am blown away by you," he told her.

But the day was only beginning. Their folksy caucus moved next to a senate hearing room. Senator Migden's bill was to be heard that afternoon.

Joe and his group gathered in the hall outside room 4204 to strategize. Their signs and posters were lined up. Speeches were rehearsed. Suddenly Siu-Mei exclaimed, "Look who's here!" It was Father O, bounding toward them, his face flushed from rushing. "I wouldn't miss this," he said, catching his breath. For several minutes, he talked and told stories, offering jokes to ease the tension.

He was happy the committee had moved into a new arena, beyond the church sphere and beyond the legal sphere. "We have gone from the Vatican to the archdiocese to the secular," he said with a laugh. He was optimistic on this day because the measure to protect St. Brigid was supported by influential people.

It was time for them to be heard by the senate committee. They filed into the room and took seats. Siu-Mei bowed her head in prayer, too nervous to watch.

The semblance of a truce with the archdiocese had collapsed, and the parishioners believed that Migden's bill was a lifeline being thrown to St. Brigid. They had agreed they could not let go of that lifeline simply because the archdiocese had asked it of them.

The first to speak were members of the San Francisco archdiocese, who had just announced that while they still had no plans to reopen St. Brigid, they would agree to require any buyer of the building to wait at least ten years to tear it down.

"We see this as a noble gesture on the part of the archdiocese," George Wesolek said. "And it provides time for everyone to cool down."

He was joined in opposing Migden's bill by a handful of clergy leaders. He said that the archdiocese was quickly garnering support from dozens of religious organizations across the state and that the interfaith leaders saw the bill as a "serious threat" to religious institutions in California and an intrusion into the governance and mission of their work. He had also been taken aback by what he saw as the vicious attacks on the Catholic Church by political leaders. He felt Migden and others were using the clergy abuse cases as a way to slam the church whenever possible.

The parishioners said that they saw the archdiocese's ten-year promise as a crafty ploy to get Migden to withdraw her bill.

"If they were sincere about preserving the building, they would preserve it in perpetuity, not for ten years," Joe said.

Bebe St. John said, "The Catholic Church has time on its side. We don't have time on our side. I've seen what ten years has done to the building. We do what we can to care for it, but there has been neglect. In another ten years, it will be in worse shape. And there will be fewer people who have an intimate connection to the church."

Joy Duffy, a St. Brigid parishioner for twenty-five years, said she no longer trusted the promises of the archdiocese. "They are making this offer because they believe we will fade away," she said.

The testimony was followed by a fusillade of questions. Then it was time for a vote. The parishioners, filling a long row of seats—

with Father O in the middle—clasped hands. It felt as though every step of the way had led them to this point. The bill to protect St. Brigid was approved by a 9–3 vote. It would go before the full senate within a month.

The committee members applauded and breathed sighs of relief. Siu-Mei raised her head, tears in her eyes. She smiled at Joe, who was already up and heading out the door—intent on talking to the senators who had voted no.

Out in the hallway, Carole Migden told the group, "This is a good first step. This is a historic site. It was built more than a hundred years ago. It's a place where people like [former San Francisco mayor] George Moscone took their sacraments. But this is just the beginning. We have some formidable opponents in the San Francisco archdiocese. We cannot underestimate them."

After treating everyone to a quick bite to eat, Joe reminded the group that they needed Migden's bill to pass *and* historic preservation status to be granted.

Back in the city, Lorraine found a parking spot in front of St. Brigid. Joe told everyone to rest up. They had another big day—starting first thing in the morning.

Early Wednesday, parishioners were back in their St. Brigid sweatshirts, holding WE LOVE ST. BRIGID signs, and toting enormous posters of their church. But this time, they were packed into a room at San Francisco City Hall. Their application to have St. Brigid declared a historic landmark was about to be heard.

Committee members again offered testimony, and again they listened to opposition from the San Francisco archdiocese. They brought with them eight hundred cards in support of Migden's bill, plus the nineteen thousand signatures they had collected over the years calling for the reopening of St. Brigid. They had architectural historians lined up to speak on the importance of the Romanesque building and on the role played by the early Irish immigrants in constructing the church.

Joe spoke first, saying, "We'd like to put up pictures of our church so you can see what we're talking about."

"Your time is running," a commissioner said.

"I understand that more than you know," Joe said. "We are in a race here. For eleven years, we've been trying to get this church reopened and preserve it forever. It doesn't matter to any of us that the archdiocese came in 1994—after it was shuttered—and said the church is no longer sacred. They said they desanctified it. It doesn't work that way. It is still sacred. A place is made sacred because of what it means to people and to families. As Senator Migden said yesterday in Sacramento, this is one of the most emotional issues she's dealt with in her career."

Next up was Nelly Echavarria, the seamstress who had attended St. Brigid for twenty-seven years, wearing her black beret. "This church lives deep in my heart," she said. "This is one of the more beautiful buildings in San Francisco. I pray every day, 'Please give that magnificent building this status. Please save our church.'"

Father O again faced a panel on behalf of his flock. "St. Brigid is one work of art, inside and out," he said, adjusting the microphone. "There are people who say, 'Trust us, we will make sure the building is taken care of.' But I have concerns when nothing is written down on paper. With St. Brigid, there is an even higher level of attention and respect needed. There is an integrity to the structure. I come from the old city of Cork, Ireland. It is my belief that it's important to keep the old with the new, the ancient with the modern. It is my belief that contracts are needed even between the best of friends. We need something in writing to protect St. Brigid for the ages."

Next, Eleanor Croke told the commission: "My grandparents came from Tipperary, Ireland, and this church was built by Irish people who put all of their savings and work into it. They did this for posterity—not to have it torn down to pay for the abuse of priests. This is stealing our religious culture and heritage."

Glenn Corino, the athletic director at St. Brigid School, said,

"Just stand at the corner of Broadway and Van Ness and look at the building. You don't need to be religious to see it needs to stay there."

Officials from the archdiocese said they wanted to sell St. Brigid at fair market value and were opposed to the committee's bid for landmark status.

"The archdiocese cannot commit several million more dollars of its increasingly scarce resources to retrofit and reopen a parish such as St. Brigid's, which was not viable as a parish even a decade ago when it was closed," said Wesolek. He added that giving landmark status to St. Brigid would make selling the property "extremely difficult" and would cut "the value of the property in half." He noted that funds were needed for the archdiocese to compensate the victims of clergy sexual abuse.

Siu-Mei again sat with her head in her hands. Now it was time for the Landmarks Preservation Advisory Board to vote. Joe was calm. It was how he felt in high-pressure moments. Driven by deadlines, he was confident now that the vote would be in their favor.

It was unanimous: 6–0 in favor of recommending St. Brigid for historic landmark status.

"Hell yes!" yelled a parishioner from the back of the room, causing others to break into laughter. "We did it!" Joe exulted. "We really did it." Father O said, "We need a celebration. A decade of fighting and we have a victory." Lorraine Kelley stretched her stiff legs and chuckled. "The race is not to the swift, nor the battle to the strong," she said.

Joe loved seeing the committee members smile. The victory was all theirs. For a moment, he closed his eyes and said a prayer of thanks. As the room emptied, he told them that the measure would be heard next by the Board of Supervisors before it reached the desk of Gavin Newsom, their longtime supporter who was now San Francisco's mayor.

Out in the hall, Wesolek found himself confronted by the diminutive Echavarria. Wearing a tweed skirt suit and hat, the seamstress—who came up to Wesolek's thick chest—shook her fist at him and said, "The archdiocese has done a terrible thing in closing St. Brigid. You should be ashamed of yourselves!"

Wesolek knew by now to listen without trying to reason. He had learned that all of the archdiocese's arguments about demographics and economics and rational things went nowhere with these parishioners. It was as if they didn't hear what he was saying; it wasn't what they wanted to hear.

Entering the hallway, Joe said he was taking everyone out to lunch to celebrate. As they were leaving, he tried to catch the attention of Wesolek, who was still under siege by Echavarria. Joe briefly caught his eye, but Wesolek looked away. Joe had a feeling that something big was developing behind the scenes, that the archdiocese still had its own hand to play. It had been more evasive and elusive than usual.

Joe was right.

Within days, the archdiocese made an announcement that shocked the city and reverberated across the globe. Archbishop William Levada had been named by Pope Benedict XVI to lead the Vatican's Congregation for the Doctrine of the Faith, making the San Francisco archbishop the highest-ranking American in church history.

Levada, still being dogged by allegations of abuse case cover-ups in his former diocese—as well as his lack of oversight in his current diocese—would replace the man who had ascended to the papacy, his old friend, the former Cardinal Ratzinger, who had his own track record of ignoring or keeping quiet allegations of abuse. Levada would take over as the preeminent protector of Catholic teaching, one of the top two cardinals at the Vatican.

Joe sent a message to the committee: "At one level, maybe Levada will bring back the bacon for us. On another level, no one really knows what it will mean to San Francisco. We will have made it through three archbishops: Quinn, Levada, and whoever this new guy is. I know there is general unease over this news. But as usual, there is also a sense of hopefulness. The new archbishop will have a fresh clean slate. And, we are still here, with our own victories to celebrate."

News of the committee's victory made its way from parishioner to parishioner, from those still in San Francisco to those who had moved across the country.

David Hansell got word while listening to talk radio. He whistled to himself and said, "Well, I'll be darned. They are actually getting somewhere." To him, it was time for one more important fix-it job. Every time David worked on one of the doors, washed the steps, or plucked weeds from the church grounds, his gaze was drawn upward to the figure of the Savior and the Greek monogram above the main door, IC XC NI KA, meaning "Jesus Christ conquers."

Now, as the reopening of St. Brigid felt possible, he was eager to ready the sleeping beauty. It was time to tackle the bas-relief medallion-like frieze of Jesus above the main door. For several months, he had been going from church to church, in San Francisco and Marin County, studying the statuary and religious displays. He studied them for shading, and he studied them for just the right hue of white.

Early one morning, not long after hearing the committee's good news, David carried his thirty-two-foot ladder to the steps of St. Brigid. He spread his drop cloth at the base and checked his paint-splattered satchel to make sure he had what he needed. Climbing the ladder, he paused halfway to admire the work he'd done on the front door, with its ornate wrought iron. He was pleased. The shades of gray he had mixed blended well with the cloudy stones of the church and the leafing framing the door.

Continuing upward, he eyed the Savior, who had seen better days. He looked like hell, David said to himself. Jesus' cloak was dirty, his peaceful face and wavy hair were a dusty gray, his crown a muted brown. David's favorite prayer had always been the Lord's Prayer. He said it every day, typically at night. It went through his mind now as he began to work: *Our father, who art in heaven.* Like the sanding he did, the prayer had a lulling quality. The morning air felt good.

He had briefly considered using 14-karat gold leafing for Jesus' crown, but he reminded himself he was a painter, not an artist. Besides, he couldn't afford it. So he found a straightforward, clean-looking white paint for Jesus' cloak and would use regular gold paint for the crown. He cleaned the cloak with harsh solvent and used steel wool to sand away the old paint. As he sanded, he continued his prayer: *Hallowed be thy name. Thy kingdom come. Thy will be done on earth as it is in heaven.*

David opened a can of paint and reached under the ladder, feeling for the hook. It amazed him that more than a decade had passed since St. Brigid was closed. He was seeing his son infrequently now, as his boy was a man of twenty-three and—he liked to give him a hard time—was "living in sin" with a woman who had also been raised Catholic but wasn't practicing. He hoped that his son would one day return to the Church, and that the time he had spent inside St. Brigid, soaking up the traditions, rituals, and Scripture, would resurface as it had with him when he needed it most.

He had started with the Savior's feet and worked his way up. *Give us this day our daily bread, and forgive us our trespasses, as we forgive those who trespass against us.* As he mulled the words, David knew he hadn't forgiven the trespasses of the church leaders, whether those in San Francisco who had closed St. Brigid or those across the globe who had turned their backs on victims of abuse. He looked at the serenity of Jesus' smile. The Church had failed him. Remarkably, his own faith felt untroubled. Continuing to work, he finished the Lord's Prayer: *And lead us not into temptation, but deliver us from evil.*

After his work on the Savior was done, he made his way back down the ladder, set his things aside, and went and stood across the street from St. Brigid. He wanted to evaluate his work, and hoped he hadn't fancied up Jesus too much. He liked what he saw. Jesus was pristine.

He returned to the steps and collected his things. Walking down the street, carrying the ladder, drop cloth, paint, and his grip, he smiled to himself. The morning traffic was picking up and a new day beginning. He hoped this would be the last time he would need to work on the church while it was closed. Before turning the corner from Van Ness onto Union, he took one more look back at the church. He could still see the white cloak of Jesus.

"Not bad for a simple housepainter," he told himself.

51 *Something Unusual to Propose*

JOE WAS GETTING things done, but at the expense of his personal life. He was supposed to be working on stories on gay marriage for the *Washington Post* and the *Bay Area Reporter,* but all of his time was consumed with St. Brigid. For Joe, there was irony in working so hard for the church that had been the bane of his youth.

At the usual weekly committee meeting at Holy Trinity, Joe had something unusual to propose. First, though, he wanted to congratulate them on their hard work.

"If you can say we've taken one step forward in eleven years, it's happened in the last few months," he said. "The diocese has said, 'We will not tear down this church.' That's a biggie. That means it's very limited in terms of what they can do. A church is a church is a church. It's got stained glass. It's got angels. It's got a whole bunch of pews facing an altar. It's a church."

Antsy with adrenaline, Joe shot up from his seat and left the room, returning from the kitchen with a giant box of champagne-filled chocolates to pass around. He wanted to keep the committee's momentum going, to keep that sense of "Hell yes!" It was about time everyone let loose.

"We have achieved a lot, but we have a lot of work ahead of us," he continued. "We need to build on our victories, to deluge Governor Schwarzenegger's office with faxes and phone calls about Senator Migden's bill. We need to follow up with his legislative aide. We need to get ten thousand phone calls pouring into his office. Siu-Mei is working on our website so it will show this as our number-one action item. We'll e-mail our list. We'll do a big mailer. We'll do handouts. We need to mobilize like we have never mobilized."

Joe said he planned to write thank-you notes to every person who had contributed in recent weeks—more than $5,000 had been donated. Siu-Mei and some of the others exchanged knowing glances; Joe's unreadable handwriting was now an inside joke.

"We have the attention of the city, of our elected officials, and finally, *finally,* of the archbishop on his way to Vatican City," he said, passing the chocolates around.

Lorraine Kelley raised her hand and said, "August thirteenth is the going-away party for Levada. It's $150 per person."

"I think we should crash it," Joe said, eating chocolates like popcorn.

Siu-Mei noted, "Tomorrow is the archbishop's birthday."

Joe asked, "Who is it in our group that writes the great birthday cards?"

Everyone chimed in: "Eleanor."

"I already wrote him a congrats letter," Eleanor Croke said. "But I can write him a birthday card too."

Finally, Joe started in on the subject he was reticent to address. He mentioned that he had received a call that day from Senator Migden's office. He reminded everyone that she had stepped in to save St. Brigid. Now she expected something in return. He said that she was feeling intimidated, now that Levada had been named the number-two man at the Vatican.

"Senator Migden told me, 'The stakes have gotten higher in this,'" Joe relayed. "I responded, 'You are telling me something I don't know?'" The point of his story was that she was putting her neck on the line and wanted the group at St. Brigid to show support for her. Joe had considered not broaching the subject, but the truce with the archdiocese had long since faded, and the wall of silence was back up. Migden was their best hope. So after more stalling, after fiddling with his bracelets and taking a deep breath, Joe suggested that it would be a good idea for them to show their support for Migden by marching together and carrying signs backing her and promoting their cause—in the San Francisco Gay Pride parade.

By now, Joe was sure the committee members were aware of his sexuality. They heard him make occasional references to a certain friend, and they read stories he wrote for gay newspapers. But they never asked about his love life.

Helen Piscevich was the first to speak. "I don't think that is the right place for us to be," she said. "Joe, let's cut this short."

Lorraine again raised her hand. "I don't think we can *not* be there. It's great exposure for us. And Migden wants and deserves our support."

In an attempt at levity, Joe said, "We have the choice of being next to a transgender group or a leather manufacturing booth."

There was silence.

Joe tried again. "Actually, our booth would be on religion row. There will even be a group from the Boy Scouts."

There was more silence.

Joe knew that acceptance came slowly for some—if at all. His mother had accepted him, but only because her love was all-forgiving. His father had treated him like a pariah. His former wife's anger felt undiminished.

After a brief discussion, the committee members saw little choice but to have a contingent in the parade. But as Joe started out on his bike ride home, he doubted that they would actually show up.

Joe biked to the corner of Howard and Spear streets early on the morning of Sunday, June 26, 2005, the day of the Gay Pride parade. It was a beautiful day in the city, but Joe's mood was dark.

He chewed nicotine gum, wishing for the umpteenth time that he hadn't sworn off cigarettes. He repeatedly checked his cell phone, convinced that the committee members would call to say they couldn't make it.

He searched the staging area and saw no one from St. Brigid. He was surrounded by men in neon tights and colorful balloon headdresses. Drag queens in circus-bright makeup sashayed by. The lesbian motorcycle group Dykes on Bikes was a few blocks up.

At nine-thirty, just as the parade was about to start, Joe spotted Siu-Mei, Bebe St. John, and Jan Robinson. They were the first to arrive. He let out a sigh of relief. They were there not only for St. Brigid but also for him. Bebe said she had been up late the night before making the heart-shaped signs: SAVE OUR LANDMARKS, SAVE ST. BRIGID, and THANK YOU CAROLE. She had enlisted the help of her mother and sister. Siu-Mei apologized for being grumpy. She had given up her favorite part of the week: Sunday morning horseback riding lessons in Marin County. Jan said that she was missing a solemn Mass at St. Dominic's.

Migden and her entourage showed up. Joe made a point of saying hello so she would know that the St. Brigid crew was there. Not long after the parade began, they were joined by Father O. There he was, wearing his collar under a sweater and marching with the St. Brigid contingent in one of the biggest gay parades in the world. As he marched along, holding a SAVE ST. BRIGID sign, he smiled at the crowd, taking in the spectacle and cheers of support.

The group made its way slowly up Market Street where thousands of people lined the way. The sky was a brilliant Matisse-blue. Others from the committee were busy in a booth at the corner of Larkin and McAllister, across from the gilded dome of City Hall. They had been there since 7 A.M. to set up and begin gathering signatures of support for Migden's bill.

Lorraine Kelley, wearing a long cotton skirt, a white blouse, and orthopedic shoes, stood at the edge of the St. Brigid booth and tried to catch the attention of passersby. "You want a cup of coffee, sir? Help us landmark our church." She looked around, her eyes growing wide. Directly across the way was the Hot House Entertainment booth, with posters of videos with titles including *Screw* and *The Hard Way*. Bare-chested men in leather walked by. "I'm competing with that," she said with a grin.

Margaret Sanderson, in a powder blue windbreaker and cap and her matching eye shadow, said to Lorraine, "Did you see those two fellows wearing barely-there underwear? You know, I don't think I would ever have come here if it weren't for Joe. I guess I'd thought I was just too old." There was a hint of satisfaction in her voice. She returned to the work at hand, repeating her mantra of "Help us get our church open!" to the crowd streaming by.

Lorraine, who had lived in San Francisco all her life, also had never attended the gay parade. "San Francisco is a very in-ter-est-ing city," she said slowly, her eyebrows arched as she watched the throngs of people, many dancing to techno music blasting from a booth nearby. "Every single block is different. Life is pretty wonderful. When you're older, you think you've seen it all. It's nice to get a chance to be surprised."

As the day wore on, Lorraine managed to smile through the constant discomfort of her arthritis and bad knees. "My knee is giving out," she told the others, but she refused to sit down. Several hours into the event, she had gathered more than two hundred signatures. Margaret had her fair share, too, as did Bill Van Way. They offered paradegoers cookies, caramel squares, Hershey chocolates, and hot coffee.

When Joe arrived at the booth, he was overcome with emotion. The weeks before had been filled with happy surprises and unexpected victories. Today was another one. For so many years, he had been ashamed of being gay. He had constructed a tenuous web of lies, wishing it were otherwise, trying to make it something else. Now, surrounded by the intrepid believers and his revered priest, Joe no longer felt like an outsider.

This was his family now.

52 *Then He Got the Call*

By late July 2005, Joe was confident that the bill to save St. Brigid would pass the senate and assembly and make its way to the governor's desk. He knew more lobbying was ahead but felt proud of the committee's efforts. He had visited Sacramento so many times that he had gone from having a shelf in Migden's office to having a desk.

And the threat from the archdiocese had abated. Shortly after Archbishop Levada was named to his vaunted position in Rome, Les McDonald had assured Joe: "Absolutely nothing will happen to St. Brigid until a new archbishop is installed." Joe had managed to reach him one day by chance when McDonald picked up his own phone.

Everyone on the committee was charged with various tasks. Bill Van Way would contact Republican clubs. John Gregson and Dennis Conrad were to lobby Irish groups and call members of the prominent Phelan clan, whose relatives had attended the church from its inception. Ken Epley said he would contact San Francisco's supervisors. Lorraine intended to rally support from the Italian Catholic Federation and said she was making progress in reaching Governor Schwarzenegger's wife, Maria Shriver.

Thank-you cards were sent to supervisors, state legislators, and anyone else who had helped them. And committee members were sending letters to the governor daily. Clementina Garcia wrote on July 20, saying, "St. Brigid involves so much artistic detail that only barbarians would destroy so much beauty! Please preserve St. Brigid. Future generations will be glad you did and will be forever grateful!"

Joe found himself smiling about St. Brigid. Every time he drove or biked by the church, he said out loud, "Hang on for a bit longer. We are going to save you."

Then, on Friday, August 12, Joe got the call. Siu-Mei was barely making sense. Between anguished gulps she delivered the news: St. Brigid had been sold. Really sold. Out from under them.

The buyer was the Academy of Art University, a San Francisco art school with extensive real estate holdings. The church was unloaded for $3.7 million—in a red-hot real estate market where a single condominium could go for that and an assessed land value twelve years earlier of more than $17 million. The academy said it planned to do $7 million in restoration and seismic upgrades, including readying the sanctuary for school and community events and using the basement gymnasium for its athletic program.

"I'm flabbergasted," Joe said. "What about a religious use of the building?"

"Apparently not," Siu-Mei said.

"How can I not take this personally?" he asked, not expecting an answer. "St. Brigid is a part of me. I know it's a part of so many people. It's a part of you. How are we supposed to continue to believe? Was the archdiocese doing an 'Art of War': keeping their friends close and enemies closer?"

Joe hung up the phone. The church had over a century of history, over a decade of tenacious struggle trying to save it. Under his watch, the grand old sanctuary now belonged to an art school. Not even an esteemed art school; this one plastered its ubiquitous buses and buildings around town with its red AA logo.

Later in the day, Joe called Siu-Mei, realizing he had basically hung up on her. He needed to make sure she was okay. He called her at work. He called her cell. He e-mailed her. He even went to her apartment. Finally, it dawned on him. She was a block away, sitting on the steps of St. Brigid, next to the candle she had kept lit—every night, night after night—for eleven years. Her face was streaked with tears.

Across town, in the quiet offices of the San Francisco archdiocese, there was relief.

Archbishop Levada, in one of his last acts before heading to Rome, issued a statement saying he approved of the deal because of the art academy's "proven track record in preserving a number of San Francisco historic buildings and using them for purposes that benefit the entire community."

Monsignor Schlitt, holding court in his office, said, "Now St. Brigid is the Academy of Art's problem." Schlitt was pragmatic in both his work and his life. He had grown up poor. His father, an auto mechanic, had died when he was young. By the age of thirteen, he knew he wanted to be a priest. In his mind, suffering, like joy, came and went. The past decade had been tough. Churches were being closed, protests launched. Bad priests were exposed. Good priests were guilty by association. "It has been a very raw period," he said. "Abuse cases have gotten more and more prominent. When you wear the collar, you get painted with the same brush." It didn't help matters, he said, that the Committee to Save St. Brigid was always "harping, harping, harping," even before they "got the politicians involved." In recent weeks, Schlitt had told McDonald: "Les, do *not* take Joe's calls. You have a job to do."

Wesolek's reaction was tempered. The sale seemed like the best solution, given all of the challenges. It would keep the church as a physical presence, but it would not be a place where people worshiped. He was dismayed, though, by the sale price. "The financial part of this is terrible," he was the first to say. "Just terrible." And he felt melancholy about the building itself. He drove by St. Brigid on his way to work. He understood better than most how much love there was for this place of souls. "In one sense, when people get so attached to their church, it shows that the Catholic Church is doing its job," he said. "A church is a very special place—a place of faith and reverence and community. It makes it so painful when there is this kind of separation."

Sitting back in his chair, Schlitt was far less measured. "St. Brigid has been the fight that wouldn't die," he said. "When you're in this job, you deal with challenges. What reward is there in closing St. Brigid? What reward is there in selling it? If there is a reward, maybe it is that it will get rid of these parishioners."

53 *"We Have Come a Long Way"*

THE NEXT DAY, Joe stood on the foggy, windswept hilltop of Lafayette Park in Pacific Heights. It was Saturday, August 13, and he was joined by dozens of parishioners and the leaders who had preceded him—Father O and Robert Bryan.

Their mood was as bleak as the summer afternoon. The recent victories had raised them up, made them believe eleven years of working, praying, marching, and lobbying had paid off. The occasion was the group's annual outdoor picnic Mass, held the same time each year. Under wool blankets, the faithful huddled for warmth on park benches.

Joe nodded to Father O and to Robert. The parishioners looked at one another with a sympathetic sadness, as at a funeral.

Lorraine Kelley approached Joe. As she began to speak, she broke into tears. "How deceptive," she said, her hand clutching his shoulder. "How absolutely deceptive. The church teaches us not to lie. They teach us to tell the truth. When you look back at this whole thing, you know they were not telling the truth. It will take a hundred years to recover from this. There's so much that's gone into St. Brigid."

Standing nearby, Tillie Piscevich shook her head and said, "Oh

God, I guess this is finally the end. It never occurred to me that our church would be gone. We were really good parishioners. It just doesn't seem real."

Eleanor Croke remarked, "I can't imagine the Academy of Art needs so many buildings. Now they want to grab our church? Well, they grabbed it. This is a big blow. I don't know how we can proceed from here."

Jan Robinson nodded. "It's a bombshell. I can't believe it's sold to the Academy of Art. They already own half of San Francisco."

Carmen Esteva said that it had become clear to her that church officials viewed them as the enemy. "But we did nothing wrong," she told those around her. "Church leaders have turned their backs on us."

Tillie, taking a seat because she was feeling weak from her radiation treatment, said that after all of the struggles of the Catholic Church of late, with the clergy abuse cases and closed churches, she would hope that the Church would have learned to involve parishioners more. "It cannot remain top-down autocratic," she said. "This younger generation won't be as accepting as we were. It would've been nice to feel a sense of unity with our leaders, even if the end result of the church being sold was the same. We could have gone through it together."

Robert stood nearby. Like Father O, he had stayed close to the group, helping whenever he could. No one felt blame toward him or anyone else. They all had brought their own talents. For Robert, it was a tense and high-stakes legal crusade, and he had given a decade of his life to St. Brigid. On this day, he wrapped his arms around his daughter, Auda Mai, who was leaving the next day for a boarding school in London. Robert was no longer surprised by anything the archdiocese did. He had believed from the beginning that the church would be sold to pay for abuses by priests. They had spent all those years denying it—only recently admitting the truth. He saw the Catholic leaders as far removed from the everyday faithful.

"I never got the impression that the bottom line for the archdiocese was doing the right thing," Robert said. "To the contrary, it was always money, money, money. There was a total disregard for the community, the history, and the people of San Francisco."

Jan had a letter she had written to the committee years earlier, a letter that resonated now. "We don't have our beautiful church in which to celebrate," she read to the others. "But during this time St. Brigid has come to mean so much more than a building. St. Brigid is Joe slaving over the latest newsletter. It is all of Robert's legal filings. It's Nelly's speeches and Lily and Carmen's prayers. It's Siu-Mei's photography and computer skills. It's Helen and Tillie, otherwise known as our 'branch office,' and it's John Gregson's building reports. It's Bebe's minutes and planning skills. It's Robert and Norma Head, who take care of our marketing and just about everything else. Most of all, it's our best friend, Father Cyril O'Sullivan, who has put aside everything to help us."

She continued: "It's everyone who has held together these past years in an extended and sometimes dysfunctional family known as the Committee to Save St. Brigid. We can take pride in the fact that we have come together in a crisis and have shared our abilities and talents to try to do something right about something that is wrong. One thing is for certain. The parish we were in is vastly different than the parish we have become. Imagine what we could do if given four walls and a roof over our heads!"

The normally ebullient Father O stood behind his makeshift altar. He had been hit hard by the news. Before anyone from the committee could tell him of the sale, someone had left a gloating message on his voice mail at the rectory. "St. Brigid was sold," the caller, who didn't give his name, said gaily.

Father O had come up with a saying for this Mass: "Out of Doors. Full of Faith." The Mass began. Anger deepened Father O's lilting voice. The merciless wind extinguished two white candles and almost toppled a gold chalice. His dark curls, now dusted with gray, framed his wind-chafed face. He wore a white linen robe with a long, thin scarf embroidered with gold crosses on each side.

"When I heard the news that the church was sold, I was embarrassed and ashamed," Father O said. "The mentality of the Catholic Church today can be very cold. It can be aloof. It can be analytical. It's like a boardroom. This is a pretty poor performance of the diocese against its people. My mother taught me to think better and act better than the diocese has acted. This is the antithesis of relating to one another as brothers and sisters. It is mind-boggling that after eleven years, this is the way it's come down, that they would go outside of our people. To me, this is the ultimate betrayal. It is a betrayal to the good people of St. Brigid. It is a betrayal to the priests who have served there for a century. It is a betrayal of faith."

Finally, Father O softened his tone. He noted that the deal between the Academy of Art and the archdiocese was in escrow and had sixty days to go through.

"I will wait for sixty days," he said. "I do believe in miracles. I hope that the art college will change its mind and do the right thing and allow the church to be a church. But I know that I certainly will never regret anything we have done as a committee. I'm sure every single person here has asked, 'Is this worth it? Is all of this effort futile?' My answer is that I've been in soccer games where you're two to three goals down and you have minutes left and you still come back. Of course this is a low point. We are close to a finale. But we still have sixty days.

"We can be proud of what we have done," he continued. "We told the diocese that what they were doing was not right. We will bring our beliefs to the grave. You are the representatives of true faith. You have the courage and conviction to be St. Brigid parishioners to the end."

He urged them to remember that the problem was never with them. "Right up until this point, there has always been a small possibility that that church could be returned," he said. "For all of these years, it was never a completely closed door. The unfortunate part is that the people who made the decisions that closed St. Brigid were not humble enough to admit they were wrong in ordering the closure. But they dug their heels in. They entrenched themselves to where they could never be budged. There was never fairness to discuss it in open dialogue. It wasn't that the church had no hope, but it's that there were men who were not willing to admit that they had made a mistake."

He looked at his friends. "I have seen incredible transformations in all of you over the last ten years," he said. "I saw people who were shy or reticent, who wouldn't articulate their needs, grow into leaders. You may not even see that in yourselves. But I can see, from where you started to where you are today, that the changes are profound."

Hands were joined together as they prayed in unison. *We pray for all of those here who have great sorrow or pain. We pray the Academy of Art will change its mind and St. Brigid will be used as a church, as it was designed. We pray that over the next sixty days there will be a miracle.*

Then all eyes turned to Joe. As he began to speak, it felt as though even the busy city streets stood still. Joe reminded the group that he had been in constant communication with the archdiocese and there had been no mention of a potential sale. Not only that, he said, there were assurances that the archdiocese would do nothing until a new archbishop was installed.

He stood up straight. His trademark slouch was gone.

"Let me ask," he said, his voice booming. "Is there anyone from the diocese here today? Please raise your hands. Make yourself known." As soon as he had heard that St. Brigid had been sold, Joe had called the archdiocese to ask if they would send someone to speak at their picnic Mass. Scanning the crowd, he said, "Again, no one from the diocese thought we were worth speaking to. But we have ourselves," he went on. "We have each other. We have come a long way. In January, the archbishop said he planned to demolish St. Brigid and build high-rise condos there. But he realized we would not let him do that. For that, we can congratulate ourselves."

He applauded their impact and tenacity, reminding them that when their fight began, Bill Clinton was president, John Paul II was pope, and the Roman Catholic Church had not yet been hit by the scandal that was shaking it to its core. They had endured so many challenges—going through every one of them together.

Joe asked, "How many of you came to our very first picnic in the park, eleven years ago?" Nearly everyone's hands shot up. "Well, I am confident that we will continue our fight. We will make certain St. Brigid is preserved, at the very least physically."

The fog brought in a fine silvery mist, an oyster-gray light. Branches rustled in the wind, sending leaves fluttering down. The dozens of parishioners stood in a tight circle, clasping hands.

"I have to tell you something," Joe said. "You are a group, one like I've never known, that has realized its potential to genuinely care about one another. You do it in a way that you just don't see anymore in society. You comfort and cheer one another. You are an enormous extended family. You have taught me: You don't just get love. You have to open your heart to it. You have made that possible for me. I have found a home, here among homeless Catholics." His voice breaking with emotion, his dark eyes shining, he declared, "Whatever happens in the future, I can say this for sure: I love you. I do. I love every one of you."

A chorus followed: "We love you, too, Joe."

54 *Party Crashers*

MORE THAN TWO THOUSAND partygoers in dark suits and cocktail dresses swept past the protesters in front of the Marriott Hotel in downtown San Francisco. The politicians arrived in shiny black Town Cars, the cardinals and bishops in their colorful vestments. Police kept a watchful eye on the group holding signs and handing out leaflets.

It was the farewell bash for Archbishop Levada, triumphantly heading to Rome. Joe and the others from St. Brigid were near the front door, bearing signs and posters: SAVE ST. BRIGID CHURCH—NOT ST. BRIGID ART COLLEGE and ARCHBISHOP LEVADA, WHY HAVE YOU FORSAKEN THE FAITHFUL FROM ST. BRIGID? They were interviewed by television reporters but ignored or sidestepped by passersby.

It was the night of August 13, just hours after the emotional picnic in Lafayette Park. The members of the committee had made it home in time to clean up and change before heading back out. Inside the grand ballroom, Joe joined Carmen, Siu-Mei, Bill Van Way, and Lorraine and Donald Kelley, who had purchased a table for the event. Joe didn't remain seated for long. There were politicians to confront, religious leaders to corner. He wanted to know why all of the people he had spent months befriending had told him nothing of the sale of his church—of the city's church, the people's church.

Supervisor Aaron Peskin saw Joe heading his way. At his table were Supervisor Michela Alioto-Pier and other city officials. Alioto-Pier held up her hand and was the first to say, "Joe, I want you to know one thing: We had no idea this was coming." She added, "The Committee to Save St. Brigid is an extraordinary organization. I'm aware that you've been in my office pleading the church's case at least three times a day for a long time. I know this is very frustrating for parishioners. But it's your group that has saved the church from demolition." Peskin nodded.

Joe squinted at them in disbelief. "You knew nothing of the sale?" he asked. Again, they assured him that they too had been caught by surprise.

After a brief discussion, Joe spotted Mayor Gavin Newsom across the room and maneuvered his way back through the crowd. Without saying hello, he asked Newsom point-blank, "Mayor, I hope you're not behind this."

Newsom said, "I've discussed the possible sale of the church with [the folks at the Academy of Art] twenty times, but I didn't know this was coming right here right now. I had discussed it with them as a last resort."

Out in the lobby, Joe ran into George Wesolek, whom he hadn't talked to since the sale was announced. He hadn't seen him since their high-stakes meetings in Sacramento and San Francisco. It was Wesolek who, months earlier, had encouraged Joe to bring developers in who could draw up plans for the land around the church.

Wesolek looked surprised to see Joe and made a nice-to-see-you overture. Joe was in no mood for platitudes.

"How did this happen?" he demanded.

"You could have made an offer, too," said Wesolek, who was stuck in the ten-deep line at the bar.

Joe shook his head. "George, that's not true. I brought you two sets of developers and you told me to go to Les. Then Les told me not to do anything until we had a new archbishop."

Wesolek said he was sorry.

Joe shook his head.

"George, you had such potential to pull in the best Catholic allies for life," he said. "All of these people from St. Brigid, the ones you obviously thought were the enemies, love being Catholic. All we've wanted all this time is our church back. That's all we ever asked."

Wesolek accepted Joe's anger and understood. But he knew that he had tried, again and again, to make the distinction to Joe and the others that while the diocese was open to saving the building, it was unlikely the church would ever reopen as a church.

Inside the ballroom, Archbishop Levada's entrance was greeted with a standing ovation. Mayor Newsom presented him with a cable car bell, saying, "With all the bells you hear in Rome, I hope this bell will remind you of San Francisco." Senator Dianne Feinstein and U.S. Representative Nancy Pelosi paid tribute to Levada, as did Cardinal Roger Mahony of Los Angeles and Bishop George

Niederauer of Salt Lake City, a friend of Levada's for fifty-five years. President George W. Bush and his wife sent a letter of tribute and congratulations.

Finally, Levada gave a short talk. He called San Francisco a city that is "always reinventing itself. We have an example in how to go about reinventing ourselves in the example of our patron, Saint Francis. Look at his love for the poor; how he spared nothing to be a part of the mission of Jesus. In Saint Francis we have an example to lead us forward.

"I'm going to go [to Rome] to do my best, to serve him [Pope Benedict] and to serve the local churches throughout the world. I ask God to bless all of you, the wonderful loving Church of the Archdiocese of San Francisco, for years to come." In closing, he said he especially appreciated the presence of so many parishioners from all over the city.

The members of the Committee to Save St. Brigid managed to smile at one another. No matter what, they were still St. Brigid parishioners.

When the program was over, as chairs were being piled on top of tables, the group from St. Brigid remained—to plot their next moves. On the back of the program, they sketched out a plan of action. It was simple. Get the city to landmark both the interior *and* the exterior of the church, a possibility now that the building was in private hands. After all, Joe pointed out, how could you put in an art school if the whole church had to remain a church?

55 *Risking Arrest*

Mary Baynes frantically dialed Joe's cell phone. She was calling from the parking lot of St. Brigid. "St. Brigid is being looted," said Mary, the member of the committee who worked in the school cafeteria and kept an eye on the church.

"There are security guards taking things out of the church. You need to get here as fast as you can."

It was early on the morning of Friday, October 21, 2005. Escrow had closed earlier in the week on the sale of St. Brigid Church to the Academy of Art University. The San Francisco Planning Commission had told the committee the day before that the chances of landmarking the interior and exterior of St. Brigid were good, but the issue needed to be heard in coming weeks by the Board of Supervisors.

Joe threw on his clothes. "Unbelievable," he said to Mary. "Absolutely unbelievable. They continue to astound me. They are removing relics before the issue of interior landmarking can reach the Board of Supervisors." Leaving his house, Joe called Siu-Mei and asked her to alert the troops. Within twenty minutes, Joe was at St. Brigid. Committee members lined the sidewalk. "Let's go," Joe said, jumping out of his Miata. "We have to stop them. They're hauling things out of our church. A truck is apparently pulled up on the other side, workers are inside, and religious artifacts are being carted off."

The gates on each side of the church were locked. Joe said they could reach the back of the church through St. Brigid School, where they were always welcome. Siu-Mei sprinted beside Joe; most of the others walked as best they could. Tillie, who had been on bed rest for weeks following radiation for her breast cancer, walked cautiously but determinedly.

"Oh, my gosh, I hope I make it," Tillie said, Helen staying by her side.

"Carmen, you stand guard at this door," Joe yelled from up the street. Carmen took her position, her face peaceful, her arms crossed. The diminutive woman who had never attended a meeting before joining the Committee to Save St. Brigid was ready to stop workers from leaving the church. Robert Head, who sped from home when he heard that objects were being hauled away, agreed to stake out the front door.

Joe, passing quickly through the school, reached the churchyard and ran to the open sacristy door. A security guard from the Academy of Art stopped him from entering. Peering around the guard, Joe could see a handful of workers inside the church. They were vacuuming, cleaning, and taking the beautiful stations of the cross from their positions high above the pews into the sacristy, where they were lined up like fallen soldiers on the carpeted floor. A loading van was next to the door.

Helen and Tillie caught up with the others. Tillie told the stone-faced security guard that this was their church. She asked if she might be allowed to just look in.

"Lady, this is private property," he said.

Suddenly, Helen gasped. "Oh, no," she said, getting a glimpse inside. "That's my Saint Anthony. He's down. Oh, no. That's my statue. There he goes. I used to say, 'Tony, Tony, look around, something's lost and can't be found.' If I lost an earring, or feared losing something really important, I would say that and things would be found and prayers answered." She sighed and turned away from the door. "You know, I'll be glad when this is over, one way or the other. They never had the courtesy to talk to us and say it's sold. Now we have to watch this piece-by-piece destruction of something we love."

She asked Tillie, "What are we going to do?"

Tillie responded, "Watch it go?"

"I wonder where my Virgin Mother statue is," Tillie said, trying again to make her way past the guard, who blocked her way with a beefy arm. "I just want the rosary around the statue of the Virgin Mother," she said, getting no response.

Minutes later, the door was closed in the parishioners' faces.

"Do we have all of the doors covered?" Joe asked. Everyone had a cell phone. Everyone reported back to Joe.

Joe had already phoned the city's building department and left a message saying workers were inside the church—despite a stop-work order because of suspected asbestos. In his message,

Joe explained that the Planning Commission had voted the day before to give landmark status to the exterior of the church and favored—without yet voting on it—preserving everything inside.

The building inspector arrived at the same time Les McDonald walked onto the parking lot shared by the school and the church. "First of all," McDonald said, holding up his hands, "I'm no longer the owner of the church, and there is no one in the church."

Joe scoffed. "Starting first thing this morning, they've been carting relics out of the church. The door was just slammed in our face."

The inspector said, "I'm concerned about asbestos. I was told there are people inside, using a vacuum, without masks."

"The building is locked," McDonald said.

Joe gestured toward the door. "Les, come on," he said. "We had the door slammed on us. We saw people walk in. That is not the truth."

"That's a nasty comment," McDonald shot back. "You're saying that you don't believe me? God bless you."

Joe shook his head and almost laughed. "*God bless you? You are telling me that?* Les, I've learned that, unfortunately, I can't trust you."

Robert Head told the inspector: "There is a question of whether these items belong to the archdiocese or the people. In my mind, the property belongs to the parishioners, and the archdiocese should wait until this is decided by the Board of Supervisors."

Suddenly, the door to the sacristy opened. Workers were lined up, ready to move the relics.

"We won't let them take these things out," Joe said, running to physically block the door. One worker managed to cart out one of the stations of the cross. Joe, Siu-Mei, and Robert Head then locked arms and stood in the doorway, forming a human chain. The other parishioners stood nearby in a show of support.

Within minutes, the police arrived.

San Francisco Police sergeant Dan Linehan listened to representatives from the archdiocese, the Academy of Art, the building department, and the Committee to Save St. Brigid. He advised Joe and the others that they would be arrested for trespassing if they didn't move.

They didn't budge.

In an effort to win the officer over, Joe smiled and extended his hand, saying, "We're with a group called the Committee to Save St. Brigid. May I just explain the situation a bit better to you?"

"No," Linehan replied. "As I said, you folks are going to have to move."

Joe was by now inured to "no."

"It's so stressful to see these things being removed," Joe said, standing in the door. "It's like seeing your childhood being removed. We are trying to preserve the exterior and interior of the church. It's not like it's just a few statues. This is a holy place. These are holy statues."

Siu-Mei sat down in the doorway, talking with another police officer. She explained that the building department had said in recent weeks that no one was allowed inside the church because of asbestos. The officer said that the Academy of Art apparently gave workers from the archdiocese permission to come in and take out the items that were not a part of the sale. He told Siu-Mei that they really were going to be arrested if they continued to block the door.

Siu-Mei pleaded with the officer: "We have been trying to save our church for almost twelve years. We don't want to be arrested."

A female police officer who had been listening stepped in. "My sister was married at St. Brigid," Michele Aschero said, adding that she had attended St. Brigid School and was a parishioner at the church before it closed. She looked at the other officers, shook her head, and said if they arrested these parishioners, they were all "going straight to hell."

Not far away, Tillie and Helen talked animatedly with Les Mc-

Donald. After a few minutes, Tillie returned to the group and told Joe: "Les agreed that he is going to give us the rosary that was around the statue of the Virgin Mother. That's something, at least." She said she had called his office at least three times before, explaining to the secretary that she was interested in the fate of the statue and rosary. She hadn't received a call back.

"Les took my information and said the statue was going to reside in the school, and that he had the rosary in his drawer at work and that he would get it to me," Tillie said, smiling at the bit of good news.

Hours later, with the standoff continuing, another building department inspector arrived with another stop-work notice. By midafternoon, workers for the archdiocese unexpectedly closed the door to the moving van and drove off.

Linehan told the committee, "The archdiocese has agreed to leave everything in here tonight and come back and readdress this at another time."

"You mean they're going to come back and readdress this when they think we're not looking?" Joe said.

"I don't know what tomorrow is going to bring," the officer said, walking away.

Beginning that Friday night, members of the committee and their friends staked out the church. They camped out in cars parked in front of St. Brigid. They knew someone with an apartment overlooking the back of the church. They devised a schedule so that the church would be guarded around the clock.

All was quiet—until 6:30 A.M. on Monday, October 24.

Siu-Mei was on duty, sitting bleary-eyed and cold in her old Honda, when she saw men with flashlights moving quickly across the courtyard behind the church. She had been there for hours, and as the weekend wound down, she had started to believe that the archdiocese would wait until the matter was decided by the Board of Supervisors. She watched several men go into the church. Then she saw them coming out with large objects. She called Joe.

She called the police. She took pictures. She ran as close as she could get and yelled at the workers to stop. But they continued, removing precious relics as Siu-Mei watched helplessly from behind the locked gate.

Helen and Tillie waited several days before calling Les McDonald about the rosary. Tillie was excited to have it, to hold it and pray to the Virgin Mother. Her breast cancer prognosis was good, and she wanted to keep it that way. She called McDonald's office at the archdiocese but never made it past the secretary. She again told the woman the story of the rosary, saying that McDonald had it in his drawer and wanted to get it to her. After several more calls, the secretary finally told Tillie that it was nowhere to be found. It had been "misplaced," she said.

Tillie wasn't about to leave it at that. She sat down at her kitchen table and wrote a letter: "Dear Mr. McDonald: We are very disappointed that we haven't heard anything about the Rosary you promised us. You told us the Rosary was in your desk and we could have it. When we called recently, we were told it was misplaced. I would be interested in knowing what has happened to the Rosary." The letter included a photo of the Blessed Mother with the rosary around her neck.

Not long after, McDonald called Tillie at home. He told her that it was true. He didn't have the rosary. But he said he had another rosary, a very special rosary, that he would send to her. He said this very special rosary had belonged to Archbishop Levada and had been blessed by the pope.

"Mr. McDonald, I thank you for the offer," Tillie said evenly. "But I'm not interested. I can always get a rosary. I was interested in *that* rosary, which went with the Virgin Mother statue. You told me you had it, that it was in your drawer, and that you were going to give it to me." Hanging up, she said to Helen, "I've been a Catholic all my life. I've given all of my extra time and money. Was it too much to ask to get this one rosary?"

56 *Tears of Joy*

On a Sunday morning in May 2006, Joe arrived at Most Holy Redeemer Catholic Church in the Castro, about three blocks from the center of San Francisco's gay community. He was perspiring, having biked from home. He walked his bike past a group of men praying. Their refrain was familiar: "*Hail Mary, full of grace. The Lord is with you. Blessed are you among women, and blessed is the fruit of your womb, Jesus. Hail Mary, mother of God, pray for us sinners, now and at the hour of our death. Amen.*" The Hail Mary and the praying of the rosary had a way of pulling Joe into a trance. It silenced his body and drowned out the world.

Joe locked his bike and hustled up the stairs to Most Holy Redeemer, or MHR, as people called it. At the top of the stairs leading into the sanctuary was the Reverend Steve Meriwether, there to greet parishioners. The church was packed, and Joe found a seat in the second-to-last row. He settled in at the aisle, next to two men with a toddler.

Sunlight beamed into the newly renovated building through a skylight above the altar. The choir, as his mother would have said, sounded "just magnificent!" He had started attending MHR, telling friends, "I'm trying to be a practicing Catholic—in that I desperately need the practice." On a more serious note, he had said, "I've become more and more aware of my Catholic faith because of St. Brigid."

The congregants sang:

> Longing for light, we wait in darkness.
> Longing for truth, we turn to you.
> Make us your own, your holy people,
> Light for the world to see.
> Christ, be our light!
> Shine in our hearts.

Shine through the darkness.
Christ, be our light!
Shine in your church gathered today.

Joe used a handkerchief to wipe his brow. His taut body relaxed, and the corners of his mouth turned up in a slight smile. He looked at the crowd. Nearly all of the parishioners were gay or lesbian. The church was overflowing with people every time he visited. He was starting to recognize many people by face and knew quite a few by name.

Reverend Meriwether delivered his homily, which was followed by more singing. The time passed quickly. The warmth and joy made Joe think of what St. Brigid could be. He still believed that the old church could be a beacon for disenfranchised singles who had been reared Catholic but who had fallen away and longed to return. He was not giving up his dream of making sure the church reopened—somehow. He smiled at the men next to him, who took turns chasing after their two-year-old son.

"Lord Jesus Christ, you said to your apostles: I leave you peace, my peace I give you. Look not to our sins, but on the faith of the Church, and grant us the peace and unity of your kingdom. Let us offer each other the sign of peace."

At many churches, the ritual of peace and handshake felt perfunctory to Joe. But here it was an opportunity for effusive and prolonged greetings. Father Meriwether went from row to row, saying hello to those he knew, welcoming those he didn't. He knew Joe and greeted him warmly. They had talked before about many things, including the elevation of Cardinal Ratzinger to pope, about the pontiff's stated views on homosexuality—that it was an "intrinsic disorder"—and Joe's struggles to be gay and Catholic. Joe knew the passages of Scripture, such as Romans 1:24–27, that condemned homosexual acts as *"a serious depravity."*

In a recent conversation, Joe had told Meriwether, "The most important thing that religion gives me is, 'Love God, love your neighbor.' I'm a cafeteria Catholic. I take parts. I take the fundamental teachings of loving thy neighbor. I'm not sure how what goes on in Rome influences me. It is so far removed from my day-to-day life. Do I want to reform Pope Benedict's beliefs on homosexuality? No. Do I want to live like a Christian? Yes."

Meriwether responded, "If the church is destroying your spirit, then you've got to get out of it. But if you're in a good local church, then you've got to stay and fight."

The words reminded him of Father O. Joe had never gone to him for confession, instead confiding in him as a trusted friend. Father O knew that Joe had been living a wild life. And he knew that Joe was trying to find his way morally. He had seen Joe progress. He saw him centering his life. He felt Joe was almost there.

Joe had told Father O that for many years, he didn't feel fit to receive the Eucharist, that somehow he would be sullying the central mystery of the Church. He had lied to his family and friends. He had never fully "gone through adolescence until he was thirty-seven," he said, and so became promiscuous to make up for lost time. He had to forgive himself, and he had to ask for God's forgiveness. He had learned, he told Father O, "that all good relationships come with the truth." He also told Father O of his dread of confession, for all that he needed to say, and because of the memory from childhood of being reprimanded for failing to remember the Apostles' Creed. "I have not been back to confession since," Joe said. "Also, it feels so impersonal. Here you are, revealing your innermost thoughts, and you don't see the person you're talking to."

Father O had told Joe that his decision to take communion came down to where he was in his own conscience. He said that before Joe accepted the Eucharist, he needed to be at peace with himself. "In my view, every single person is a child of God," Father O said. "And every single person has a right to worship and to talk about and experience the divine in their lives. Gays are children of God as much as anyone else."

On this Sunday morning, when it was time for the breaking of the bread, Joe no longer felt unfit. He bowed his head in prayer. In his own way, in his own time, he had repented.

57 *Tragedy Strikes*

A MONTH LATER, on the morning of June 29, 2006, Mary Dignan yelled at her dad that they were going to be late—again. She was in San Francisco for the summer, attending school. Thursdays were especially hard, as she had to be in English class by 8 A.M. She woke her dad.

"Dad, I need cash," she said, "for the bus and lunch."

"I just gave you money," Joe moaned.

"That was a couple of days ago," she replied, shadowing him as he tried to get ready. Reaching for his wallet and keys, he said he would go to the bank quickly, taking George with him.

As soon as he returned, Mary raced out the door to catch her bus.

"Bye, Dad," she yelled.

"Bye, Mary," Joe said sleepily.

Mary was irritated that she always had to ask her dad for money. But she could see that he was even more preoccupied than usual. He said something to her about needing to write a speech on St. Brigid to give the next day. She knew he had a meeting with the people from the Academy of Art University and that he had learned only the day before that their lawyers would be there.

Joe sat down at his computer. He felt overwhelmed. Since the announcement in August—now nearly a year before—that the church was sold, he had turned his attention from calling the archdiocese to calling the Academy of Art. He wanted to meet with the school's director, a woman who had inherited the empire from her father, but was met instead with an all-too-familiar wall of silence. It had taken nearly a year to set up the meeting for Friday, June 30. It happened to fall on the twelfth anniversary of the closing of St. Brigid.

At 8:40 A.M., Joe sent an e-mail to Siu-Mei asking for her to-do list for the next day's meeting. "There seems to be no will among supervisors for preserving St. Brigid as we know it," he wrote. "I feel very shaken. Elisa Stephens [the owner of the Academy of Art] won't even see us. I'll be surprised if she's there tomorrow. On the one hand I'm tempted to declare success and go home. We've saved the building. Isn't that good enough? But for some reason the answer seems to be no."

The committee continued to work aggressively to get the Board of Supervisors to approve the legislation landmarking St. Brigid's exterior and interior, including the stained-glass windows, pews, and statuary. The academy opposed the measure, saying it would "subject the university to greater scrutiny," and had asked the committee to trust them to care for the church in perpetuity.

In the days leading up to the meeting, stunned committee members had learned that lawyers for the art school had filed a request with the California Office of Historic Preservation to have St. Brigid removed from the National Register of Historic Places and from the state registry. This would make landmarking on a city level next to impossible and allow the new owner to do whatever she wanted with the building. The attorney for the school wrote that there were "substantial errors in the 1995 nomination report which should make the building ineligible for national register and the California register."

Joe was supposed to be working on several freelance stories but again put his writing on hold. He spent two hours on the phone talking to aides in supervisors' offices. He was trying to get a sense of the agenda from the other side. As he was waiting for one of the supervisors, he read something that brought a smile to his face. Written by Siu-Mei years earlier, it had been included in a booklet, *What St. Brigid Means to Me.* It was filled with diary-like entries on how the closure of St. Brigid had affected its parishioners. Siu-Mei wrote: "It has been years since I entered this magnificent church. I still remember vividly how, every time when the doors gently closed behind me, it closed off the madness of the world where only materialism matters. I was so proud of my home church, St. Brigid. It is not just a church for our neighborhood. It is a 'universal' Roman Catholic Church, welcoming anyone, Christians, non-Christians, historians, architects, fatigued tourists, homeless—anyone who needs a peaceful place to reflect."

Shortly before noon, feeling he needed his own place to reflect—and to be reinvigorated—Joe decided he would get in a quick workout at World Gym on De Haro Street, about six blocks from his home. He called to George, who still had to go everywhere with him. They arrived at the gym, and Joe tied George up in his usual spot, telling him he'd be out in an hour.

Inside, Joe got on the treadmill. He would go over the meeting in his mind while jogging. He wanted to convince the Academy of Art to at least consider opening the church for weekend Mass. He also needed to make it clear that the Committee to Save St. Brigid was not backing down on its landmarking push. After what he'd been through, he was not about to trust someone else to take proper care of St. Brigid.

He set the time and began to jog.

Shortly before 1 P.M., Mary finished her English and math classes for the day and walked to her godmother's house, a few blocks away. She spent the afternoons there, so her dad could work. She was happy to be in San Francisco for the summer. It was where she felt most at home. Two months shy of her fourteenth birthday, Mary no longer cared that her father was gay. She joked about the weird guys he dated, especially his on-again, off-again relationship with a man he called "Bambi." She had recently told him, "Dad, I love you no matter what."

Siu-Mei was at her South of Market office, where she was a programming analyst for the city and county of San Francisco. She was worried. She had sent Joe an e-mail first thing in the morning asking for *his* agenda for the meeting and responding to his query for her to-do list. She had not heard back from him. One of the questions she wanted Joe to address was how the art school would be able to hold events inside the church without having done any seismic upgrades.

She had been unable to reach Joe over the phone. She called again but was sent directly to voice mail. She returned to her project, but her mind remained on Joe. He should have called her by now, if only to yell at her.

By midafternoon, Siu-Mei still hadn't heard from Joe. She decided to call yet again. This time a man picked up. It wasn't Joe. Siu-Mei apologized and said she must have dialed the wrong number.

"Are you looking for Joseph?" the man said. "Joseph Dignan?"

"I'm calling for my friend Joe," Siu-Mei said, the words coming out slowly. "Who is this?"

"I'm an investigator with the coroner's office," the man said.

"Where is . . . What happened to Joe?"

Mary was walking up the driveway to her godmother's house when she spotted her dad's friend from childhood, her "Uncle Phil" Bailey. He wasn't smiling. Mary wondered why he was there and why he had such a weird expression.

It was an unusually hot day. Phil looked gray and was perspiring. He walked up to Mary, knelt down, and held her arms. It seemed like minutes before he said anything. Finally, he spoke. At first he couldn't get the words out. He wiped his brow. Then he said, "Mary, your dad has died. He had a massive heart attack."

Mary stared at him. "You're lying," she said. "That doesn't happen. My dad is healthy. He was at home this morning. You're lying. This doesn't make sense. I just saw him this morning. We fought over stupid stuff."

Phil was crying. Then Mary was crying. She didn't understand. All she could say was "No."

Siu-Mei walked the eight blocks from her office to the coroner's office at 850 Bryant. She asked whether she could see Joe, if she could see Joseph Howard Dignan. She said he had turned forty-nine ten days earlier.

She was told what had happened. Nearing the end of his workout, Joe had stepped off the treadmill and sat down. His head was in his hands, and he began to shake. Then he collapsed. A firefighter working out nearby ran to his side. CPR was performed, but it was too late. Joe had suffered a heart attack. He was pronounced dead at 1:13 P.M.

Siu-Mei wandered the gritty South of Market neighborhood, finally sitting down on the sidewalk in front of a row of bail bonds shops. She began to sob. She called Father O, who tried to comfort her. Sometime later, she made it back to her office. She typed an e-mail to those who were planning to attend the meeting the next day, including supervisors and members of the Academy of Art.

She wrote: "Our very dear friend, Joe Dignan, died today."

Late in the afternoon, Mary was headed to her dad's house to pick up her things when she remembered George. The dog would have gone to the gym with her dad. He would have been tied up outside, waiting for him to emerge. With her godmother driving, the two went to the gym, but there was no George. Mary went to the rail where George was always tied and felt the metal, hot from the afternoon sun. How long, she wondered, did it take for someone to notice George and to make the connection to what had happened? Did George start to howl? Did he see an ambulance come and go, with people racing on the way in and taking their time on the way out? Could he have caught a glimpse of Joe on the stretcher? Would he have pulled at his leash, as he did on walks? Still holding the rail, tears streaming down her face, she wondered whether George could have felt as alone as she felt now. She had been left at the railing, too.

Her godmother, who had gone inside, was told the dog had been taken to the animal shelter a few blocks away. Mary was gently steered back into the car. They retrieved George, and the three went home. Mary walked slowly into her dad's office. He was supposed to be there. His coffee cup was there. She felt its cool sides. His glass of water was there. His computer was turned on, the screen black. His papers and notepads were everywhere.

George searched for Joe too. Finally, he came to the desk where Mary was and looked up at her.

Mary picked up a card from his keyboard. It was something he had written for the tenth anniversary of the closing of St. Brigid, two years earlier. She read his words: *Ten years. A decade. The time it takes for a child to grow up, for a grownup to grow old. The Second World War took half as long, the Great Depression, about the same. At midnight on June 30, 1994, the bell in St. Brigid's tower rang for the last time. Then the front doors of our beautiful church slammed shut behind us, and they haven't opened since. That night we, the parishioners of St. Brigid, stood outside the locked doors and looked up. We encouraged each other ("Don't worry, it won't be for long"); we sang ("We shall overcome, some day"); and we prayed ("Deliver us from evil. Amen"). The archdiocese called the police. That night, we went home, but we haven't given up. We meet every week. We work to keep our parish community together. We come back to renew our determination that we will see our beautiful church reopened.*

Mary placed the card back on the keyboard. Next to it was a stack of papers. At the top of the pile was a St. Brigid to-do list.

58 *Honoring Their Leader*

THE COMMITTEE MEMBERS MET in the basement of Holy Trinity. The seat Joe had occupied at the long table remained empty. The portrait of the unsmiling priest was still on the wall. But there was no clicking of bicycle spokes. No black bracelets. No gossip. No laughter. No friendly admonishments for their leader to behave. They talked about holding a memorial service in Lafayette Park, the site of the summer picnic Masses. They talked about having it at Holy Trinity, where they had spent so much time. They talked about St. Dominic's, a Catholic church across town, with the Saint Jude shrine for desperate causes.

But they knew there was only one place to honor Joe.

Siu-Mei sat in her apartment on Van Ness Avenue. Having a memorial service at St. Brigid seemed impossible, but Siu-Mei would try—for Joe. She called Father O on his cell phone. Before long, other committee members were making calls to the Dignan family, the Board of Supervisors, Senator Migden's office—and the Academy of Art, which held the keys to St. Brigid. Siu-Mei made her way to the steps of St. Brigid. Her tiny figure dwarfed by the ornate front door, she prayed: "You have to help me with this. Please, Joe."

The art academy knew when to set aside differences. And they understood how these Catholics felt about their church. On July 11, the day the Board of Supervisors honored Joe Dignan, the Academy of Art announced that friends and family were welcome to use St. Brigid for a memorial service.

Word spread quickly. It was what everyone wanted, and what no one wanted. After twelve years, they would be back inside.

59 *Divine Discoveries*

LORRAINE KELLEY held her breath as she entered the church. She scanned the sun-dusted sanctuary, anxious to see whether it had changed. She looked from the nave to the altar, from the organ loft to the marble pillars. She was relieved. St. Brigid was more resplendent than ever. The soaring coffered ceilings had been brightened with a fresh coat of paint. The solid oak pews were newly polished. Her gaze settled back on the altar, on a portrait of Joe.

Carmen Esteva walked up the right aisle, past the "poor boxes" for offerings. She blinked at the brightness of the sanctuary. The stained-glass windows glistened from a recent shine. Helen and Tillie Piscevich made their way slowly up the steps of the church, pausing under the archway of the door.

It was July 20, 2006, and the doors of St. Brigid, closed for twelve years, were opened. Joe's memorial service was soon to begin. Hundreds of people packed the church. Far different from when they had attended before, the parishioners knew one another now. Their lives were woven together. At the altar, beside Joe's image, was a bouquet of brightly colored flowers gathered by his friend Dane Devoil from his mother's garden. The flowers were his favorite—and Eleanor's—the dahlia.

Helen looked at the archway inscribed with the names of saints. She scanned the sanctuary. "I'm surprised at how I feel," she said to her sister. "It's strange, but I feel that I've actually gotten more religious in fighting for this place for all of these years."

Tillie nodded. "We certainly developed friendships we wouldn't have had otherwise."

"Yes, it's been interesting to get to know the people we knew by face or name only before," Helen said. "I guess church was more routine before. We went to church every Sunday. We went home. It was automatic—until it was taken away."

Lorraine fidgeted in her old familiar pew. It was beautiful, but not the same. She and her husband had stopped attending Mass regularly. The breaking point was when the Catholic Church started closing and selling churches to pay for priest abuse cases. But to anyone who asked, Lorraine would say, "Am I still a Catholic? Yes. That's like asking me if I'm still Italian."

Everyone settled into their seats. Helen and Tillie were near the front on the right, Lorraine and her husband near the stained-glass window dedicated to the memory of her late grandfather, Carmen was one row back, and Eleanor Croke was close by. Siu-Mei took a mental inventory: The Sacred Heart statue was there, but the Virgin Mother and Saint Anthony were gone, along with a small statue of Mary and the infant Jesus. The rugs, candles, and some donation boxes were missing, as were the red cushions at the communion rail. The confessional was broken, though Father Hanson's name remained on the door. The holy font was there. The stations of the cross were gone—carted off that morning in October as she stood helplessly behind the gate.

Siu-Mei's gaze rested on the portrait of Joe. She had asked God, "Why take Joe away now, when everything seems to be coming together for him?" Joe was at last defining faith for himself, tending to his mother's home, making sure Mary was enrolled in a good Catholic school. He was closing in on himself. Since his passing, Siu-Mei would find herself walking or driving and would hear his voice or feel his presence. It was the one thing that buttressed her, lifting her spirits and telling her it was going to be okay.

Robert Bryan sat across the aisle, in his usual pew off to the left. The death penalty attorney remained bitter toward Catholic officials. If not for the integrity of Father O and the devotion of people like Joe and Siu-Mei and so many others, Robert would have formally renounced his Catholicism years earlier.

Parishioners had come to him over the years, even recently, telling him how they had pleaded with the archdiocese to open

St. Brigid—just for a few hours, for a funeral Mass for a wife, a father, a child. The answer was always no: a flat no; not an apologetic no. He told his wife wryly, "Now that the church is out of the hands of the archdiocese, the doors reopen?" He added, "Today should have been a day of rejoicing. We finally made it back inside. There is joy in these people, not in this place."

Janie Yee sat in a pew about halfway to the altar. She had always prayed that her family—particularly Lily—would be returned. Now, in one way, being back inside felt good. But in another way, it was like returning to a childhood home that belonged to someone else. She looked at the walls, where the stations of the cross once hung. The paint was a lighter shade where the statues had been, reminding her of body outlines at a crime scene. She looked at the altar, where the priests used to prepare communion, where her children had their baptisms, confirmations, and concerts. The table was gone. There was no incense. She looked to the front and back of the church. The prayer candles that Lily lit were no more. Still, the old church held its beauty. It was where her sister had blossomed.

Carmen had last been inside St. Brigid with her tall, dark, and handsome Jess, but she hadn't attended daily Mass for over a decade. Looking up to the heavens, to Jess and the other angels she believed watched over her, she said, "My soul feels safe." Her prayers were more abundant now, more a part of her everyday routine. Her housekeeping was offered in prayer. Her interactions were offered in prayer. The struggle to live with God was moment to moment, but more real.

Minutes before the memorial was to begin, Carmen told Lorraine that she had approached Archbishop Levada not long before he left for Rome. "I used reverse psychology on him and said, 'Archbishop, I know you are one of those who want to gather the parishioners and not scatter them.' He held my nametag and looked at my name—I was wearing a nametag to this event—and he said, 'Carmen, what parish do you belong to?' I said, 'St.

Brigid,' and he dropped my nametag." She smiled as she recalled the story.

"This is so overwhelming," Lorraine said, nodding at Carmen.

In a pew at the front of the church, close to the portrait of her father, was Mary Dignan, looking pretty and grown up in a black sleeveless dress. This was her first funeral. So many people had been touched by her dad's life. Holding the memorial program, she stared at the cover, with a picture of Joseph Howard Dignan and his life span: June 19, 1957—June 29, 2006. Inside the cover was a quotation written by Father O, the writer of slogans, to sum up Joe's philosophy: "I've lived my life as I understood it. Right or wrong, I came to terms."

Senator Carole Migden, small and wiry with curly grayish blonde hair, arrived. She saw the portrait at the altar and remarked, "In life, Joe couldn't get in here. In death, he's in."

Father O entered his church, pausing to look toward the altar. He closed his eyes to take in the scent. It was still St. Brigid, but it was changed—like everyone here. He gazed up at the ornate rose window, its outer petals portraying redemption and the immortality of the soul. This was where he had liked to take in the spectacle of Mass, to reflect on its reassuring rhythm. This was where he had been the morning of November 13, 1993, when Father Hanson had announced that St. Brigid would close. There was stunned silence that day, and there was the explanation that it was "God's will."

Slowly making his way up the aisle, clasping the hands of Joe's friends and fellow parishioners, Father O was inside St. Brigid for the first time in twelve years. In fewer than three years, the Irish priest had eulogized Joe's mother and father. Now it was Joe. Restless Joe. Sweet Joe. Troubled Joe. Serene Joe. The Joe who as a kid plotted to escape from this church. The Joe who as an adult envisioned a new beginning for St. Brigid.

Father O found his usual place at the altar. The corners of his mouth turned down. "When I heard the news that Joe had passed on, I simply froze," he began, the room growing still. "Joe was such an active, energetic human being. It tears your heart open." Gesturing at the beauty surrounding them, he said, "Joe stood up to save this magnificence. He took on the Catholic hierarchy. He said to them, 'You are not leading us. You are misleading us. You are not sanctifying us. You are desanctifying us.' He lived these truths until the very end. He was working on St. Brigid until the moment he died."

Father O continued: "This struggle for St. Brigid has been full of disappointments, full of humiliations. I don't know how many nights Joe went to bed disappointed. But he got up the next day and was not discouraged. I have nothing but honor for Joe. His kind of dignity is my kind of dignity. His kind of Catholicism is my kind of Catholicism. His friendship is my friendship. His leadership is my leadership. So much is owed to this one man."

Before the service ended, Father O played "An Irish Lament" on his flute. The melancholy notes moved like a gentle wave from the front communion rail to the back pew. A hush fell over the sanctuary. For a moment, St. Brigid was a church again.

After the service, the parishioners lingered below the steps of St. Brigid, just as they had done on the church's final night in 1994. The heavy front door was again pulled shut, this time by security guards from the Academy of Art University. Unlike on that night, the bell of St. Brigid did not ring on this day. It had been Joe who had sneaked up the church tower after the final Mass to ring the long-dormant bell. He had climbed the narrowing stairs until he reached a tall and wobbly ladder. He hesitated briefly but forged ahead—only to find that the rope used to pull the bell was missing. He put his hands on the enormous wheel and began to pull. The bell screeched through years of rust, finally ringing out with baritone force.

On the steps, the committee members smiled as they shared stories, including some from the last picnic Mass in Lafayette

Park almost a year earlier, the day after they had learned that St. Brigid had been sold. They recalled how Joe had stood in the center of the group on that cold and windy day. They remembered his calm and certitude. They remembered his words.

"I have to tell you," Joe had said, "I have never had a more moving Catholic experience than in this park with you. It is the place where I have—for the first time in my life—come to understand faith."

The fog had settled in, and Joe opened up to them.

"It is where I have come to understand that faith is within us," he had said. "This understanding of faith came to me when no one was telling me I had to be in church. It tested the nature of faith. It asked: 'Is your faith worth standing freezing in a park for? Is it worth having Mass in a parking lot?'"

Joe's eyes had welled with tears that day.

"What I've come to learn," he said, "is that my faith has nothing to do with the gold chalices or big cathedrals. It is deep inside."

Epilogue

San Francisco's former archbishop, William Levada, is now one of the top officials at the Vatican, and the highest-ranked American in Church history. He is prefect of the Congregation for the Doctrine of the Faith—a position formerly held by Cardinal Ratzinger, now Pope Benedict XVI. Before leaving San Francisco, the archbishop publicly acknowledged that proceeds from the sale of St. Brigid could be used for sex abuse settlements. He also said the proceeds would go in part to build a new gym for its school. That never happened. Children from St. Brigid School are bused to a gym across town.

As the scandal around the Catholic Church has widened in recent times across Europe, and the pope himself has been criticized for his handling of abuse cases, Cardinal Levada wrote an article that was posted on the Vatican's website. In it he criticized the media for finding fault in Pope Benedict's oversight of sex abuse by clergymen. He wrote: "I am not proud of America's newspaper of record, the *New York Times,* as a paragon of fairness."

Since 2003 the Archdiocese of San Francisco has paid more than $67 million to settle a hundred clergy abuse cases. Despite Levada's statement that the proceeds could be used for sex abuse settlements, the archdiocese says now that payouts have come instead through its insurance programs, its reserves, and real property sales. Monsignor Patrick O'Shea, who was convicted of grand theft and fraud and put on probation, was never convicted on molestation charges, due to expired statutes of limitations.

Nationally, nearly fourteen thousand molestation claims have been filed against Catholic clergy, according to the U.S. Conference of Catholic Bishops. Internationally, hundreds of new cases have surfaced. Abuse-related costs for the U.S. Church have reached more than $2.3 billion.

Hundreds of parishes across the country are being closed and consolidated, due to a shortage of priests, the high costs of maintaining aging churches, demographic changes, and the fallout from the sexual abuse scandal. In some cases, dioceses filed for bankruptcy just as civil suits against them were going to trial. These include dioceses in Portland, Oregon; Tucson, Arizona; Spokane, Washington; Wilmington, Delaware; Davenport, Iowa; San Diego, California; and Fairbanks, Alaska. An umbrella group, the Council of Parishes, was formed to help organize vigils to resist church closings, aiding in four parish occupations in and around Boston. Those vigils have lasted for more than six years. The council helps with appeals to the Vatican, civil lawsuits, and raising public awareness.

Despite the demoralizing—and still widening—scandal, Catholicism remains the biggest religious denomination in the United States, accounting for about 23 percent of the population, a proportion that has held steady. There are more than 1.2 billion Catholics worldwide.

In San Francisco, the city supervisors have unanimously approved landmark status for the exterior of St. Brigid. The Committee to Save St. Brigid continues to push for landmarking the interior of the church.

When St. Brigid was closed in 1994, the retrofitting costs were placed at between $5 million and $7 million. Around the same time, the archdiocese had a second, lower estimate of between $3 million and $4 million. In 1995, the Committee to Save St. Brigid commissioned its own engineering report, which concluded the seismic strengthening costs for St. Brigid to be at around $700,000. The Academy of Art said in July 2005, when it purchased St. Brigid, that it planned to put $7 million into the restoration and seismic upgrades of the building. In a recent filing with the San Francisco Department of Building Inspections, the Academy of Art said it expects to spend $800,000 on seismically upgrading St. Brigid and making both the church and basement handicapped accessible.

The Academy of Art has replaced the old sign ST. BRIGID CATHOLIC CHURCH with a new one: ACADEMY OF ART CHAPEL. Photography and film classes are held in the sanctuary, and pews are loaded with portable desks. A large movie screen is at the altar, and films by contemporary directors, including Quentin Tarantino, are studied by students.

Lawyers for the school who at one point tried to have St. Brigid deemed ineligible for the national and state registry of historic places eventually dropped their proposal after the Committee to Save St. Brigid, along with members of the city's Planning Department, rebuked their arguments.

Bishop George Niederauer of Salt Lake City, Archbishop Levada's friend for fifty-five years, became San Francisco's eighth archbishop after Levada's departure for Rome. Archbishop Emeritus John Quinn, who presided over the closure of parishes in San Francisco in 1994, is retired. The Reverend Gregory Ingels, the former canon lawyer who represented the archdiocese against the committee's legal appeal, was accused of child molestation in 2004. The charges were eventually dropped—despite a taped admission of guilt—because the statute of limitations had expired. Father Daniel Keohane, installed by Quinn in 1994 to oversee the closure of St. Brigid, was recently put on administrative leave after allegations of sexual abuse surfaced. Keohane was associate pastor at St. Cecilia Church—the same church Monsignor O'Shea had led in the early 1990s.

George Wesolek is director of public policy for the San Francisco archdiocese. He says lessons were learned from the process of closing churches. "We were really the first archdiocese in the country to be dealing with these closures," he says. "There was no template. What I learned is that this is not an easy thing to do. It's very, very painful. I learned there really isn't any way to do it without having significant opposition from groups of people. Now, so many years later, every kind of approach has been tried with these closures. What you can't avoid is the issue of people's emotional attachment to their church. It's not a rational thing entirely. On the positive side, the fight over St. Brigid and elsewhere shows just how attached people are to their faith, and to their churches. The people of St. Brigid are good people. They're not bad people who had a bad motive. They worked hard. And, to be honest, to see their commitment fifteen years later impresses me. That kind of commitment you don't see often—in anything, anywhere."

Robert Bryan still represents inmates on death row. He has not attended church regularly for more than a decade. He remains a Catholic because of the people he met working to save St. Brigid. His daughter, Auda Mai, also doesn't attend Mass regularly but still calls herself a Catholic, as does his wife, Nicole. "What I saw with the committee was powerful," Auda Mai says. "The amount of faith they had and have is incredible. They basically reinforce my faith in humanity." Robert says that all of his early suspicions about what he deemed as lies around the closure of St. Brigid were proven true. One of the main reasons stated was the high cost of retrofitting. Reading the report filed with the Planning Department by the Academy of Art, he said, "This is more proof of the lies. Originally, the archdiocese said it would cost between $5 million and $7 million. Today, with far higher building costs and inflation, it is only $800,000? What the church leaders did to the people of St. Brigid is criminal."

Father Cyril O'Sullivan is pastor of two small churches in Nicasio and Lagunitas in Marin County. One of the churches, St.

Mary's, was built in 1867 and seats a hundred and thirty people. Father O enjoys the assignment, as it reminds him of some of the close-knit parishes he knew in rural parts of Ireland. "You get the seasons, you get the farming life," he says. "It's a different pace." In the years after the closure of St. Brigid, Father O was ostracized by other priests in the archdiocese. Many refused even to sit with him at retreats. Recently he has begun to hear words of support from other priests, who approach him to say he was right to stand up for St. Brigid. He continues to coach the St. Brigid men's soccer team and supports the Committee to Save St. Brigid. He believes in his heart: "As long as St. Brigid remains in the structure of a church, there is always the possibility of its one day becoming a church again."

Lily Wong and Janie Yee's mother, Dymphna Wong, who was born on November 15, 1909, passed away on April 16, 2008, at the age of ninety-eight. She was survived by nine children, twenty-two grandchildren, and nine great-grandchildren. By the time of her death, she had become a devoted Catholic. Lily and Janie on occasion attend the Chinese Mass at Saints Peter and Paul Church in North Beach. Janie says, "It's very grand and nice, but it's not St. Brigid." She adds, "It's okay, though. My belief is no longer in the Church or the building. It is in Christ alone." Lily says, "I just go and attend Mass and come back. I need someone to go with me. I'm not familiar with the building." But she is at peace, saying, "Whatever happens in the moment is not important. What happens for my soul is what's important."

Joe Dignan's ashes will one day be scattered in the San Francisco Bay, along with the ashes of his mother. Mary Dignan attends a Catholic girls' school, which had been selected by her father before he died. She says she was comforted after his death by letters from the members of the committee. "They mailed me so many letters," she says. "It was nice knowing they were there. They had known my dad for so long. They had known me since I was a baby." The group pooled their money and sent Mary a gold necklace of the St. Brigid cross, whose original design was of plaited straw, with a diamond in the center. Mary says she does not go to church but considers herself a Catholic.

The Dignan home on Lombard Street—San Francisco's "crookedest street"—has been cleaned and organized. An estate sale was held, with certain items listed, including: "Limoges vases, period furniture, an elaborately painted piano." The garden is flourishing, thanks to Dane Devoil, and has a prolific Ponderosa lemon tree, a bougainvillea that has created a fuchsia canopy from the garden to the roof, redolent rosebushes, and—of course—big and bold dahlias. The home is in a trust in Mary's name.

Polly Dignan, who is remarried and goes by Polly Magoggin, says she feels gratitude and sadness when she thinks of Joe. "As much tumult and fighting as Joe and I had over Mary, I did love him very much at one point in life. We were together for ten years. I am eternally grateful to him for Mary. I just wish he could see Mary now. She has gone through her hard teenage times. She turned out to be the most wonderful young woman. Joe would be so proud of Mary."

George, the basset hound, lives with a family on a horse farm in Petaluma.

Helen and Tillie Piscevich bought a rosary to be placed around the neck of the Virgin Mother statue that for decades had been inside St. Brigid. The statue now resides in St. Brigid School.

Carmen Esteva remains the spiritual leader of the Committee to Save St. Brigid. She is no longer fearful for the safety of her soul, believing that doing good deeds is as important as going to Mass.

David Hansell attends church regularly but hasn't become a parishioner anywhere. His son seems open to one day returning to church. Hansell says that while his faith in the Catholic Church has been diminished, his belief in God is stronger than ever. From time to time, he walks by St. Brigid, slowing to check on his handiwork. "I have no regret about doing the work," he says. "It was a genuine gift that remains genuine today."

Every year on June 29, Father O, Siu-Mei Wong, Jan Robinson, Helen and Tillie, and Bebe St. John meet at the House of Prime Rib, a block from St. Brigid, to pay tribute to Joe. The House of Prime Rib was chosen because it was Joe's favorite restaurant as a child. They share stories, laugh, and raise their glasses—Cosmopolitans with extra lime are served in Joe's honor. They marvel at the passage of time: The next day is June 30, the thirteenth, fourteenth, fifteenth, or sixteenth anniversary of the closing of St. Brigid. When they leave the restaurant, they hug one another and say they will see each other on Tuesday—at their regular committee meeting, when their SAVE ST. BRIGID CHURCH sign will go back up on the iron gate.

Members of the Committee to Save St. Brigid, who met at least once a week for fourteen years, meet biweekly in the basement of Holy Trinity Cathedral. They gather a few minutes early to pray for the departed. They pray for Joe's soul. They continue to pray for a miracle—that, despite the odds, St. Brigid one day will reopen as a house of worship.

The struggle for St. Brigid is considered the longest-running parish protest in Catholic America.

The faithful from St. Brigid have not joined any other parish.

From time to time, a candle can be seen burning on the steps of St. Brigid.

AUTHOR'S NOTE

I began working on this story in late 2004. I have interviewed more than seventy-five parishioners who attended St. Brigid Church or School. I attended dozens of meetings of the Committee to Save St. Brigid and reviewed thousands of pages of notes from committee meetings and agendas dating from early 1994, as well as legal pleadings. In addition, I reviewed parishioners' journals, daily planners, photo albums, home movies, and letters from the period. I went with the group to hearings at City Hall, and in Sacramento. I attended outdoor vigils, masses, picnics, and demonstrations held by the committee.

Several members of the Committee to Save St. Brigid kept exhaustive notes and records of everything from meetings and correspondence to donations and e-mails. Special thanks to Siu-Mei Wong and Robert Bryan for keeping methodical records and for exhuming them to help with this book.

For the archdiocese's perspective, I interviewed George Wesolek, the public policy director, the Reverend Monsignor Harry Schlitt, head of administration, and Maury Healy, communications director. Archbishop John Quinn declined several requests for an interview, as did Cardinal William Levada.

ACKNOWLEDGMENTS

I'd first like to thank Ken Conner and David Lewis, my talented editors at the *San Francisco Chronicle,* who helped me bring the story of St. Brigid to life in the newspaper. For more than a year, they listened to me talk about the parishioners and their plight, about their personal histories and the life of the old church, situated on one of San Francisco's busiest corridors. On countless mornings, I would arrive at work after meetings or events of the Committee to Save St. Brigid and say, "You won't believe what's happened now." I would marvel at the parishioners' tenacity, at the interplay of personalities, and at their innocence. They seemed from another time, even another place. Ken loved the fight being waged by these parishioners without a parish and soaked up the details. David loved the challenge of making structural sense of their story, which includes dozens of people and spans more than a decade.

Next I'd like to thank my literary agent, Joe Veltre of the Gersh Agency in New York, for seeing the potential of the newspaper series to become a book. He worked with me closely on my proposal, and his faith in the project never faltered. I'll never forget the day he called to say there was interest from editors at major publishing houses. The interest that fit came from a talented and well-respected editor, Susan Canavan, at Houghton Mifflin Harcourt. She got the story—and the challenges of telling the tale—from the beginning, and her direction has been inspired. My appreciation also to the staff at Houghton Mifflin Harcourt, including Shuchi Saraswat, Michelle Bonanno, Ayesha Mirza, and Beth Burleigh Fuller, who kept track of deadlines and walked me through the process of turning a manuscript into a book, and to my copy editor, Luise Erdmann.

This book could not have happened without the parishioners of St. Brigid, who brought me into their lives and their struggle. I want especially to thank those who spent the most time with me: Robert Bryan, Father Cyril O'Sullivan, Joe Dignan, and Siu-Mei Wong. Also, I am grateful to David Hansell, Carmen Esteva, Lily Wong and Janie Yee, Helen and Tillie Piscevich, Jan Robinson, and Bebe St. John. They put up with my relentless presence and questions over many years. They are all gracious and heroic, in different ways. My thanks also to the Reverend James Bretzke, a professor at Boston College, who helped me better understand Church hierarchy and traditions. And I want to thank George Wesolek of the San Francisco archdiocese, who explained and brought to life the Church's side of the struggle.

Finally, there are friends and loved ones who helped me: M.aar, Heather, Jane, David D., George R., my brothers David and Kevin Guthrie and their families, and my late father, Wayne Guthrie, a voracious reader who would have loved this story. There is no one, though, who has been more supportive of me than my mother, Connie Guthrie. She has drawers full of newspaper stories I've written—stories that go back fifteen years to the start of my career in journalism. Thank you, Mom. And while my young son, Roman, doesn't know it yet, he inspires everything I do.